Risk and Ruin

AMERICAN BUSINESS, POLITICS, AND SOCIETY

Series editors: Andrew Wender Cohen, Pamela Walker Laird,
Mark H. Rose, and Elizabeth Tandy Shermer

Books in the series American Business, Politics, and Society explore the relationships
over time between governmental institutions and the creation and performance of
markets, firms, and industries large and small. The central theme of this series is that
politics, law, and public policy—understood broadly to embrace not only lawmaking
but also the structuring presence of governmental institutions—has been fundamental
to the evolution of American business from the colonial era to the present. The series
aims to explore, in particular, developments that have enduring consequences.

A complete list of books in the series is available from the publisher.

RISK AND RUIN

Enron and the Culture of American Capitalism

Gavin Benke

PENN

UNIVERSITY OF PENNSYLVANIA PRESS

PHILADELPHIA

Published in cooperation with
the William P. Clements Center for Southwest Studies,
Southern Methodist University

Published by
University of Pennsylvania Press
Philadelphia, Pennsylvania 19104-4112
www.upenn.edu/pennpress

Printed in the United States of America
on acid-free paper
1 3 5 7 9 10 8 6 4 2

Library of Congress Cataloging-in-Publication Data
Names: Benke, Gavin.
Title: Risk and ruin : Enron and the culture of American
    capitalism / Gavin Benke.
Other titles: American business, politics, and society.
Description: 1st edition. | Philadelphia : University of
    Pennsylvania Press, [2018] | Series: American business,
    politics, and society | Includes bibliographical references
    and index.
Identifiers: LCCN 2017054844 | ISBN 978-0-8122-5020-6
    (hardcover : alk. paper)
Subjects: LCSH: Enron Corp. | Energy industries—Corrupt
    practices—United States. | Business failures—United
    States. | Accounting—Corrupt practices—United States. |
    Capitalism—United States—History—20th century.
Classification: LCC HD9502.U54 E57225 2018 | DDC
    333.790973—dc23
LC record available at https://lccn.loc.gov/2017054844

For Stephanie

CONTENTS

Introduction

The men did not stand a chance in Houston. Kenneth Lay's company, Enron, had become a potential embarrassment for the Texas city after the corporation collapsed in 2001 amid a shockingly elaborate and expansive accounting fraud. Blame for this fiasco largely fell on Lay and Jeffrey Skilling, who had transformed the company over the course of the previous decade. Now, at the start of 2006, the two men were facing criminal charges. Some former Enron executives had already agreed to jail time, but the trial of these two men was especially symbolic—and the mood was ugly. "They don't even deserve a trial," one potential juror put it. "Let all the people they ruined have at them."[1]

The anger and outrage in the jury pool should not have surprised Lay. The word "Enron" was already a pithy reference for corporate wrongdoing. The company's story had been told and retold by journalists, filmmakers, ex-employees, and others, powerfully shaping public opinion. Many of those in the jury pool had even read a book or seen a movie about Enron. Lay's attorneys argued it was absurd that he should stand trial in Houston, but their effort to get their client away from that Texas courthouse was unsuccessful.[2] In February, the soft-spoken Lay appeared alongside Skilling as a prosecutor told the jury that Enron's collapse was "about lies and choices."[3]

The trial went on for months, and as a hot Texas summer loomed in late May, both men were found guilty. The verdicts read like veritable laundry lists of white-collar crime, including wire fraud, securities fraud, conspiracy, insider trading, and making false statements to banks and auditors. After the convictions, though, their fates parted. Lay died of a heart attack less than two months later, launching conspiracy theories variously involving suicide, foul play, or a faked death. Skilling, for his part, began a lengthy prison sentence and equally long legal battle to get out of jail early. Rich and powerful men had been held to account. However, the trial of Ken Lay and Jeff Skilling did not deliver high courtroom drama. It was mere epilogue.[4]

Before the trial, Lay, Skilling, and others had already joined the rogues' gallery of disgraced American businessmen who have periodically disrupted an otherwise optimistic story about American industrial ingenuity and entrepreneurialism. Much as earlier outrageous business episodes gave Americans notorious characters—from the Gilded Age's "Jubilee Jim" Fisk and the "Mephistopheles of Wall Street" Jay Gould, to the "Junk Bond King" Michael Milken in the Reagan era—Enron provided the public with yet another cabal of villains wearing suits and ties. The particulars of the energy company's fall might have been new, but the root cause was older than the Republic. Enron was a story "best told in an English literature class" to help "explain what hubris is all about," a Houston lawyer told the *New York Times* shortly after the collapse. The remark was prescient.[5]

Enron's history is most often written as a tragicomic story about deeply flawed people undone by their own arrogance and greed. To be sure, the pen (or camera) could transform Enron's management team into fascinating characters. Ken Lay, the firm's chairman and chief executive officer, was both a deeply religious self-made man and a natural schmoozer who traveled in the rarefied circles of the political and corporate elite. Jeff Skilling, the man most responsible for molding an entirely new corporation out of the old one, was at once brash and brilliant. Authors rarely missed an opportunity to comment that Skilling declared himself to be "fucking smart" during a recruitment interview for Harvard Business School.[6] Rebecca Mark, the executive who led Enron's disastrous attempt to run a water company, a Texas-based journalist wrote, preferred a "slightly trampy look" and relied on sex appeal to advance her career.[7] Andrew Fastow, the architect behind the balance sheet fraud hiding in the details of Enron's financial statements, was ethically rudderless and immature, slipping *Star Wars* references into the names of the financing schemes. Little wonder, then, that more than one book about the company included a "cast of characters" in the front matter. What's missing from these morality tales is the larger view of how Enron typified the nature of American capitalism at the end of the twentieth century.

The story itself began in 1985, when Enron was created through the combination of two older natural gas companies with Lay taking on the role of chairman and CEO. In order to illustrate a chronic ineptitude at the company that would play a part in the company's eventual collapse, many authors noted that the first postmerger name—Enteron—was a synonym for the gut. The firm was quickly renamed, and a greater folly lay ahead, but only after an astonishing triumph. At the end of the 1980s, Jeff Skilling joined the company and developed an entirely novel approach to gas transportation. His insight was to see how complicated financial products could be used to navigate the natural gas industry's new regulatory landscape. Success came fast, and in the hopes of repeating it, Enron moved away from operating as a traditional pipeline company and entered into a number of different ventures. By the end of the 1990s, Enron resembled an Internet company in style and an investment bank in substance. The business press (as well as financial analysts) hailed the transformation and celebrated Skilling's genius. Amid the fanfare, though, Skilling and Lay were guiding the company toward disaster.[8]

A combination of arrogance and incompetence frequently resulted in ill-advised deals and management decisions. In Teesside, England, for example, Enron's managers built the world's largest natural gas cogeneration power plant and then signed bad contracts that led to lawsuits and lost profits. Teesside, though, was a negligible misstep compared to Rebecca Mark's audacious but disastrous power plant project in India, which even the World Bank refused to fund. Noting Amnesty International's and Human Rights Watch's complaints about labor abuses during construction, as well as the ultimate inability of India's government to pay for the electricity, authors chronicling Enron lingered over the failure of the firm's leadership to anticipate the myriad problems they confronted in India. In these books, the plant's fate was bound up with descriptions of Mark's personal vanity. *New York Times* journalist Kurt Eichenwald, for instance, set the scene by describing Lay and Mark in a limousine cutting a path through abject poverty on the streets of India, while Bethany McLean and Peter Elkind, authors of *The Smartest Guys in the Room*, wrote about Mark "zipping around Houston in a ruby-red Jaguar XK8 convertible" after completing the deal.[9] Likewise, many authors attributed Skilling's push for the company to enter electricity markets to his personal arrogance. Mimi Swartz, a Houston-based writer, and Sherron Watkins, one of the many insiders to publish their own accounts, wrote that the executive "scoffed" at the suggestion that the company should stay away from such business as "just the kind of arguments they heard when they were fighting gas regulation."[10] Electricity, though, was just the beginning.

Enron, the story goes, was a company characterized by a lack of discipline, unchecked hubris, and boorishness. Approval forms for multimillion-dollar deals went unsigned. Sensible thinking and established business practices were routinely dismissed as uncreative. Extramarital affairs were commonplace.

In many books, the head of Enron Energy Services, Lou Pai, came to represent this culture at the company because he led all-male employee excursions to Houston's strip clubs, and eventually left his wife after impregnating one of the dancers. Such abominable ethics and thoughtlessness were on display in Enron's ruthless exploitation of California's newly deregulated electricity system. Enron traders gleefully profited during the state's energy crisis in 2000 and 2001. To great effect, the film director Alex Gibney used tapes of traders swearing and laughing about the state's woes as the soundtrack to images of automobile accidents caused by darkened traffic signals.

Fatefully, it was this same brash overconfidence that led Skilling and the board of directors to allow Andy Fastow to set up and run the multiple corporate structures called "special purpose entities," or SPEs, to do business with Enron, which ultimately destroyed the company. In what writers would later regard as poetic justice, the SPEs had become essential for propping up some of the very deals and new businesses that the press fawned over in the late 1990s. But these were late revelations. Enron may have been a con, but it was a con that worked for years. Incredibly, as Skilling led the firm into uncharted territory, as Andy Fastow introduced convoluted financial schemes that masked failing businesses, and as Rebecca Mark bought and built massive (and doomed) water and power projects around the world, nobody—including the company's top managers—stopped to ask questions.

In the judgment of these writers, Lay seemed more interested in cultivating a public image than managing a complex, global corporation. Famously, the executive was close with the Bush family. As the Texas journalist Robert Bryce saw it, after fund raising and donating to George H. W. Bush's political campaigns in the 1980s, Lay had become a "Big Shot in Houston."[11] The poor kid from Missouri, the story went, was now hobnobbing with the global elite. But there was far more at stake than Ken Lay's personal ambitions. Lay would push for a new baseball stadium in Houston because he supposedly coveted nothing more than to build a personal legacy in Houston. "When did Ken Lay even have time to run Enron?" McLean and Elkind asked in their book.[12] Vanity, though, was not his only problem. Beyond his pursuit of the spotlight he was uncomfortable with conflict. After divorcing his first wife to marry his secretary, Linda, many authors noted that Lay spent holidays with both women in an effort to avoid unpleasant realities. This personality trait was also evident in his management style. Lay was simply unfit to run a large, complex organization.[13]

Enron was unstable, and it couldn't go on forever. The pressure of keeping the shaky scheme from toppling altogether would eventually prove too much for Skilling, who fell into depression and quit after becoming Enron's next CEO. Following Skilling's departure, Lay and others realized that the SPEs Fastow engineered were a potential disaster and attempted to "unwind" them, but it was too late. Some journalists and financial analysts were already growing skeptical about Enron's operations. In the fall of 2001, the company issued a number of public financial restatements and provided a more accurate—and much less flattering—picture of the company. In the wake of this new scrutiny, Ken Lay's deft political maneuvering failed him. In an exchange that would find its way into every Enron narrative, he read aloud an anonymously submitted question asking him if he was on crack.[14] The man's word wasn't worth spit, and the firm's stock price and credit rating soon crashed. The company declared bankruptcy at the end of the year. At the time, it was the largest business failure in American history. Enron made for good story material, and these stories have powerfully shaped how the company is remembered and studied.

Echoing these popular narratives, writers of a scholarly bent studying business and law have pointed to the all-too-human problems of arrogance, greed, and negligence in their own attempts to make sense of Enron's collapse. They have also broadened their focus to poor incentives and a lack of internal controls. There is certainly merit to such an analysis. The board of directors, for example, was shockingly derelict in its responsibilities. They rarely met apart from the management team and in general did not dwell too deeply on issues that should have given them pause. In addition to faulting the board of directors, some studies have found a similar negligence from Enron's accountants at Arthur Andersen, their lawyers at Vinson and Elkins, financial analysts at investment banks, and business journalists.[15]

In contrast to the attention journalists and professional studies have given Enron, historians have done little more than offer an occasional comparison to the Gilded Age. To some extent, this lack of attention is understandable. Despite being so spectacular, the firm's collapse had an oddly ephemeral quality. As one journalist put it shortly after the bankruptcy, "not a single light flickered" when the company fell apart. To be sure, individual retirements were ruined, but the episode's consequences seemed to end there. Besides, how could one fit the rare and strange personalities that concocted accounting frauds as complex as Escher prints into a broader historical pattern? Because of this legacy, Enron occupies an uncomfortable middle ground—extensively documented, but underanalyzed. However, framing Enron as a case of catastrophic oversight failure or a Shakespearean tale of hubris obscures many of the larger economic, political, and cultural shifts that played a role in this company's fate.[16] These larger shifts are at the center of this story.

The culture of capitalism and business in the United States at the end of the twentieth century informed Enron's history in profound ways. The company—in both its development and its demise—was shaped by a moment in time when business and political leaders adopted new attitudes toward regulation, found an abiding confidence in market mechanisms, and enthusiastically embraced new ideas as the pace of business quickened. Enron, in other words, is a product of this distinct moment in American business when old processes, logics, and assumptions no longer seemed to apply.

Corporate fraud is nothing new, of course. Many of the hallmarks of the Enron collapse—accounting fraud and the complicity of investment banks—are about as old as the large-scale American corporation. Still, the details of each scandal can be unique to their moment. In retrospect, it might seem obvious that Enron was sliding into fraud, but many of Lay and Skilling's choices were made in the context of a world that seemed to be in the midst of fundamental change. As several historians have noted, corporate fraud is often found in markets that are full of frenetic, entrepreneurial activity and innovative experimentation. Such a dynamic could easily be found at Enron, a company that labored to craft its public image around the word "innovative." The firm's collapse may have involved outright criminal activity, but that illegality was informed by larger shifts in the global economy. Chalking up Enron's collapse as a strange and aberrant episode is to pass up a particularly rich case study about the odd, uncertain path that capitalism took at the end of the twentieth century. Indeed, it was the peculiar culture of American business during these years that facilitated the specific contortions of strategy and structure, as well as word and image, that ruined Enron.[17]

In the twentieth century's final decades, rising economies around the world, the breakdown of once-dependable assumptions about the postwar economy, and the emergence of new technologies meant that U.S. corporate managers had to rethink organizational structure, basic strategy, and the firm's relationship with a number of different stakeholders. This economic tumult loosened what were previously fixed assumptions about the way the world worked. The 1970s offered the first glimmerings of a new and far more interconnected world. As America's unchallenged industrial and economic power dissipated at the start of the decade, policy makers and economists increasingly looked to market mechanisms to manage economic conditions. A palpable feeling that the global economy was becoming more tightly knit together and that conventional economic wisdom was irrelevant sent American policy makers, corporate executives, and city politicians searching for a new path forward.[18] The particular set of political and economic solutions that emerged from this difficult period has come to be called "neoliberalism." With the "market" as a guiding metaphor, trade policy was liberalized, industries were deregulated, "market incentives" replaced regulatory controls, social services in cities were slashed, unions lost ground, and, perhaps most important, the financial services industry became an increasingly powerful economic force. This "financialization" of the U.S. economy meant that the center of economic power in the United States shifted away from industry and toward Wall Street, forcing dramatic changes in corporate strategy that both responded to a more dynamic stock market and capitalized on the profit-making opportunities that accompanied the proliferation of new financial instruments. During the final decades of the twentieth century, neoliberalism's market-based philosophy became something close to common sense—an inherited and unexamined set of beliefs.[19] The term itself refers to an ideal conception of a world that is a unified and unregulated space that capital can move through unimpeded, as well as to the policies and practices intended to create this ideal environment. These shifts began amid the crisis of the 1970s, but the transformation of American business did not end there. In a process that would eventually be called globalization, international trade and business began to cross formerly impermeable national borders aided by advances in communication and transportation. As globalization became a more visible process during the 1980s and 1990s, politicians, corporate managers, and business writers all reimagined the role of the city, the function of government, the implications of new technologies, and corporate responsibility toward the environment. As a major energy corporation, Enron was not sheltered from these changes.[20]

The shifting political, cultural, and economic terrain of neoliberalism and globalization powerfully influenced the ways in which Lay and Enron played a public role in Houston and how the company responded to environmental worries, and it determined what new markets the company would enter. Just as important, Enron was an active participant in shaping these

new ideas. Enron's story also reveals how American business successfully cemented a new sense of cultural prestige at the end of the twentieth century.
The 1990s were a time of furious change, and the company was heralded as
revolutionary in the business media and rewarded by the stock market
because managers like Lay and Skilling seemed to have mastered the era's
complex dynamics. Jeff Skilling in particular turned Enron into an example
of what corporations could become if they managed this new world properly. This very celebration made Enron's ignominious demise all the more
shocking. The firm's collapse was a genuine crisis of legitimacy for this new
style of business thought.[21]

Consequently, Enron's history highlights the points of intersection
among these different trends over the course of the 1990s. By looking at
Enron, we can understand how an unlikely coalition supporting a new baseball park in a Texas city's downtown was connected to management books
being authored by business school faculty, how Houston's recession in the
1980s was connected to California's 2001 energy crisis, how concerns about
global warming were connected to the expansion of new derivatives, and
how fraudulent accounting might be justified using the language of Silicon
Valley. Looking at Enron, in other words, helps us understand the complex
way that corporations were both objects and agents of neoliberalism and
globalization.[22]

Illustrating how this culture of capitalism facilitated Enron's development requires telling the firm's story in a new way. Unlike the popular narratives that call attention to unique personalities at the company, my retelling
assigns greater weight to the larger forces that pushed Enron toward fraudulent activity. At the century's end, policy makers and business leaders faced
a profoundly unstable business environment. Just as significant as the global
turn that business took during these years, a growing financial services sector
and the introduction of new information technologies forced businesses to
rethink formerly static concepts such as value, assets, and strategy. Throughout this book, I chart several interconnected themes across Enron's history.
First, I examine the changing fortunes of Houston, Texas, where the company was headquartered as the city felt the reverberations of a shifting global
political economy after 1970. Second, I track the rise of a new approach to
business strategy that emerged at the end of the twentieth century. Third, I
chronicle a change in attitudes toward regulation and the function of the
market among policy makers and business leaders. Fourth, I document the

evolution of an expansive business lexicon and visual aesthetic that accompanied and encouraged these broader political and economic changes. Enron's managers found themselves deeply enmeshed in and sometimes at the forefront of many of these trends. Considered against such a backdrop, Enron's history looks different.

In order to reveal how these broader forces set the stage for this very public business fiasco, the narrative arc of this book is longer than Enron's own relatively brief decade-and-a-half existence. My accounting of Enron's history does not begin with the firm's creation in the mid-1980s but opens instead on Houston, where political economy resonated in particular ways during the second half of the twentieth century. A long tradition of business elites who played a large role in Houston's affairs, as well as the centrality of oil and gas to the region's economy, meant that by the second half of the century Houston was both unmistakably Texan and inextricably linked to the global economy. These unique circumstances drew both Ken Lay and Jeff Skilling to the place just before the topsy-turvy world oil market decimated the city's economy, Wall Street became newly invigorated while domestic manufacturing sputtered, and the natural gas business was faced with an uncertain future after national deregulation.[23]

From this point, I chronicle how policy makers' understanding of the post–Cold War era had a dramatic effect on Enron's strategy and structure. In particular, a sense of environmentalism was central to policy discussions about how an increasingly interconnected world should operate. Because energy and the environment were so intertwined with one another, this same attention to environmental sensitivity was also central to Enron's marketing and government relations. Gradually, though, a more abstract idea of a world market characterized by networks of finance and information liberated from backward-looking regulation replaced earlier, more environmentally conscious ideas of globalization. Lay, Skilling, and Rebecca Mark advanced, rebuffed, and adapted to these changing attitudes toward the environment, an increasingly empowered Wall Street, and a quickly integrating global economy. These adaptations and confrontations led Lay to push for changes to Houston and for increased deregulation across the country, and led Skilling to fashion a new approach toward business that creatively (and ultimately fatefully) combined these different strands.

The second half of the book tracks the evolution of Enron from the symbol of new economy success to easy shorthand for corporate fraud. During the latter half of the 1990s, the company enjoyed widespread praise in various business outlets. Enron's managers were spokespeople for this new world of business. The appearance in the late 1990s of the "new economy" style celebrating brains over industry that accompanied the Silicon Valley technology boom provided Enron with the rhetorical and symbolic tools to represent and communicate its newer businesses. While the "new economy" sensibility did not allow Enron to precisely define its new business, it presented the company with an opportunity to more aggressively promote different aspects of its preferred political-economic model, especially deregulation. It did not hold this position for long, however. To put it mildly, the way the business press, Wall Street analysts, and politicians talked about the company changed substantially from 1997 to 2001. Two separate debacles in 2000 and 2001—the California energy crisis and the revelation of accounting fraud—transformed the company into a symbol for all the ills of the deregulation that Lay and Skilling had championed for so long. However, Enron's cultural significance became apparent only after its bankruptcy at the end of 2001.

Much in the way the book opens with Houston and the gas business before 1985, it concludes in the post-Enron era by exploring the voices, debates, and modes of understanding that cemented a particular version of Enron's history in American memory. Though Enron's collapse was a political crisis and threatened the new style of business, what emerged from a brief but furious period of cultural production about Enron was a story of personal failings and deliberate deceit.[24] This story served to limit the implications of Enron's failure for American capitalism writ large.

Enron is the subject of this book, but its concerns move well beyond this one corporation. Rather, this case study uses Enron as a lens to examine wider currents and interconnections that not only helped to make Enron but are in many ways still fixtures of contemporary political economy. As one historian has recently pointed out, corporate failures can be just as "transformative" as corporate successes.[25] This was not the case with Enron—but it could have been. Public outrage after the firm's collapse was swift and reveals that the incident tapped into a wider discomfort with what had become of the U.S. business system. The quick flood of Enron stories all invoked old and well-burnished stereotypes about American business that have long been an important part of the nation's cultural discourse. Still, a newer ideology built around a hazy, expansive notion of "innovation," an abiding confidence in corporations as the most trustworthy stewards of an increasingly interconnected world, a suspicion toward regulation, a stout faith in new technologies, a widespread investment in the stock market, and the stranger varieties of financial instruments all survived the Enron debacle and came to a catastrophic climax in the 2008 economic crisis. Examining the narratives both around and about Enron—during and after the company's life—helps explain why such a public implosion failed to produce substantive change.

CHAPTER 1

Enron Emerges

Because his upbringing made him an attractive literary subject, in the books that appeared after Enron's collapse, authors tended to introduce Kenneth Lay as a child, growing up poor in Missouri. The journalist Loren Fox, for instance, wrote about a young Lay sitting atop a tractor and daydreaming about business.[1] The well-known *New York Times* business reporter Kurt Eichenwald opened his book on Enron with a scene that could have been taken from *The Grapes of Wrath*, with the Lay family moving across the country in a jalopy.[2] Bethany McLean and Peter Elkind, the *Fortune* journalists who cowrote *The Smartest Guys in the Room*, chose to be direct, stating that Lay "grew up dirt poor" and that "the Enron chairman's history is a classic Horatio Alger story."[3] The contrast between such humble beginnings and the revelations of wanton excess at Enron in the late 1990s let these writers cast Lay as a man doomed to ruin. Other authors, such as the *Texas Monthly* journalist Mimi Swartz and Sherron Watkins (the Enron "whistle blower") considered Lay to be an enigmatic presence.

Still, even if "Enron was a story with a mystery at its center," Swartz and Watkins also insisted that "no one could understand Ken Lay or the company he built without understanding Houston."[4] Despite its obvious importance to Enron's story, though, writers found themselves struggling to make sense of the relationship between Enron and Houston. Robert Bryce, writer for the liberal-leaning *Texas Observer*, for example, called Houston a "city of irrepressible optimists" but also judged that Enron's habit of "buying" politicians at the national level was simply an extension of Houston's business culture.[5] Such conflicted feelings about the city's role in Enron's story is understandable. The company came together at a moment when the city was in the midst of a deep structural change. Perhaps, then, the best point to begin unraveling Enron's collapse would be in 1967.

That September, Ken Lay was a young man writing to his former professor at the University of Missouri, Pinkney Walker, about his doctoral exams in economics at the University of Houston. "If they are successful," he wrote to Walker, "maybe I can get a thesis underway while in the service."[6] It must have been an anxious time for the twenty-five-year-old. Though he was entering the armed forces in the middle of the Vietnam War, Lay did not know if he would end up in the air force or the navy, because "befitting the slow-moving military animal, a number of minor problems" had slowed his application "to almost a halt."[7] Walker, a conservative economist, surely appreciated Lay's mild annoyance with an apparently inefficient government bureaucracy. Much like other letters the young man sent to Walker, news of a likely military commission was typed on letterhead for the Humble Oil and Refining Company of Houston, Texas. One of Walker's favorite students, Lay had moved to Houston in 1965 to work for Humble as an economist and speechwriter.[8]

By the next January, Lay was in Naval Officer Candidate School in Rhode Island, which even decades later he remembered as being "very, very cold" in comparison to the city he had just left. After being commissioned, the newly minted ensign spent the next three years at the Pentagon, during which time he finished his degree. Lay may not have relished leaving Houston, which was still in the midst of a long boom following World War II. Though he would eventually return to Houston, in the interim, the city, the energy industry, and the global economy underwent profound transformations—such as the rollback of regulatory frameworks across the country, the rise of an emboldened financial services industry, and the first stirrings of a new round of economic globalization. It would not be the first time that wider forces played a crucial role in the city's development.[9]

The area's geography helped shape Houston's long and important relationship to the world economy. The Buffalo Bayou, a curving body of water, wound its way through the north of what would become the city's downtown, eventually emptying out to the east in the Trinity Bay and the waters of the Gulf of Mexico. Early Houstonians were well aware of how important the bayou would be if the city were to last. The Port of Houston was established in 1842, not long after two brothers from New York state, John Kirby and Augustus Allen, founded Houston in 1836. The modern Houston Ship Channel, though, was not completed until 1914, providing a crucial link that tied Houston to an international cotton market. In addition to early boosters like the Allen brothers, Houston's growth during the second half of the nineteenth century was influenced by larger regional trends.[10]

The city itself had originally been divided into different wards, though the ward system ended during the twentieth century's first decade. Fourth Ward, just south and east of the central business district, had long since been settled by African Americans, many of whom arrived in Houston after the Civil War in a neighborhood that would eventually be called Freedman's Town. Ultimately though, African Americans settled in other parts of the city as well. French-speaking creoles fleeing the Great Mississippi Flood of 1917 also migrated to Houston and settled in Fifth Ward, which was north of the Buffalo Bayou. Across the water in Second Ward, a Spanish-speaking Mexican and Tejano community grew in the twentieth century's first few decades.[11]

At the edge of Second Ward, a grand railroad station had been built in 1911. Indeed, railroads were a major part of Houston's economy in the early twentieth century, as well as a major employer of Fifth Ward creoles. Both the Ship Channel and the railroads were a cause of pride for the city's elite. A 1928 booklet printed by the city's chamber of commerce entitled *Houston: Where Seventeen Railroads Meet the Sea*, hinted at the business community's ambitions to connect to wider markets. While cotton was crucial to the city's fortunes, during the twentieth century, a different commodity would come to dominate Houston's economy.[12]

After oil was discovered at nearby Spindletop in 1901, Houston was guaranteed a unique and important place in terms of international trade. However, it would take a number of developments in the twentieth century to make the city synonymous with energy. Even in the few decades after the Spindletop discovery, cotton remained the city's dominant economic force. However, the New Deal and Second World War proved to be a sea change in the area's economy. The transformation that began during the Depression years was expertly shaped by Jesse H. Jones, a powerful New Deal administrator and the owner of the *Houston Chronicle*, the area's paper of record. As the head of the Reconstruction Finance Corporation, Jones was able to direct federal money toward Houston to be used for infrastructure improvements.[13]

The United States' entrance into World War II further added to the region's fortunes. Because of the area's shipping channel, the city quickly became a center of petrochemical refining during the war. As a part of the war effort, the federal government also provided assistance to develop manufacturing facilities around the area to produce materials like airplane fuel and also built the "Big Inch" and "Little Inch" oil pipelines. These projects would provide the city and its businesses with a major boost after the war, transforming Houston's political economy. Indeed, the massive federal investment in infrastructure helped petrochemicals become the central fact of economic life in the city.[14]

Oil, of course, was the commodity most associated with Houston, but in the 1940s, the natural gas business was also entering a phase of dramatic expansion. Since the nineteenth century, both coal and natural gas had been used for heat, light, and fuel. Interstate pipelines, though, emerged only in the 1920s, when huge stores of gas were discovered in the American Southwest and pipeline construction became much sturdier. As a relatively new industry, natural gas firms became entangled with the excesses of the booming 1920s. Assembling massive utility holding companies that combined electricity producers with gas pipelines, men in the power business, such as the notorious Samuel Insull, displayed a decided flexibility when it came to both the law and finance. Shares of utility holding companies were among the hottest stocks in a frenzied period on Wall Street, and when the market crashed in 1929 and the country fell into depression, utilities quickly became a focus of outrage. Out of concern that a rapacious and monopolistic "Power Trust" was developing, the Federal Trade Commission (FTC) had launched an investigation of these businesses a year *before* the crash. When the FTC published its findings in a huge report in 1935, unemployment was at 20 percent, and the country had already seen some of the Dust Bowl's worst storms. Americans were hardly willing to tolerate revelations of stock manipulation and shady financing. Industry regulation was a certainty.[15]

In 1935, the same year the report was released, President Franklin Delano Roosevelt signed into law the Public Utility Holding Company Act, which took aim at the threat of monopoly power, and split natural gas operations from electricity companies. Other New Deal actions that focused on the world of finance, such as 1933's Securities Act, as well as the Securities and Exchange Commission's creation, also had implications for the power industry.[16] Finally, 1938's Natural Gas Act located the industry's regulation at the federal level, with prices set by the Federal Power Commission (FPC). In contrast to the free-for-all that characterized the power business during the 1920s, the FPC would now grant access to markets and set prices for pipelines based on a "just and reasonable" rate of return. The commission also began breaking apart natural gas companies. Soon, the natural gas industry was split into three different segments—producers, pipeline companies, and local distribution companies. In this way, the shape of the natural gas industry moved in a parallel fashion with much of the U.S. economy. Through the trauma of the Great Depression and policy experimentation of the New Deal, an emphasis on stability emerged, meaning regulation for large portions of the economy. Laws, such as the Glass-Steagall Act, which separated commercial and investment banking, reflected this impulse. Even after the Depression's end, industry regulation and a Keynesian approach to managing the business cycle through "countercyclical fiscal policy," dominated the federal government's economic and industrial policies. Despite deliberately exercising more government control over economic activity, in the immediate postwar era, U.S. pipelines grew. Not only did construction increase, but other pipelines—including Houston's Big Inch and Little Inch—were converted to transport natural gas. These pipelines were to play an important role in Houston's development.[17]

Two brothers, Herman and George Brown, who had operated the Brown and Root construction company since 1919, purchased the Big Inch and Little Inch pipelines from the federal government after the war, enabling the creation of the Texas Eastern Transmission Company, a natural gas pipeline operation.[18] Gaining control of the pipelines and establishing the gas company ushered in the brothers' heyday in the postwar era, when they "just formed one corporation after another."[19] No doubt the Brown brothers and other businessmen seized on the opportunities presented to them, but these opportunities would not have existed without an emerging political economy that was running on fossil fuels, as well as the stuff's abundance around Houston. George and Herman Brown were at the center of a group of businessmen who exerted tremendous power in the city. Just as he had during the New Deal and the war, as both a politically connected mover and a powerful local businessman, Jesse H. Jones helped usher in the city's postwar boom. Downtown, at the Lamar Hotel, which Jones owned, local business interests including Jones and the Brown brothers would meet in Suite 8F, which was leased to Herman Brown so he could have a place to stay when he was visiting from the state capital in Austin.[20]

The suite itself was expansive, consisting of two bedrooms, a living room, a dining area and a kitchen. During the city's postwar heyday in the 1940s and 1950s, when the Lay family was struggling to stay afloat in the Midwest, the Brown brothers and the other members of the 8F Crowd, including a local judge, James A. Elkins, and businessmen, including Gus Wortham, Jim Abercrombie, and William A. Smith, cemented commercial and social ties over drinks, exercising power through "interlocking directorates." Because they served on the boards of each other's companies, the business affairs of these men were all intertwined. Similarly, united by a common sensibility when it came to city affairs, the men of Suite 8F pursued measures to create a friendly business environment. For these men, business and civic interests were perfectly aligned. The group's political influence was also formidable. Some historians have likened a local politician visiting the Lamar Hotel as the equivalent of a job interview. In addition to their local power, the 8F group's influence also extended to Washington. In particular, the Brown brothers had close, long-standing ties to two Texans in D.C.—then senator Lyndon B. Johnson and the Speaker of the House, Sam Rayburn. Nor was the group's clout limited to the hard worlds of business and politics. In addition to their shared business interests, the men also got in the habit of supporting each other's local charities and other activities around town. Because of this, much of Houston's postwar development was directed from 8F in the Lamar Hotel.[21]

Iconic symbols of Houston's midcentury ruling class, the members of the Suite 8F Crowd saw themselves as working to raise Houston's profile nationally and generally contributing to the city's greatness, though the manner in which the group worked was inherently undemocratic. These men did not concern themselves too much with garnering public support for their plans but masterfully exercised power and pressure behind closed doors. Accounts of the meetings in Suite 8F emphasize drinking and playing cards. The men also hunted together on excursions outside of Houston. Hard-drinking, gambling, hunting, cementing deals in the privacy of a hotel room, entirely white and male, the Suite 8F Crowd seemed to be the very definition of an "old boys" club.

This mix of fraternity and privilege was often reflected in the specific issues the group championed. It was a conservative group of men, and the city grew in a way that reflected their values. Unsurprisingly, the group also pursued anti-union activities, lobbying aggressively for the state to adopt right-to-work laws, though the Houston men were hardly unique in this respect. In their politics, the 8F members were like other Sunbelt business elites who found themselves at odds with the economic scene generated by New Deal politics and were determined to build a movement that championed "free enterprise." Though the men played roles in the creation of the Texas Children's Hospital and the development of Rice University, and pushed to bring a modern airport to Houston (even though that put them at odds with the mayor), critics note that while they held sway, the city hardly developed in an equitable manner. For much of the twentieth century, systematic disenfranchisement of the city's African Americans was a part of Houston life. Indeed, while the 8F Crowd was intent on improving Houston's business environment and, through charitable projects, raising its national standing, racial inequality in the city continued to persist. Like other places in the South, Houston was a Jim Crow city that left behind a legacy of disenfranchisement that business elites like the men drinking and playing cards in that hotel room seemed uninterested in addressing. The giant oil and gas companies that continued to grow alongside African American neighborhoods that were more or less neglected by city government revealed a lopsided prosperity. Indeed, Houston's progress during the middle of the twentieth century was an ambiguous record.[22]

Though the 8F Crowd was irrefutably Texan, midcentury Houston was in other ways emblematic of the way many car-centric cities developed after the war. The absence of any significant public transportation along with a good deal of highway construction meant that Houston became an extremely low-density area, exacerbating both racial and class segregation. This pattern was shaped by a number of midcentury developments that could be found in other southern cities. Aided by air-conditioning and automobiles, growth in Houston sprawled out in every direction away from the city's core. In fact, Houston was unique among big American cities for a complete lack of zoning laws, which allowed the city to evolve in strange ways. This sense of an emptying center and absence of planning would be one reason the metropolis began to seem formless as it grew over the next few decades.[23]

Still, if Houston's growth at midcentury was chaotic, it also signified a boundless sense of economic good times. The city's growing economy mirrored (in broad terms) a sense of nationwide postwar prosperity. Indeed, Houston was not alone among Sunbelt cities in the southern and western United States that benefited from military and federal spending, as well as businesses relocating to parts of the country where labor unions were weaker. The 1940s and 1950s were marked by American business power. Facing little competition from overseas, American corporations grew after the war. However, postwar growth was a far cry from the overheated bull market of the 1920s. When the accounting firm Arthur Andersen began training clients to use new mainframe computers, or when an editor at *Fortune*, William H. Whyte, worried about the social consequences of too many American men climbing the corporate ladder to middle management positions in *The Organization Man*, they were reflections of the stability that characterized corporate life during the American era. In the 1940s and 1950s, a new form of corporate organization—conglomeration—began to take shape as well, as firms began to diversify into new and different markets. Along with older companies such as General Electric and DuPont that moved into new lines of business, by the mid-1960s, newer conglomerates like LTV and Gulf and Western typified this sort of business organization. The natural gas business was no different.[24]

Pipeline companies had also started diversifying in the second half of the 1950s, though the reasons were unique to the industry. In Wisconsin, politicians had become concerned about the monopoly power held by Phillips Petroleum, a major gas producer in the region, and by the early 1950s, a legal dispute between Wisconsin and Phillips began winding its way through the American legal system. The case eventually reached the U.S. Supreme Court, which in 1954 ruled that Phillips Petroleum could be considered a natural gas company subject to price regulation. The implications of the Phillips decision were enormous, giving the FPC the authority to set the price at which producers could sell gas to pipelines. Though it would take decades before most Americans felt it, the Phillips decision created a major problem. While gas prices had been stabilized and demand increased, the ruling had also disincentivized production around the country.[25] Instead of investing in more pipelines and gas-producing operations, natural gas companies began investing capital in other, and sometimes unconnected, businesses. Despite the Phillips decision, however, in the 1950s and 1960s Houston showed no signs of the looming natural gas crisis. On the contrary, the city's growth continued.

In 1958 NASA chose the city to build the Johnson Space Center, and in 1965 (the year Ken Lay moved to Texas), the Houston Astros played their first baseball game in the Astrodome, a massive stadium that was a veritable monument to postwar affluence. The next few years, however, would bring a tremendous amount of uncertainty. The disincentives for companies to expand gas exploration in the wake of the Phillips decision meant that gas production was declining. In fact, in 1968, the discovery of new gas sources fell below production. The supply, in other words, was running low. Though politicians began looking for a way to relieve the problem, by the start of the 1970s, a solution had not materialized. If the dwindling gas supplies portended trouble, other sectors of the U.S. economy were also hurting. Beginning in the late 1960s, the unprecedented prosperity of the postwar years seemed to be at an end. Since 1967, economic growth had been slowing, and the rate of inflation began to rise. Apart from a declining domestic economy, the global economy was changing in other ways.[26]

Because the industrial capacity of other nations had been ripped apart by the Second World War, the United States found itself at the center of an effort to stabilize the global postwar economy after the smoke of the battlefields lifted. Planning began in July 1944, when attendees of the United Nations Monetary and Finance Conference in Bretton Woods, New Hampshire, most notably John Maynard Keynes, called for the creation of the International Monetary Fund, the World Bank, and the General Agreement on Tariffs and Trade. Even beyond establishing institutions that could bolster faltering economies, Keynes was also determined that controls be put on capital flows because of the complications they could create for individual economies. One of the most important features of the Bretton Woods meetings was the inauguration of fixed currency exchange rates based on the U.S. dollar, which was then convertible to gold. The Bretton Woods conference was Keynesianism on an international scale and placed the United States at the center of global economic stability. It was, in other words, a powerful indication of American economic dominance. Throughout the Bretton Woods era, the government sent U.S. dollars abroad to aid Europe's recovery. American industry was so dominant that the United States entered into lopsided agreements with struggling countries to help them recover their industrial capacity and economic health as part of a Cold War strategy to blunt the spread of communism throughout the world. Facing scant international competition, the U.S. economy could easily bear such burdens.[27]

By the late 1960s, however, the stability that defined the "American era" came undone. By then, other nations had recovered from war, and other areas of the world, such as Latin America, were emerging and placing new economic pressures on the United States. So began a long stretch of declining American industrial might. Indeed, during the 1970s, American manufacturers ceded much of their share of the global manufacturing market to other areas of the world. The Keynesian political economy of the postwar era seemed to be failing. What is more, the Bretton Woods system guaranteed that the U.S. dollar would be a strong currency for much of the postwar era, meaning that U.S. exports became too expensive to compete with products coming from recovering economies around the world. By the time Richard Nixon took office, the United States was running a trade deficit. In 1968, the year Nixon was elected, natural gas consumption outpaced gas discovery, and

Lay began his navy career, investors outside of the United States began exchanging dollars for gold—a sign of waning confidence in the American economy. In response to deteriorating conditions, Nixon, with the backing of his Texas-raised treasury secretary, John Connally, announced in August 1971 that the United States would no longer link the dollar to gold.[28]

Additionally, geopolitical events seemed to yank the nation out of a sense of complacency. Most dramatically, when OPEC members stopped exporting oil to the United States to protest American support for Israeli military action during the 1973 Arab-Israeli War, fuel prices skyrocketed. The oil shock caught the Nixon administration off guard. Not only was it unthinkable that smaller states, such as the OPEC members, could have such a huge impact on the U.S. economy, the postwar sense of the United States' ability to act autonomously on the world stage no longer seemed feasible. Most immediately, the steep rise in oil prices exacerbated the inflation already hurting broad sectors of the American economy. However, the enormous profits that OPEC members reaped in the process meant a massive amount of money—petrodollars—was set loose in the global financial system. Indeed, the 1973 oil shock sent the price of oil through the roof. As gas lines formed at service stations around the country, the outsized profits that OPEC members enjoyed entered international money markets just as political leaders failed to reestablish the Bretton Woods system of fixed exchange rates after Nixon had ended the dollar's convertibility to gold two years earlier. Crucially, currency exchange rates would now float. With newly variable exchange rates and more money sloshing through the international banking system, the door had been opened to the creation of a much more dynamic world of finance.[29]

Within a few years, financial derivatives that allowed investors to hedge against currency exchange rate fluctuations began to appear. When the economists Fischer Black and Myron Scholes published their options pricing model in the May 1973 issue of the *Journal of Political Economy*, for example, it signaled a steep increase in complexity in the financial services sector. Derivatives contracts had a much longer history—grain futures, for instance, were essential to agriculture in the nineteenth century. Rather than merchants directly examining individual bushels of grain, the stuff was grouped into broad categories. In places like Chicago, merchants and sellers would then work with slips of paper instead—buying and selling grain and claims on the following year's crop throughout the day without ever laying eyes on the material itself. However, the new financial derivatives were far more

complex because risk was now priced using sophisticated mathematical techniques to determine the price volatility of an asset—which might now be the
relationship between two different national currencies instead of something
as tangible as a bushel of wheat. If this new way of pricing financial derivatives was an impressive intellectual feat, it was also an acknowledgement of
new levels of global economic instability. The American experience with a
globalizing economy in the 1970s was an unpleasant one that shook national
confidence. At the start of the 1970s, it seemed like the economy was simply
winding to a stop.[30]

By contrast, Houston boomed. Though the region grew steadily in population and physical infrastructure during the postwar era, the 1973 oil
shock provided the city with a big boost. As the price of oil rose throughout
the decade, so did the city's fortunes. Increased oil exploration and drilling
in response to the rising price of oil was also good for the city's economy.
Likewise, services related to petrochemicals were in demand during the 1970s.
In the first half of the decade, the city's population grew by over 19 percent.
By 1976, the Houston metropolitan area had a population topping two million. Befitting Houston's sprawling development, the vast majority of this
growth did not take place in the city's center, but in suburbs like Conroe and
Missouri City. In some ways, Houston's petroleum and debt-fueled boom
in the 1970s was indicative of a changing city. Passenger rail service out of
Union Station downtown near Second Ward ended in the middle of 1974. By
the mid-1970s, oil and gas unambiguously anchored the city's economy, with
petrochemical refining being a major source of employment—over eighty-
five hundred jobs by the middle of the decade. Other industries connected
to petroleum, such as oil field equipment manufacturing, added to the region's prosperity. Even beyond the manufacturing jobs in the city, Houston
also had a thriving managerial class in the 1970s.[31]

Though the 8F Crowd's zenith was the 1940s and 1950s, and though key
members of this group had died in the intervening years, Houston in the
1970s was still a product of their era. A 1976 article from *Texas Monthly*, a
faithful chronicler of the Lone Star State, even opened with a scene of George
Brown walking over to the Lamar Hotel every afternoon to take a nap in 8F,
which, according to his wishes, had been left untouched even as the rest of
the hotel had received a makeover. Opening in this way, the article's author,
Harry Hurt III, signaled a changing of the guard and the passing of an era,
casting a nostalgic eye to 8F's heyday, when the now-napping Brown and the
other members of the group "called the shots on most major business and

political developments in Texas." Times, though, had changed. As Hurt put it, "The government, economy, and population of Texas have grown too large and become too diverse to be controlled by a hotel-room clique." Rather, Texas was now a "modern, urban state." Despite traffic, air pollution, and flooding problems that accompanied the city's growth, all in all, life was good for many Houstonians.[32]

If the 1970s was a period when Americans experienced the first stirrings of economic globalization, *Texas Monthly*'s survey of power in the state also reflected this subtle shift. Significantly, Hurt noted that the state's largest company, Shell, was part of an international conglomerate, Royal Dutch/Shell, that had "primary concerns" that were "national and international."[33] Despite persistent economic pessimism throughout much of the country, the area's unemployment rate was consistently a few points lower than the national average in the second half of the 1970s.[34] With Houston's fortunes rising, it was of little wonder that in the mid-1970s, an ambitious young man might find himself in Houston after college. In fact, it was exactly where Jeffrey Skilling wound up—working for First City National Bank—after graduating from Southern Methodist University in Dallas.

Though he graduated with a bachelor's degree in applied science, at SMU, Skilling had become fascinated with the business world. While Skilling did not like his engineering classes and did not distinguish himself academically, he also took some business classes and was "fascinated" and soon earned the nickname "AB"—"all business."[35] Later, he would recall favorably comparing the warm weather in Dallas to the chilly Midwest where he grew up. Indeed, Texas was a special place for Jeff Skilling. In other ways, though, Skilling's college career was emblematic of a growing trend in the Sunbelt. Although university students had come to regard corporations as part of a "sick society" in the unrest of the 1960s, at the start of the 1970s, organizations such as the Foundation for Economic Education sought to rehabilitate business's reputation among college students and met with a measure of success. At Sunbelt schools, like SMU, majoring in business became increasingly popular in the 1970s. The Dallas college was even among the schools that had put together courses on entrepreneurship during the decade. Taking the business classes that caught his interest much more than those in his own major, Skilling was one of a new generation about to enter the white-collar workforce who regarded the world of business as something that could be studied and learned as a set of skills apart from what any one business itself was actually doing. Nor were these courses politically neutral. Indeed, many of the classes on entrepreneurship and business were taught from the perspective of free enterprise. It was also through this new business curriculum that the idea of "entrepreneurship" was fashioned as a noble and brave course to chart. Indeed, SMU was one of many schools that emphasized the nobility of the entrepreneur.[36]

Skilling didn't stop with a few classes at the undergraduate level but soon applied to graduate business school. Though he kept the University of Houston open as a possibility, he also applied to Harvard Business School and was accepted. Texas had long agreed with Skilling, but he also "loved" Harvard Business School. Later, he described his time as an MBA student as "probably some of the best years of my life." It was at Harvard where Skilling became more fully enmeshed in business *as a discipline*. Skilling would happily recall his education as filled with learning "all sorts of new things, exciting things, about business." Much like the college courses in business that he took in Dallas, his time at Harvard further helped professionalize Skilling as a businessman—a process that was completed when he took a job at the consulting firm McKinsey and Company and returned to Houston in 1979. Skilling's education and early career were expressions of a changing political and business environment.[37]

Since the start of the postwar era, conservative intellectuals and businessmen had been laying the groundwork for promoting the "free enterprise" system. These men were hostile to unions and regulators alike but knew that their ideas were well outside the mainstream of economic thinking. However, over the course of the American era, this network of economists, writers, and businessmen developed the idea of the "market" as an all-encompassing concept that could be contrasted with the regulatory impulse that dominated postwar industrial policy. While policy makers had been in many ways unsympathetic to their attack on a regulated economy—Nixon had, after all, declared himself to be a Keynesian when it came to the economy—in the tumult of the 1970s, their arguments began to pick up steam. The Keynesian stumble opened up a space for new and radically different economic ideas. An intellectual tradition that had been building at the margins of philosophical debate and commonsense politics now moved to the center of economic thought. Along with these shifts in large-scale economic thinking, the idea of what a corporation should be was changing as well. When, in 1970, the conservative economist Milton Friedman wrote in the *New York Times* that corporate executives should be focused solely on making "as much money as possible while conforming to the basic rules of the society," because a manager was, in the end, a mere employee of the stockholders, it both signaled a break with the logic of the regulatory era, as well as hinted at an increasingly *financialized* idea of a corporation.[38] Indeed, thinking about a corporation in financial terms had been one development to grow out of the era of conglomeration. Managers began to regard the different companies that conglomerates owned as something closer to a stock portfolio instead of parts of a unified corporation. This shift in perspective gave rise to a number of financial techniques that corporations would undertake to produce profits. Provocative statements such as the ones Friedman made in the pages of newspapers, as well as arcane financial techniques in the boardrooms of conglomerates, were early signs of a structural transformation taking place in the U.S. economy. This reorientation toward the market inside corporate boardrooms had a parallel in policy circles.[39]

In the second half of the decade, when Jimmy Carter took office (and Skilling relocated to a booming Houston), deregulation moved to the political center. The postwar regulatory era now came under pressure from both the political right and the political left. It was Ted Kennedy, for instance, who led the effort to force price competition for travelers by deregulating the airline industry. Even some liberals outside of government, like the consumer advocate Ralph Nader, fought for regulatory repeal. In an era when the fresh memory of Watergate ushered in a wave of suspicion toward the government, Nader was just one of several critics who saw regulatory bodies as having long since been captured by the industries they were supposed to regulate. Other serious critics of regulation, such as the economist Alfred Kahn, had the president's ear. By the end of the 1970s, ideas that had once been seen as definitively conservative were now accepted as mainstream and common sense.[40]

Significantly, as the production and consumption imbalance in the industry became apparent, natural gas would be one of the focal points of deregulation during the Carter years. During the winter of 1976 and early 1977, a shortage in gas for power generation and heating was so severe in the northeast that schools and industrial plants shut down. A state of emergency was even declared in New York. The gas shortage was the reason that Carter appeared before the country in early 1977 wearing a sweater in one of his first public addresses as president. It would not be the only time the president would have to talk about energy with the country. On an evening that April, a grave-looking president sternly told Americans in a televised address from the Oval Office that it was time for an "unpleasant" conversation about energy. Carter declared the "moral equivalent of war" and laid out his National Energy Program. As part of this broad strategy, Carter's office released a more detailed plan two days later that called for natural gas price deregulation as one of several measures. The next year, in 1978, the president signed the Natural Gas Policy Act into law, inaugurating a process of deregulation spanning over a decade. Not only did the act reconfigure and expand the Federal Power Commission and rechristen it as the Federal Energy Regulatory Commission (FERC); the law also created a number of different price categories for gas based on a number of factors, such as how new or old the gas was. Despite such actions, problems with the nation's energy supply continued to frustrate Carter's tenure.[41]

The nation was hit with a second oil shock when the new Islamic revolutionary government in Iran suspended exports to the United States in the last few days of 1978.[42] The long gas lines were back. The 1979 shock, which Jimmy Carter believed had plunged the nation into a spiritual crisis, only added to Houston's good fortune.[43] There would be very little malaise in Houston. On the contrary, some worried about the consequences of too much optimism in Texas. As a report by the Bureau of Business Research at the University of Texas put it: "As energy becomes more scarce, the question again arises whether or not a booming Houston economy can continue its growth if it is so highly dependent upon oil and natural gas."[44]

The Creation of Enron

It was in the midst of such euphoria that Ken Lay returned to Houston to serve as the president and chief operating officer at Transco Energy Company, which operated natural gas pipelines, in 1981. His years away from Texas had provided Lay with a number of invaluable experiences. At the start of the 1970s, he was stationed at the Pentagon, working for the assistant secretary for financial management. Lay planned on returning to Houston after leaving the navy, but his old professor Walker was now a part of the Federal Power Commission and wanted his prize student working for him. Lay wound up staying "about a year and a half" before being "persuaded to go over to the Department of Interior and become deputy undersecretary of interior for energy."[45] Despite his misgivings, the Interior Department was a good place to spend time for someone, like Lay, who was a budding expert in the energy business. In the years before the creation of the Department of Energy much of the country's energy policy came from the Interior Department, and in a sign of a more confident conservative movement, some in D.C. were beginning to advocate for petroleum deregulation. After Enron's collapse, a number of writers would point to Lay's time in Washington as a formative period that allowed him to hone his political talents and stoke his ambitions. Still, Lay returned to the private sector in 1974, taking a job with Florida Gas Company as vice president of corporate development. He was well suited for the career change. Like other Sunbelt businessmen in the 1970s, Lay was committed to both his Christian faith and the principles of free enterprise. At Florida Gas Company, Lay thrived. In short order, he became president of the company's pipeline unit, Florida Gas Transmission Company, which transported gas throughout the state. It was here that Lay spent the rest of the 1970s.[46]

Lay did not remain in Florida for long. In 1984, sensing that he could not assume the leadership role he wanted because his boss did not intend to retire, Lay moved to Houston Natural Gas, taking on the roles of the company's chairman and chief executive officer. He returned to Texas seasoned by adulthood—already balding and remarried to Linda, his former secretary, after his first marriage ended in divorce. Though he was now in charge of a large company, his first year on the job was a difficult one. Early that year, Coastal Corporation, a natural gas company headed by Oscar Wyatt, Houston's highest-paid business executive, launched a hostile takeover attempt of Houston Natural Gas. Lay steered the company away from that danger, but the experience was "painful"—and a harbinger of things to come.[47]

Wyatt's takeover attempt was emblematic of the period. In the 1980s, the shift toward finance that had begun in the 1970s took off with a greater force. The emphasis on shareholder value and the market had evolved into a frenetic merger movement in which even the largest publicly traded companies were suddenly vulnerable to unwanted takeovers. Led by raiders like Michael Milken, investors and financial figures went hunting for companies that seemed weak and bloated, but full of unlocked potential. Wall Street in the 1980s made for good storytelling, and the rise of unruly finance reinvigorated American business journalism. Not only did business magazines such as *Fortune* and *Businessweek* see their circulation numbers rise, but book-length business narratives detailing the excesses of the Wall Street era, complete with their generic conventions, began to emerge. Apart from the outrageous stories the era produced, though, they marked a profound economic transformation. Wall Street concerns for shareholder value were increasingly setting the

terms of business in the United States. Even companies that faced no imminent takeover threat took preemptive steps to appease shareholders.[48]

Though financial services had clearly become the most important sector of the economy, the energy industry was not immune to the changes
being ushered in from places like New York. At times, the mix between a frenetic banking sector and the energy business could prove to be combustible.
In 1984, for instance, Continental Illinois became the country's largest-ever
bank bailout after regulators worried about a wider fallout if the investment
bank went under. Continental Illinois had reached the brink of bankruptcy
in large part because it had done too much business with an Oklahoma
bank that had developed extremely risky practices lending to companies
involved in oil and gas exploration. Continental Illinois ultimately survived,
and later in the decade, a young man named Andrew Fastow went to work
there as an investment banker. Even apart from the mergers and acquisitions
activity being conducted on Wall Street, gas pipelines underwent a massive
reorganization as FERC continued its long process of regulatory restructuring.[49]

Though both the supply and price of new gas increased after the Natural
Gas Policy Act, when the price of oil dropped in the early 1980s, gas ceased
to be an attractive alternative fuel source. While the average price of gas at the
wellhead rose from eighty-four cents per thousand cubic feet to $2.59 be-
tween 1978 and 1983, the price of U.S. crude oil dropped from $31.77 to $26.19
per barrel between 1981 and 1983. Aside from shifting economic conditions,
take-or-pay contracts, which obligated pipelines to pay gas producers for a
minimum amount of gas (over 70 percent), were a growing problem. Pipeline companies were caught in a bind. Once FERC issued order 380 in the
spring of 1984, which allowed both local distribution companies and industrial facilities and producers to buy and sell gas directly to one another, "spot
markets," complete with brokers connecting buyers and sellers, emerged.
The three-tiered structure established during the New Deal was breaking
down. Another FERC order, 436, pushed the transition even further by
creating a huge incentive for pipeline companies to operate as carriers of gas
that had already been sold on the spot market, instead of buying and resell-
ing gas. Within a few years, carrying gas, as opposed to buying and selling it,
became the primary function of gas pipelines. Along with all the regulatory
change, the nature of pipeline corporate organization began to morph.
Throughout the 1980s, pipeline companies began combining with one another,
creating far more substantial systems than had previously existed.[50]

Enron emerged in this moment of reorganization and shift away from regulation. Under Ken Lay's leadership, and perhaps informed by Wyatt's takeover attempt, Houston Natural Gas began to return to its original business. So began a period of selling businesses that weren't related to energy while also buying more gas pipelines, including the old pipeline division of Florida Gas that Lay had once run, and the Transwestern pipeline, which supplied gas to California, from Texaco Eastern. However, the most dramatic change for Houston Natural Gas came from an outside offer.[51]

The Omaha-based InterNorth approached Lay and Houston Natural Gas (HGN) in 1985 about combining the two companies. Even though Lay had expanded Houston Natural Gas's pipeline capacity, the Nebraskan company boasted a far more expansive network. Buried underneath the continent, the ethereal fuel moved through steel pipes snaking out every which way. As Lay remembered it, InterNorth's pipelines started in East Texas and ran north "through Kansas" to serve the "big markets in the upper mid-west like Minneapolis." InterNorth was also the operator and an owner of the Northern Border Pipeline, which connected Canada and the lower forty-eight states. The combination would complement and extend HNG's reorganization. Indeed, when the merger took place, the result was dramatic.[52]

The new company, HNG/InterNorth, now boasted a pipeline network that ran vertically up and down the continent "from the Mexican border all the way to Canada" as well as from coast to coast.[53] This impressive geographic scope helped to create a powerful new force in the natural gas industry. Now the country's most extensive natural gas transmission system, the network was moving about 20 percent of the U.S. natural gas supply. Both companies also had other energy operations, including production and exploration. Even though the combined company shed a number of assets, the new firm was a substantial, vertically integrated energy enterprise. Indeed, the merger created a new company, one that required a new corporate identity, and HNG/InterNorth would soon trade its inelegant and unwieldy title for a pithier one, and on April 10, 1986, a press release went out over the news wires announcing that HNG/InterNorth was changing its name to Enron.[54]

Despite the impressive pipeline system, the company was in such a weak position after the merger that before long it was facing an existential threat from another hostile takeover attempt. This time, the attempt was led by Irwin Jacobs, who had earned the moniker "Irv the Liquidator" for his early takeovers and subsequent liquidation of those companies.[55] In 1986, Jacobs had managed to get hold of an 11 percent stake in the company. Fearing the takeover, the company bought the shares that Jacobs held back from him at a premium. While Irv the Liquidator walked away from the company making a tidy profit, Enron was cited in the business press for being a victim of "greenmailing."[56] In the context of Wall Street in the 1980s, Jacobs wasn't necessarily going to look like a villain. Drawing on the logic of shareholder value, corporate raiders like Jacobs justified their actions by arguing that they were strengthening the nation's business system. Indeed, T. Boone Pickens (a Texan who *Texas Monthly* would soon proclaim to be infinitely more powerful than Ken Lay) even put out a press release for the express purpose of declaring Enron's management team a glaring example of corporate weakness. Pickens, a notorious corporate raider much like Jacobs, was using Enron as an example of how inefficient corporations had become. So egregious was the Enron case, Pickens declared, that he predicted the episode would be "remembered as 'Black Monday'" by Enron's shareholders.[57] He was wrong, of course; there were far worse days for the company's shareholders ahead. Still, Lay's response to the episode revealed both the calm, stately demeanor that anchored his public image and nodded toward the direction that the business community was moving in. Speaking at a meeting that was organized by Arthur Andersen a year after the run-in with Jacobs, Lay proclaimed that corporate raiders like Pickens and Jacobs had helped companies "rethink" strategy, and helped them refocus on core businesses. However, the financial shenanigans of the 1980s were also causing problems inside the company.[58]

In an office north of Manhattan called Enron Oil, two commodities traders had hidden trading losses from speculating on the price of oil and embezzled money from the firm. An executive based in Houston, Mike Muckleroy, worked quickly to help the company survive the potential disaster.[59] Writers would later pluck the episode from the maelstrom of corporate transformation in the 1980s to foreshadow the culture of deceit that Lay sanctioned at Enron after Jeff Skilling had fundamentally changed the company, and to mark the beginning of the rise of Rich Kinder, who would soon become the company's president and chief operating officer. Most authors dedicated an entire chapter to the incident. Bethany McLean and Peter Elkind's account also figured prominently in the 2005 movie *Enron: The Smartest Guys in the Room*. At the time, however, the *New York Times* simply reported that the company's leadership was shuttering Enron Oil "after learning that the unit had lost $85 million because of unauthorized trading in the petroleum futures markets."[60] The event passed with little notice. Indeed, the news arrived only a few days after the October 19, 1987, stock market crash, which sent stock markets reeling and raised the specter of a broader economic downturn. With calamity averted, Enron once again resumed its process of charting a new way forward in a newly deregulated gas market. It was in the midst of such upheaval in the world of finance that Enron had moved its headquarters to Houston in 1986.[61]

As Skilling remembered, McKinsey's analysis of the natural gas industry convinced him major changes were coming. Lingering issues, such as take-or-pay clauses, which required gas pipelines to buy (regardless of whether or not gas was delivered) a set amount of gas from producers, had become a huge liability for pipeline companies now that producers and users could buy and sell gas directly, without a sale to a pipeline. It was important, the consultants argued, that their client Enron relocate to Houston—indisputably the center of the energy business. From this location, the company could set about the long and difficult task of renegotiating their natural gas contracts. By the time Enron managers arrived in the city, though, the good economy Houstonians had enjoyed throughout the 1970s seemed to be nothing more than the memory of an era that had long passed.[62]

While at first Houston seemed to weather a deep, nationwide recession in the early 1980s without too much of a problem, when OPEC reduced the price of oil, the city was in trouble. Though the price of oil rose to $31.77 in 1981, nearly ten times what it had been in 1971, the following year the price began to fall precipitously, leading to a decline in petrochemical manufacturing and layoffs in the energy industry.[63] The collapse in the price of oil revealed how tightly the city's fate was tied to that specific commodity. The long boom fueled by oil came to a sudden stop as parts of Houston began to resemble a Depression-era city. Along the San Jacinto River, a tent community where over two hundred people could be found "cook[ing] on campfires and collect[ing] aluminum cans for a living" was becoming known as "Tramp City U.S.A."[64] The shantytown was full of unemployed workers who had left the north, only to find that the recession had finally arrived in Houston. Indeed, there was little sympathy for the new arrivals in a city that was beginning to feel its own unemployment numbers move up. As the energy industry struggled, it pulled much of Houston's economy down with it. By January 1986, the city was experiencing record foreclosures, with some fearing that the rate would only increase throughout what by all accounts was shaping up to be a very bad year. Later that year, the city's unemployment moved past 10 percent. Signs of hard times were everywhere: a steep decline in church collections because congregations increasingly included the unemployed offered further revelation of how badly the area was hurting and how deeply connected to oil the city had become.[65]

The continued drop in the price of oil—to less than twelve dollars a barrel at the end of 1986—did not offer any hint of relief. Throughout the 1970s, construction had continued to grow, and Houstonians had lent and borrowed all on the assumption that the price of oil would eventually reach fifty dollars a barrel. The effects of such sudden and dramatic economic change were devastating. The very foundations of the economy that Jesse H. Jones had laid the groundwork for while he headed the RFC in the 1930s seemed to be disappearing. In 1986, the *Houston Chronicle* worried that "60 percent of the machinist jobs that existed along the Gulf Coast in 1982 have disappeared."[66] By then Houston's economic collapse was worse than any downturn since World War II—anywhere in the country.[67]

Other factors besides the oil bust were hurting the city's economy, too. In 1981, close to the high-water mark for oil prices, the state loosened restrictions on thrift banks, encouraging increased lending. However, by 1988, when Houston was in the doldrums, the state led the nation in savings and loan failures as that industry tumbled into crisis. Indeed, by 1987, thrift failures in other parts of Texas were being felt in Houston. Despite the high level of abstraction of global oil prices and banking failures, Houstonians viscerally felt the downturn.[68]

Unpleasant symbols of the economic devastation peppered the city. By the mid-1980s the vacant office space in Houston topped 25 percent, up from about 10 percent in 1981. People began to worry about an office space "glut" that was preventing new construction and rents from rising.[69] "They used to call them shotgun buildings," Jeff Skilling vividly remembered years after the hard times. "You could shoot a shotgun through the office building and you wouldn't hit anybody because there was no one in them anymore."[70] Across the city, construction stopped.

The economic depression did not apply just to eerily vacant office space, but also to the heavy, industrial work that flourished in Houston because the petrochemical business demanded it. As Skilling again recalled during his trial: "They were stacking rigs, big drilling rigs. If you remember, you went out I-10 west of town, there were literally hundreds of acres that had, in some cases, brand new drilling rigs just sitting there rusting in the sun."[71] As they had in the past, the city's business elites turned toward boosterism, though campaigns like "Houston Proud" had a limited effect. One of the few bright spots in Houston was the prospect of businesses relocating there in search of cheap offices, factories, and warehouses, though the Houston Economic Development Council's advertising campaign aimed at convincing out-of-state companies to relocate to Houston failed to convince many.[72]

Still, Enron had made the move. Even though some operations were being left in Omaha (and would remain there until the company collapsed), and though it meant that a mere seventy-five people would initially be making the move from Nebraska just as ninety employees were taking an early retirement as part of a general downsizing, the company was sure to be a visible presence in Houston.[73] The firm had become one of the area's largest employers simply by relocating from Omaha, though at the time of the announcement, the company was in the process of cutting its workforce from eleven thousand people to fewer than ten thousand.[74] Still, the firm moved into a prominent skyscraper in Houston's downtown that had been built in 1983, rechristening it the Enron Building. The building had gone up the same year as Transco Tower, a skyscraper that came to dominate the Houston skyline. Still, even if another natural gas company occupied the city's most impressive building, Enron's managers left no doubt as to their ambitions. A little ahead of the official company announcement, Lay had even purchased a home that had once belonged to his predecessor at Houston Natural Gas in the wealthy River Oaks section of town.[75] Over six hundred workers from Omaha were slated to arrive in Houston by the end of 1986, and though the *Houston Chronicle* hopefully proclaimed that "Houston is regaining the headquarters of one of its largest corporate citizens," Enron was returning to a transformed city.[76]

In fact, several other energy companies were moving offices to Houston because the drop in oil prices was forcing them to close smaller offices around the country. Looking for a bright spot, the *Houston Chronicle* reported that the moves were helping to cement the city's long-standing identity as an "energy capital." Houston, it seemed, could not avoid its close connection with energy that had begun at Spindletop, but this was not old energy work suddenly making a comeback. These new jobs were white-collar administrative positions, rather than manufacturing work. In fact, as the article noted, many of the manufacturing jobs connected to energy, such as working with oilfield equipment, that had been lost in the downturn were likely gone for good. Houston would remain tied to energy, but the nature of the connection was changing. Even apart from the economic woe, Houston in the 1980s was a city in flux.[77]

By the mid-1980s, *Texas Monthly*'s assessment of Houston's sway in the state had diminished considerably. It wasn't just that most of the members of Suite 8F Crowd had died—the nature of power had changed. Personal political ties, apparently, now mattered less than ideas. A *Texas Monthly* article was blunt: "the big loser" was "Houston," while Dallas had emerged "the big winner." Indeed, the two most powerful Texans according to the magazine, Ross Perot and T. Boone Pickens, were based well outside of Houston. The city's businessmen seemed to have lost their swagger.[78]

Lay did not even appear on the list of the most powerful Texans but was singled out as an example of how power was shifting away from Houston. Paul Burka, the article's author, wrote that in the 1970s, the chairman of Houston Natural Gas was "a top contender for the Most Powerful List" in part because he "spent an average of 20 to 30 percent of his week on political, cultural, and civic affairs." Lay, on the other hand, seemed shier than most Texas businessmen about dabbling in the political world. Lay did "some Republican fundraising," but that apparently was "the extent of his involvement in politics." So meekly did Lay seem to exercise his power that Burka did not bother including him on the list of Texans to watch out for in the next decade. Even if Lay sought power more aggressively, it would not mean the return of 8F-style politics. Burka left no doubt that those days were gone. A small group of powerbrokers could no longer run Houston or Texas as it pleased. The world had changed, and Texas could not "cut itself off from the world anymore." In time, of course, Burka's assessment of Lay would seem shortsighted. Lay, more than any other corporate executive, would lead the way in forging a new position for Houston in the world. Yet when Burka published his assessment of Texan power in 1987, Houston's future remained uncertain.[79] If Houston's fortunes had declined since the 8F Crowd's reign, the city's landscape had also undergone a dramatic transformation. Houston had become one of the country's most prominent examples of urban sprawl, a phenomenon that had grown so out of control that it was deforming the shapes of cities as urban buildup began to appear at the suburban periphery of cities. Writing in 1988, the journalist Joel Garreau coined the term "edge cities" to describe how the distinction between urban and suburban space became meaningless as cities began to develop "multiple urban cores"—a change that had implications for the quality of life in these new landscapes.[80] Indeed, by the end of the 1980s most working Houstonians faced commutes longer than a half hour.[81] Though Garreau was writing about a national trend, Houston still held a special place in his thinking. "I began to see high-rise buildings erupt near my home in outlying Virginia far from the old downtown of the District of Columbia," he wrote before adding, "I knew instantly what I was looking at. This basically was Houston."[82] While the writer did confess an admiration for parts of the Texas city, such as the Galleria complex of malls, offices, and apartments, Garreau was also quite certain that Houston was "never going to be confused with the Left Bank of Paris."[83]

However, if Houston did not seem sophisticated to Garreau, it was becoming more ethnically diverse. The collapse in the housing market had made it economically feasible for a number of working-class immigrant communities to grow there. Over the course of the 1980s, people had arrived from almost every part of the world. By 1990, over 400,000 of Harris County's 2.8 million residents were foreign born. Inside Houston-area homes, families were speaking languages as various as Spanish, French, German, Chinese, and Vietnamese.[84]

Likewise, even though the city recovered from the oil bust by 1990, what emerged was a different economy. While oil-related manufacturing jobs were disappearing, the city was well on its way to becoming a "knowledge-based economy."[85] Though the area had boasted a large number of office jobs for decades, that number had grown over the course of the 1980s, while manufacturing jobs declined (Table 1). If these changes were unsettling for some, they paralleled changes taking place at Enron.

Indeed, the company itself was moving into areas that could accurately be described as knowledge work and would, in time, seek out employees suited for this type of work. Additionally, the memory of a city and its business district in decline would inform many of Enron's revitalization efforts in the 1990s. Jeff Skilling, who would soon join Enron, had introduced a radical new approach to the natural gas business at the company. In Skilling's analysis, the merger of the two gas companies in 1985 had created a unique competitive advantage in this uncertain new landscape. With its massive pipeline network, Enron could aggregate, combine, split, and move gas as needed all throughout the pipelines sprawling out into the continent. Enron's pipeline system, Skilling determined, had much more *flexibility* in moving the gas around as demand dictated.[86] Calling his idea the "Gas Bank," Skilling contended that Enron could profit from the spot market in gas prices by using a combination of the pipeline network's flexibility and offering the sorts of derivatives deals that had been pioneered in the financial services

Table 1. Changing employment in Houston

Occupations in Houston	Number of Employed: 1980 (Houston City)	Number of Employed: 1990 (Harris County)
Managerial and professional specialty occupations	310,138	397,591
Technical, sales, and administrative support	423,423	469,424
Service occupations	122,714	174,911
Precision production, craft, and repair occupations	180,435	157,027
Operators, fabricators, and laborers	184,449	169,578

Sources: 1980 and 1990 census.
Note: In the 1980 census, the occupational data was listed for Houston city, while the 1990 census organized the data by county.

industry after the collapse of Bretton Woods. In the few years since FERC had moved to deregulate the market for natural gas, thirty-day contracts were set during "bid week"—a frantic few days of matching buyers and sellers where mere pennies could mean the difference between securing or losing a contract to deliver gas.[87] By contrast, through using a variety of derivatives, the Gas Bank could offer buyers long-term supplies of gas with predictable pricing. The plan was audacious; Skilling was rethinking some of the gas industry's basic ways of conducting business, and it did not go over well. After the McKinsey team presented their idea, most of the energy executives in the room were unimpressed. As Skilling later remembered, the first executive to speak after his presentation declared Skilling's proposition of be "the dumbest idea I ever heard in my life."[88] The sentiment, it seemed, was more or less shared by most in the room.

Skilling's plan, however, was far from dead. Sharing an elevator in the company's office, Skilling recalled, Rich Kinder, then the company's president, "was chomping on his cigar, and he said as soon as so-and-so said they didn't like it," he "knew this was exactly the right thing to do."[89] Lay, too, had been impressed by the young consultant.[90] Even if most of the energy executives were cool to the idea, Skilling's plan had the approval of Enron's top two managers; so began a collaboration between the McKinsey team and Enron to put the Gas Bank into action. Crucially, what the Gas Bank meant in real terms was that Enron would now offer derivatives such as "forward agreements"—

contracts to deliver the commodity for a specific price in the future—and swaps—ongoing arrangements made up of more than one forward agreement—for the delivery of natural gas.[91] The group working on the Gas Bank, including people from both companies, began "coming up with specific contract structures" and "transportation agreements" to offer gas purchasers.[92] Though it worked initially, after Skilling and the McKinsey team left, the Gas Bank began to falter. If the approach was going to succeed in the long run, perhaps the firm needed Skilling and some like-minded people working on the Gas Bank full time. In short order, an offer to run the Gas Bank as an Enron manager—not as an outside consultant—found its way to Skilling.[93]

Still in his midthirties and about to become a father for the third time, Skilling had recently been named as a senior partner at McKinsey. Still, something about starting a completely new business inside Enron must have appealed to Skilling, because he took the offer. It was a far cry from being a senior partner with the country's most prestigious consulting firm; though he arrived to the newly established Enron Finance Corporation as its chairman and chief executive officer, Jeff Skilling was also the business unit's sole employee. Once ensconced at Enron, though, the executive set about building a team and culture that was distinct from the rest of the company.[94]

While the gas industry had conducted business according to an unchanged set of strict regulatory rules for decades, Skilling's management and economic sensibilities were vastly different from the ones that the older gas executives possessed. Among management consulting firms, Skilling's old employer, McKinsey, had been the first to emphasize corporate culture as a crucial ingredient in business success. Skilling had even joined McKinsey at the precise moment "corporate culture" became the consulting firm's calling card, and he must have been paying attention.[95] In fact, the final chapter of 1982's *In Search of Excellence*, "Simultaneous Loose-Tight Properties," introduced a management philosophy that Skilling adopted as his own at Enron. According to the book's authors and recent McKinsey alumni Tom Peters and Robert Waterman, successful companies were "on the one hand rigidly controlled" but also allowed and "(indeed, insist on) autonomy, entrepreneurship, and innovation from the rank and file." The "loose" side of this equation meant companies with "clubby, campus-like environments, flexible organizational structures (hiving off new divisions, temporary habit-breaking devices, regular reorganizations)" as well as "maximized autonomy for individuals" and "extensive experimentation." Ultimately, the authors had suggested, a successful business would buzz with "the excitement of trying things out in a slightly disorderly (loose) fashion." Significantly, the authors emphasized a "flexible" organizational structure. "The organization," the two consultants wrote, "thrives on internal competition. And it thrives on intense communication" and "on informality, on fluidity and flexibility." However, the "loose/tight" principle was not just a matter of organization.[96]

In addition to this new approach to internal structure, Peters and Waterman insisted that a company had to have the right "value systems" and "culture." The prescription that the former McKinsey men offered, it seemed, had made an impression on Skilling. Now in charge of an entire business unit, the former consultant would come to draw heavily on the "loose/tight" principle. The guidelines that Peters and Waterman outlined were essentially organizational parallels of the "flexible" options Skilling was finding in the company's pipeline network and that the derivatives traders at the heart of Enron Gas Services (Skilling's business unit) were managing. It was little wonder, then, that the emphasis on a dynamic corporate culture appealed to Skilling. From the perspective of Enron Gas Services employees, a cultural change was sorely needed.[97]

Though Skilling would have to wait a few years before he could exercise his influence over Enron's entire corporate structure, his early actions clearly signaled that Enron Gas Services was to have a culture apart from the rest of the firm, starting with the built environment. When the firm had relocated its headquarters to 1400 Smith Street in Houston's central business district, floor plan layouts were standardized and uniform throughout the skyscraper. To Skilling, though, the walls seemed too constrictive, especially for a business unit organized around "loose/tight" principles and creating flexible derivatives contracts for natural gas delivery. What Skilling wanted instead was an open floor, which he would later describe as a "bullpen." After knocking out all the walls on the floor, such a wide open space would encourage creative thinking. But, as he later recounted for a University of Virginia Darden Business School case study, "the building Gestapo didn't get it," telling him "you can't do that." Ultimately, the new executive did not wait for approval. He simply hired a contractor, and the walls came down. Now, even the office interiors reflected the cultural and strategic change Skilling sought to impose on the company.[98]

Though such actions may have seemed unusual to the other executives at Enron, Skilling was hardly alone in his management style but was also a part of a larger wave of business thinking that took hold at the end of the 1980s amid an unshakeable sense that the global economy had shifted in fundamental ways. Management advisors, including Tom Peters, adjusted their message accordingly. The looseness that had impressed Waterman and Peters in the 1982 book's final chapter had now become central to Peters's philosophy. At the outset of his follow up book to *In Search of Excellence,* Peters declared that a revolution in management was imminent. Peters titled his 1987 book *Thriving on Chaos* and in the book's very first pages declared "the times" called for "flexibility and love of change." Echoing the "loose/ tight" sentiment, Peters saw instability in a positive light. "For the wise," he declared, "capitalizing on fleeting market anomalies will be the successful business's greatest accomplishment."[99]

Likewise, by the end of the 1980s, Peters (and others) also had a lot to say about organizational structure. As Peters wrote in 1990, "top managers make lousy decisions and people fail to shine largely because burdensome structures and misaligned systems get in the way."[100] In the same article, Peters pointed to the example of Union Pacific Railroad, which had recently slashed its bureaucratic structure. "In 120 days," Peters marveled, "the massive operations bureaucracy was reduced to rubble. Eight layers of management between the Executive Vice President for Operations and the local Yardmaster were cut to three."[101] Nor was Peters alone in thinking that a nonhierarchical organization could unleash creativity and innovation. Writing in the *Harvard Business Review* that same year, Michael Hammer, who ran his own consulting firm, wrote that "the watch words of the new decade are innovation and speed, service and quality."[102] Companies had to "break away from the old rules" of organization and operations. Such a break, Hammer suggested, would mean "recognizing and rejecting" these older rules "and then finding imaginative new ways to accomplish work."[103] Such enthusiastic calls for a dramatic transformation to the American business system mirrored Skilling's emerging management style.

But these profound changes were still a few years away. Much as he had done when he first came to Houston Natural Gas before the merger, at the end of the 1980s, Lay was busy selling off assets that he considered nonessential. As the head of a company strategically peeling away divisions and assets, Lay was hardly alone. Deconglomeration and a return to basics was a reversal of the postwar trend of assembling massive business combines. Deconglomeration, often to please Wall Street desires and demands, had become so pervasive that Lay was not being hyperbolic when he proclaimed that such moves indicated a "new phase in American capitalism."[104] The financial sector was forcing changes in myriad ways across different parts of the economy. Lay's company would morph, too, responding to the changes that Wall Street was calling for. After the merger and greenmailing episode, Lay continued the approach that he had taken when he first came to Houston Natural Gas—shedding assets that were not helpful to the company's central business. Since the merger, Enron had sold nearly two billion dollars in assets the company felt it no longer needed or could afford. In truth, the move was at least in part a reflection of how circumstances were constraining Enron. If the merger made sense strategically, it had created an enormous amount of debt. Even a year later, Enron's long-term debt was over $3 billion.[105] In fact, the pressure to remove the debt would drive some major company decisions over the next couple of years. Still, Lay struck an upbeat note, proclaiming that the company was now focused on "the basic business, which we know how to run."[106] However, over the course of the next decade, Enron's managers would pioneer a new style of business that was more related to the world of Wall Street than it was to the "basics" of the natural gas industry.

In many ways, Enron was doing better by the end of the decade. Indeed, in 1989, the company had become the second-biggest business in the city and, thanks in part to the rising price of natural gas, posted a billion dollars in revenue (part of this had come from selling off Enron Oil and Gas).[107] Because Enron's managers wanted the option to expand, in 1991 the company took advantage of the depressed real estate market by purchasing another half of a city block across from its headquarters. Enron and Houston were inextricably bound to one another.[108] In a text-heavy advertisement the company ran for several years in the University of Houston's student yearbook, the firm declared that it was "perfectly positioned in the new world of energy—organized to capitalize fully on the new opportunities in a changing energy environment."[109] Despite the upbeat tone, however, the company had not made a full recovery from its darkest days, nor did it mean the company faced completely smooth sailing ahead.

Enron—despite Lay's determined effort at returning the company to its basic business—was a giant (and Lay himself was one of the highest-paid executives in the country). The centerpiece of the company, of course, was the vast pipeline network that sprawled out into the continental United States, even connecting it with Mexico and Canada. Enron needed a new identity—

both inside and out. Internally, Lay offered the first of many "visions" for the company: "To become the premier integrated natural-gas company in North America."[110] To be sure, this was an ambitious goal and would require a great effort. Natural gas was not the country's primary source of energy, and the company, despite its wide geographic reach, did not have any distinguishable corporate identity. By the end of the 1980s, Lay needed to find a way to promote both Enron and natural gas.

CHAPTER 2

Making Sense of the World After the Cold War

Though Kenneth Lay and Jeffrey Skilling had navigated Enron through the regulatory and financial turbulence of the 1980s, the decade's end did not mean a return to stability. The transition between decades was a period of rupture, from environmental catastrophe to the collapse of world powers, all of which had implications for companies like Enron. In contrast to the series of shocks that confronted Americans in the 1970s, this new phase of globalization had begun with a sense of both anxiousness and optimism. Though the 1990s opened with a global political crisis, a growing awareness of impending environmental catastrophe, and an economic recession, American politicians and business executives exuded confidence that such a challenge would undoubtedly be overcome without much sacrifice. Despite these lingering concerns, the malaise of the 1970s and a sense of limits had vanished. Both the priorities and optimism of the early 1990s characterized Enron's early experience with globalization.[1]

Over the first part of the decade, John Wing and Rebecca Mark, executives in the firm's international development unit, spearheaded massive power plant projects abroad. These gas-fired plants in Teesside, England, and Dabhol, India, were also emblematic of an optimistic and environmentally conscious ethic that in part characterized global economic development in the early 1990s. When the company touted its gas-fired plant in England as an ecologically sensitive project, for instance, it was a reaction to the unmistakable green streak in U.S. culture and politics during these years. However, the new decade was just as much an extension of the 1980s as it was a break from them. In particular, the financialization of the economy continued apace. Throughout these years, Jeff Skilling would continue to build and expand the practice of applying the innovations of the financial services industry to the energy business. In time, this novel approach to the natural gas market would come to define the whole company, but in the first half of the 1990s, Enron's strategy, structure, and corporate identity would shift and morph in response to the uncertain direction of economic change. In the span of a few years, Enron's leadership would arrive at a crossroads pointing both outward, to sustainable development abroad, and inward, to regulatory changes with roots in the government's response to environmental challenges.

Change during these years was almost never subtle. The impending collapse of the Soviet Union, which portended a major shift in global politics, was foreshadowed by globally broadcast images of throngs of Germans dismantling the Berlin Wall. Famously, the conservative political scientist Francis Fukuyama declared the "end of history"—or at least the end of struggles between two large political systems. With the fall of communism, many policy makers and economists concluded that the door was now open for a wave of global economic liberalization. As the Soviet bloc disaggregated and communist governments and their command economies fell apart, policy discussions in the West turned to how quickly and completely such nations could adopt capitalist, market economies. If OPEC's 1973 oil embargo had been an experience in international interdependence that caught American leaders off guard, now the United States seemed determined to shape and control this new global moment.[2]

It was in the middle of these changes that Ken Lay entered Houston's civic affairs. In 1990, Houston hosted the annual meeting of the World Economic Forum, which was normally held in Davos, Switzerland. Significantly, President George H. W. Bush described the forum as "the first economic summit conference of the 'post-postwar era.'"[3] The rapid liberalization and integration of world economies, along with environmental policy, was a top priority for attendees. The summit was also an important personal moment for Lay, who Bush asked to cochair the host city organizing committee. While just a few years earlier, a writer for *Texas Monthly* had scoffed at the idea that Lay might be a suitable heir to the 8F Crowd's mantle, the Enron executive now stepped onto a public stage at a pivotal moment in world history. The new world order was to be hashed out in downtown Houston, and Lay was tasked with Sunbelt boosterism on a global scale.

It was a tall order. The city had only recently recovered from the devastation wrought by the previous decade's oil glut. With a population that was now more international than it had been during the days of the 8F Crowd, and with an economy increasingly focused on energy-related services, Houston

Figure 1. President George H. W. Bush and Kenneth Lay greet World Economic Forum attendees at the Kirby Mansion in Houston. Photo courtesy of the George H. W. Bush Presidential Library and Museum.

had a unique opportunity to present itself during the World Economic Forum as a cosmopolitan, global city. The *Houston Chronicle* reported that community leaders such as Lay promised "to make Houston the world's friendliest and cleanest major city" ahead of the summit.[4] The host committee also "called on area residents to acquaint themselves with statistics on Houston's upward spiral and act as salesmen for the city."[5] Determined that Houston's Texan drawl would not be drowned out in an international cacophony, Lay did not pass up any opportunity to accentuate a local sense of place, even using a mansion that the oil tycoon John Henry Kirby had built in 1926 for the host committee's offices (Figure 1).[6] When the meeting began, the *Chronicle* reported that at the start of the forum, "the flood gates opened with a 'y'all come' invitation from co-chairman Ken Lay."[7] When not attending to their official duties, foreign dignitaries attended barbecues and games of horseshoe. However, the host committee's attempts to walk the line between down-home Texas hospitality and a more worldly identity came off as awkward at best—"cowboys who appreciate Cezanne," as one French journalist put it.[8]

Such dissonant notes, it seemed, were a constant during the summit. The mayor's use of her own gender as an example of the city's progressivism, for instance, was undercut by Ku Klux Klan members participating in antisummit demonstrations.[9] Transportation routes for visiting elites discreetly circumvented African American neighborhoods in Fourth Ward that had fallen into poverty.[10] Likewise, the city's homeless had been pushed out of downtown during the meeting.[11] One local restaurateur's remark that it would be "worth every penny" if the "only publicity we get is that Houston is no longer going down the toilet" was a far cry from the host committee's aspirations.[12] Still, the summit had given Lay a public role in the city's affairs, and a vision of what Houston could become—a unique and storied place that was also prepared for a new globally interconnected economy—had emerged in the process. If Houston's place in a new world order had not been cemented during the World Economic Forum, Lay was far more certain about how his company might respond to a renewed sense of global environmentalism in the United States.

When Lay gave a public address to a Houston audience later that year, he declared that Enron was "in the right business at the right time," explaining that natural gas would become "the fuel of the 1990s." "It's a clean source of energy," he told his audience, "contributing less than any other fossil fuel to the emissions which cause acid rain, the greenhouse effect or the destruction of the ozone layer in the atmosphere." Like others in the natural gas industry, Lay clearly regarded natural gas's environmental benefits as critical to Enron's fortunes. Indeed, to be "the First Natural Gas Major, the Most Innovative and Reliable Provider of Clean Energy Worldwide for a Better Environment" was now Enron's corporate vision. In pinning Enron's fortunes to the environment, Lay revealed a keen sensitivity to public and political sentiment.[13]

A sense of urgency over ecological peril had been building for years. The 1980s had been a bad decade for American environmentalists, who were both alarmed and galvanized by Ronald Reagan's attitudes toward their cause. During his presidency, environmental protections suffered under Reagan's broader assault on regulation. Not only was the president publicly opposed to protecting land from development, but members of his administration set about cutting budgets for regulatory agencies, and his appointees to head the Department of the Interior and the Environmental Protection Agency were hostile to the environmental movement. Still, evidence of environmental devastation grew throughout the decade. By the end of the 1980s, there was a broad scientific consensus around global warming. During the 1988 presidential campaign, the Republican candidate, Vice President George H. W. Bush, even declared he would become "the environmental president."[14]

The national mood demanded a response from large corporations, and in the late 1980s, Enron's leadership had worked hard to establish the company's ecological bona fides. The company's 1988 annual report, for instance, suggested that "renewed interest in clean air" would be good for the natural gas company.[15] The report's cover featured a gas power plant in the background with a field of flowers in the foreground. The image embodied a "pastoral ideal" that sought to harmonize the photograph's two elements—the industrial power plant and the fields.[16] Similarly, the 1989 report's cover proclaimed that natural gas was the "cleanest burning and most economical of all fossil fuels" and that it held "the promise for a cleaner world."[17] Such language reflected a broader sense in the U.S. gas industry that environmental issues would be good for business. In adopting a "green" posture in its marketing literature, the company was following industry trends. In fact, by the late 1980s, many American businesses were crafting public relations strategies built around the environment. But these were quiet changes. By contrast, and akin to how the fall of the Berlin Wall made plain a political transformation that was otherwise hard to see, the 1980s closed with a major ecological catastrophe.[18]

On March 24, 1989, an Exxon oil tanker named the *Valdez* crashed ashore in Alaska. Within the first day, over thirty-eight thousand tons of oil spilled out from the ship. The spectacular event pushed environmental concerns to the forefront early in George H. W. Bush's presidency. An American politician ignored the environment at his or her own peril. By summer, the president called for updating the Clean Air Act.[19] The following year, both media attention and public events that marked the twentieth anniversary of Earth Day in 1990 highlighted the emerging consensus around ecological stewardship. "A quiet revolution is greening the country," *Time* magazine hopefully proclaimed in its Earth Day edition.[20] This was not mere journalistic hyperbole. During these years, a majority of Americans came to self-identify as "environmentalists."[21]

This American "greening"—which included concerns about global warming and acid rain—was influencing how the public felt about energy sources. Though they remained suspicious of petroleum companies, Americans were becoming increasingly interested in solar energy, seeing it as a viable alternative to fossil fuel. A solid majority, around 70 percent, felt that the government was not doing enough to protect the planet and address ecological concerns, and most Americans were in favor of pollution controls on power plants, even if that meant the cost of energy might go up. If the experience of the 1970s was any indication, the stage was set for another round of regulatory action. Bush administration officials were attuned to the political pressure to take action on the environment, and the president seemed well positioned to get something done. Starting with his tenure as ambassador to the United Nations, Bush had cultivated a friendly working relationship with environmentalists. When he assumed the presidency in 1989, Bush deliberately sought a contrast to Reagan's antagonism toward environmental groups. Organizations used to a hostile executive branch were pleasantly surprised when members of the Bush White House began reaching out to them in the earliest days of his administration. During meetings over the details of the Clean Air Act, environmental groups found the president to be a sympathetic listener who was unafraid to challenge the claims of some of the industry representatives in the room. The president did indeed seem determined to achieve meaningful environmental legislation.[22]

However, when Bush signed the Clean Air Act into law that November, the document reflected a vastly different sort of environmentalism than had preceded it. While the environmental movement had long relied on state intervention, the 1990 Clean Air Act reflected the same market orientation that was on the agenda at the World Economic Forum in Houston, as well as Skilling's solution to natural gas deregulation. The 1990 law was a crucial moment in environmental policy, establishing a "cap and trade" scheme for harmful emissions. Title IV of the Clean Air Act, known as the Acid Rain Program, set a nationwide limit on how much sulfur dioxide and nitrogen oxide power plants could pump into the air but permitted these companies to trade pollution allowances.[23] Rather than regulatory oversight, market solutions now moved to the center of U.S. environmental policy. This new emphasis on the market as the ideal platform for environmental stewardship was also a centerpiece in Bush's National Energy Strategy. What is more, the strategy highlighted natural gas as a clean and domestically abundant resource, presenting a potential opportunity for Lay's company. Much in the way the American Gas Association was similarly optimistic about natural gas's prospects as a market-oriented environmentalism began to take shape in the United States, Lay saw this green sensibility as a competitive advantage.[24]

Echoing the National Energy Strategy, Lay framed natural gas's environmental friendliness in terms that were in no ways threatening to his overall probusiness and market-oriented philosophy. As one of several executives advising the Republican Party's platform committee ahead of the 1992 presidential election, Lay touted the resource's abundance, the jobs that it would likely produce, and deliverance from future oil shocks. More than anything, though, he emphasized the material's environmental benefits. Significantly, Lay was also sure to connect gas's promise to deregulation. Oversight of natural gas pipelines, he insisted, "stifles and discourages competitive innovation that would provide better service to customers and encourage economic growth."[25] A regulatory agency, Lay suggested, best served the public as a "watchdog for abuse" instead of a "centralized planning agency for the industry."[26] The message found a receptive audience in the GOP. Energy and the environment were not issues Republicans were shying away from. Despite its origins in 1978, conservative politicians singled out natural gas deregulation to draw a contrast between the Carter years as a period of regulatory overreach and the Reagan and Bush presidencies. A Democratic return to the White House, the logic went, would also mean a return to onerous regulation. Drawing a link between a changing international political landscape and the environment, Missouri's Governor John Ashcroft declared that environmental protections could flow only from a strong economy. This was doubly important, he reasoned, because the United States could be an example of environmental responsibility for the rest of the world. Such comments were representative of a growing connection between the new global economy and a widespread environmentalism.[27]

Alongside the implications for the company's domestic operations, environmental issues were also shaping a nascent sense of globalization. Supposedly domestic political action ultimately pointed toward international trade and business. Even the Clean Air Act had implications that transcended U.S. borders. New regulations, for example, pushed some firms to buy equipment from abroad. In more ways than one, environmental concerns and the emerging sense of globalization were linked to one another. For his part, Lay moved beyond the party's nod toward environmental stewardship.[28]

Though some prominent Republicans and petroleum executives were opposed to U.S. participation in an upcoming United Nations Earth Summit in Rio de Janeiro, Lay urged the president to attend the meeting, which was scheduled for June 1992.[29] Despite the attention afforded the environment in the National Energy Strategy, in practice, Bush was much more reluctant to address global warming.[30] Though the president had struck a balance among competing interests with the Clean Air Act, the politics of going to Rio were far more contentious. In 1992, the White House received letters urging Bush to either attend or forgo the meeting. For some, at least, the Earth Summit would set the stage for what the post–Cold War world would look like. "At a time when socialist and communistic ideals are being repudiated around the world," the Oregon Farmers Bureau wrote him, the United States could not allow such freshly discredited ideas "to be revived under the guise of protecting the environment."[31] Bush himself echoed this sentiment in an op-ed where he claimed the "fouled waters" of Eastern Europe revealed that central planning was bad for the environment.[32] By contrast, "global economic growth" and "global environmental quality" were inherently connected to one another. "Healthy natural resources and healthy people," he wrote, were "essential for economies to prosper."[33] If Bush went to Rio, his message to the world would insist on "environmental protection through market-oriented economic development and free trade."[34] Framing his approach to both the meeting and environmentalism in terms of dramatic change, Bush wrote, "This past year we have seen absolutely historic events of enormous impact and great promise across the globe," including "the fall of Communism, the forward march of democracy, the staunch defense of freedom, and the blossoming of free market economies."[35] Now, the entire world stood at the edge of a "grand new order."[36] The president's hesitation with Rio was that it might result in "government policies" that would "distort the environmental benefits of economic growth."[37]

Possibly seeking to ease any apprehension Bush might have had about Rio, Lay assured him that the summit could produce a "public policy guide, not a policy mandate" for reducing greenhouse gas emissions.[38] Lay, however, had not internalized a green sensibility, confessing that he did not "believe the oceans will boil in a few years if we don't address greenhouse gas emissions," before adding, "but I also do not believe the U.S. will suffer from economic ruin if prudent steps are taken to reduce CO_2 emissions in order to protect the global environment."[39] If unshackled from regulation, he argued, the market and natural gas would produce a cleaner environment, cheaper energy, and jobs in the United States. Lay was proving himself to be a keen reader of a growing public mood. Indeed, even if some energy executives were opposed to U.S. participation, Enron's CEO wasn't the only American who had written to Bush in support of the Rio conference.[40] Much in the same way Lay sought to present Enron's interests as being in concert with American environmental awareness, increasingly, he also linked the firm's international projects and operations with environmental stewardship. Environmentalism was not just an American issue. Rather, as economic globalization became a visible process, the ecological risks that accompanied this commercial expansion became a more pressing concern around the world. Lay's letters to Bush in support of the conference probably did little to influence decision making in the White House. Foreign heads of state had committed to the conference, narrowing the range of options for the Bush administration. He may have hemmed and hawed in public, but in the end, the president went to Brazil.[41]

Though the concept had its roots in the early 1970s, by the start of the 1990s sustainable development was given a wider currency through meetings like the Rio Earth Summit. However, the phrase "sustainable development" proved to be elastic enough that by the time Bush went to Rio, it could accommodate even his vision of preserving the natural world through the free market. Still, U.S. participation was full of discord. Al Gore, a longtime environmentalist and Democratic senator from Tennessee who would soon join his party's presidential ticket, also made an appearance—much to the consternation of Bush officials. A leaked memo intended to embarrass the head of the Environmental Protection Agency further hinted at a lack of unity. Such an equivocal and uncertain approach to the summit was significant. The United States did not sign onto multiple treaties, and the major global warming treaty, in which participants agreed to carbon dioxide reductions, was nonbinding. Rio was not a high-water mark for international statesmanship.[42]

Yet even if the international agreements fell short of environmentalists' hopes, the preamble to one of the summit's major achievements, a document titled "Agenda 21," declared that "humanity" was standing at "a defining moment in history."[43] The significance of the Earth Summit, which put the environment at the center of the global economy, was not lost on Lay. If gatherings like the World Economic Forum in Houston announced a new phase of globalization at the end of the Cold War, the Rio Earth Summit hinted at the range of possible directions that globalization might take. Though otherwise deeply ensconced in Republican politics, Lay's enthusiasm for the Earth Summit indicated how he diverged from the party as well as other business executives. While President Bush faced criticism for his initial reluctance to attend the Brazil meeting, and what some regarded as "obstructionism" in Rio's wake, Enron's CEO wasted little time in rhetorically taking up the cause of the Earth Summit. Almost immediately, acknowledging environmental risk as a *global* issue found its way into his public talks. The timing was ideal for such a rhetorical gesture.[44]

Popular sentiment meant that energy companies like Enron could not simply dismiss environmentalists' concerns, but corporations did not face the same public relations challenges that they had in the past. Rather, the summit offered Lay an opportunity to cast corporations as the most trustworthy and effective environmental guardians. Much in the way Bush's National Energy Strategy promoted market forces, the Rio summit welcomed business interests, establishing a Business Council on Sustainable Development, and more generally affirming the link between economics and environmentalism.[45] Capitalizing on this new rhetorical space, at a global warming conference in D.C., Lay slyly offered that the corporate world could provide the way forward in "the arduous work of transforming into reality the world's commitment to reducing greenhouse gas emissions and mitigating the threat of global warming." In the business world, Lay declared, "the follow-through" was "the key," and natural gas could become "the 'bridge' fuel" that would "deliver" the entire world from "the oil era" to "a renewable energy based economy." Echoing Bush's description of the globalizing political landscape as a "new world order," with natural gas, Lay told his audience, the planet stood at the start of "A New Energy and Environmental Order." "Sustainable growth in the developing countries means increased use of natural gas," he said before proudly referencing a mammoth power project the company had under way in Teesside, England—one of the world's biggest natural gas cogeneration power plants—as an example of Enron's commitment to global sustainable development.[46]

At the same time, Lay backed away from any suggestion that environmental protection and economic expansion were at odds with one another. Rather, Lay stressed how cheaply clean energy could be produced with natural gas. Always a free market capitalist at heart, Lay was sure that natural gas would become the dominant energy source in the country "if allowed to compete in a free and fair competitive market."[47] The Enron executive was even more insistent on the connection between markets and the environment than the Bush administration. Significantly, Lay's public remarks after the Rio summit implored the energy industry to look beyond the 1990 amendments to the Clean Air Act and consider power sources that helped reduce CO_2

emissions. Much like the natural gas industry as a whole, Enron's leadership
was not fighting against the era's ecological internationalism but was happily
going along with it. Such currents—cultural, social, and political—were di-
recting Enron's actions and public image. What is more, the language and
policy implications in documents such as the National Energy Strategy and
Agenda 21 provided a way for Lay to claim environmental stewardship for
Enron without significantly disrupting the firm's operations. On the contrary, the free market was a necessary condition for sustainable development. Yet Rio was not the only public platform that Lay took advantage of
that year.

When the Republican Party chose Houston to host its national convention in 1992, Lay spotted another chance to raise the city's profile. "Welcome
to the friendliest city in the world!" he greeted delegates inside the Astrodome on the first day of the convention.[48] However, Lay's sunny demeanor
was out of step with the worry that some Americans felt. Since late 1991, the
country had been plagued by an economic recession that had implications
for the presidential election. Bush did not fare well in November. By the end of
the year, Ken Lay and Enron found themselves facing an uncertain relationship with incoming president Bill Clinton. Since the company's inception in
1985, business-friendly Republicans had occupied the White House, and
Enron executives enjoyed a cordial and welcome relationship with Bush's
Department of Energy. Who knew what the first Democratic administration in over a decade would bring? After all, the last Democratic presidency
had produced the Department of Energy. Still, despite losing a personal
connection to the executive branch, the election results did not signal hard
times for the company.[49]

Just before the election, Bush signed a new energy policy into law, which
solidified many of the ideas outlined in the National Energy Strategy. The
law, which became known as the Energy Policy Act, was aimed at encouraging environmentally friendly (or friendlier) power sources such as natural
gas and represented a move toward more industry deregulation. The law's
many parts reflected both an emphasis on the environment, as well as a market approach to energy. Environmentalists, for example, could be heartened
by measures aimed at conservation and efficiency. Mirroring the cosmopolitan sensibility of the Rio conference, a global sense of environmentalism informed the law, even creating a directorship for climate protection in the
Energy Department.[50]

Domestically, the law called for promoting renewable energy sources and also cemented and extended tax credits for some renewable energy projects. This emphasis on cleaner forms of energy was also a part of the logic behind the act's call to reform the Public Utility Holding Company Act (PUHCA) in what represented a major push toward an open electricity market. The New Deal regulatory framework no longer seemed adequate for addressing the energy concerns and issues of the late twentieth century. Lay had long pressed Bush about PUHCA reform, and now that desire was enshrined in law. Such developments seemed to favor the company. Even though his friend had lost the election, natural gas had still been cited as a source of clean energy in the Democratic Party platform. Besides, by the time Clinton arrived in Washington, Enron had established a D.C.-based government affairs department.[51]

While Enron's D.C. office did not wait long in reaching out to members of the new administration, there was some apprehension about what sort of relationship the company could expect to have with Bill Clinton's first energy secretary, Hazel O'Leary. As an initial point of contact, Enron's vice president of government affairs and public policy, Terrence "Terry" Thorn, wrote to O'Leary on May 13, 1993, inviting her to meet with the heads of several energy companies so she could "clarify the Clinton administration's energy agenda." Thorn did not mince words in stressing the importance of the visit, writing: "Quite frankly, you are an unknown quantity for people in the industry." Despite this initial apprehension, though, the company's management soon found more common ground with the new administration on global environmental issues than they had with the Bush White House.[52]

Because of Republican politics, Bush had been reluctant about the 1992 Rio Summit. By contrast, Clinton was developing a different sort of Democratic politics that was distinctly market friendly. Here, too, though, the era's environmentalism played a big role in shaping these issues. Crucially, in 1992, the Clinton-Gore campaign used Al Gore's environmental credibility as a reason for supporting a controversial proposal to create a free trade zone linking the United States with Canada and Mexico. The vice presidential candidate suggested that the plan would expand environmental protections. The proposed agreement, which became known as the North American Free Trade Agreement, or NAFTA, was an important link between the Bush and Clinton presidencies. The Democratic president's support of NAFTA signaled how economic thinking had shifted. Though the proposal represented a new policy logic, Clinton and Gore also mobilized older liberal concerns in support of the largely unpopular agreement. During a TV debate with Ross Perot, Gore insisted that NAFTA's passage would help the United States enforce environmental laws and regulations across borders. To be sure, much of the debate around NAFTA focused on the potential effect such a free trade zone would have on U.S. jobs, but Gore's evocation of environmental benefits was a testament to how such issues had come to occupy a central place in the way the global economy was being hashed out. Ultimately, NAFTA's passage under a Democratic administration represented a mainstreaming of pro-globalization policy thought. In many ways, the debate surrounding NAFTA had been a proxy fight for globalization itself. Perhaps fittingly, the face of opposition to the free trade agreement had been a cussedly stubborn Texan, Ross Perot. By contrast, Lay and the Houston energy company were in a position to welcome this next wave of globalization.[53]

Though he had long been a Republican, and was particularly close to the man Clinton had defeated in the 1992 election, Ken Lay assumed a lead role in Enron's environmental efforts with the federal government. In 1993, Lay was named as a member of the President's Council on Sustainable Development—a group meant to demonstrate the new administration's dedication to the goals set out in Agenda 21 (Figure 2). Though Lay was one of twenty-five members, an article about the council in the company's employee magazine, *Enron Business*, included a number of quotes from Lay that made him sound like a longtime environmentalist. "If we keep junking up our environment through current means of economic growth and development," he declared, "eventually we will have serious problems whether it be global warming, contaminated food chains or polluted water."[54] Such forthright environmentalism did not mean, however, that Lay was advocating for more regulatory measures. Economic growth and environmental protection were "mutually compatible" with one another.[55]

The market-based sensibilities articulated in documents such as the National Energy Strategy had survived presidential and party transition. While some corporate and energy interests had mobilized to refute the evidence for global warming, Enron's leadership did not adopt such a contrarian position.[56] Instead, with an international consensus forming around measures including carbon emissions trading and offsets, and developing economies, such as India's, beginning to open up to foreign capital, the world energy market seemed ripe for more projects like the gas-fired plant in Teesside.[57]

Figure 2. Kenneth Lay and President Bill Clinton meet during Lay's membership in the President's Council on Sustainable Development. Photo courtesy of Southwest Collection/Special Collections Library, Texas Tech University, Lubbock, Texas.

Culturally, politically, and economically, the evolving post–Cold War world seemed to augur well for Lay's company, and he seized the opportunity.

For the next several years, environmental rhetoric and iconography appeared regularly in the firm's marketing literature alongside descriptions of Enron as a "vertically integrated clean energy company." For example, illustrations and photographs throughout the 1992 annual report featured all of Enron's business operations and units as in harmony with green, nature-themed backdrops—an extension of the same themes the company had been working with for years. The cover's rolling hills painted in greens were dotted with power plants, electric lines, and even a drilling rig in the water in the distance. In the foreground, a pipeline jumped out from a lettuce patch. Enron, such images suggested, was reworking the land, but not in any way that would harm it.[58] Lay's remark at the start of the decade that Enron was "in the right business at the right time" seemed prescient. The company's emphasis on a green globalization was well in line with public sentiment and was a large part of Enron's corporate identity both inside and outside the firm for the next several years.

Figure 3. Image from the May 1994 cover of *Enron Business*. Photo courtesy of
Southwest Collection/Special Collections Library, Texas Tech University,
Lubbock, Texas.

In an effort to foster such an internal culture, by 1994 the company had
introduced an "Environmental Code of Ethics." Throughout the first part of
the 1990s, the company touted its commitment to environmental responsibility in the pages of *Enron Business*. The entire May 1994 issue, for instance,
was dedicated to Enron's environmental efforts and featured a photograph
of the Teesside power plant on the cover (Figure 3).

The photograph foregrounded cows meandering in a field with a mammoth industrial structure in the background while the caption read: "Nature
and technology harmoniously coincide at Enron's 1,875 megawatt Teesside
Power Facility, which is fueled by clean-burning natural gas. The facility, located in the United Kingdom, exemplifies Enron's commitment to a better
environment worldwide."[59] Throughout the issue, article after article linked
natural gas and the environment. For example, in a piece about Enron's lobbying efforts on Capitol Hill, Terry Thorn applauded the Clinton adminis-

tration's "willingness to use market-based solutions to solve environmental problems as progressive, innovative and a step in the right direction."[60] As it turned out, Clintonian politics had hardly created problems for Enron, despite Lay's connection to the Republican Party. "Environmentalists today have basically debunked the theory that economic growth and environmental controls cannot coincide," Thorn declared.[61] The emerging consensus in American policy circles over economic issues made it easy for Enron to maintain an environmentally friendly image without accepting new regulatory measures.

This spirit of cooperation extended to global economic development. For instance, in 1994, Thorn was one of many executives who traveled to India with U.S. government officials as part of a "Presidential Mission on Sustainable Energy and Trade," and administration officials were involved in smoothing over tensions that had erupted over Enron's plans to build a massive gas-fired plant in Dabhol, an area south of Mumbai on India's west coast. A new government with nationalist rhetoric had shut down the project, and Rebecca Mark, now the head of Enron International, would spend the next several years trying to salvage it.[62]

At the end of the year, O'Leary wrote to Mark thanking her for an event that Enron had hosted in November when India's power minister visited the United States. The visit was important, O'Leary stressed, because it helped build on what she called "the evolving partnership between the United States and India to promote sustainable development in energy, environment and trade." At least partly in terms of the federal government, Lay's attempt to position Enron as an environmentally friendly company had apparently been a success.[63]

In this way, Enron also mirrored larger trends in the natural gas industry. The American Gas Association (AGA) had even formed an environmental taskforce and was involved in follow-up talks to the 1992 Rio conference. At the organization's annual meeting at the end of 1994, the environmental benefits of natural gas was the predominant theme. In rhetoric similar to Lay's after Rio, the AGA's chairman insisted that gas was the "bridge" that linked environmental responsibility and global economic growth. Throughout the year, members of the AGA were preoccupied with how to respond to a global focus on climate change. Much as the organization had done in the past, Enron was cited by the AGA as a particularly active advocate for natural gas in international climate talks. If, though, a green rhetoric was anchoring the company's public image, there were also other significant developments

taking place inside Enron that at first had little to do with corporate environmental responsibility.[64]

Further Financialization Inside Enron

Though it was detached from Lay's public rhetoric of sustainable development and "bridge fuels," as well as conspicuous projects like the Teesside
plant, Jeff Skilling's strategy for coping with the pipeline's transformation
from a regulated business to a participant in an active market was a success.
Soon after leaving McKinsey, he had begun building the Gas Bank by hiring
employees and importing a number of practices that he had learned in finance and consulting. Still, at a moment when Lay was fashioning a public
image that incorporated globalization and environmentalism, the fledgling
unit was an anomaly inside Enron—a difference that would have been clear
to stockholders and potential investors (such as pension fund managers)
browsing the firm's 1990 annual report.[65] That year, the inside flap of the
front cover folded out to reveal five photographs representing the firm's
major businesses. In this lineup, the image for Enron Gas Services (which
housed the Gas Bank) stuck out. Compared to other pictures referencing the
connections between energy and the natural world, the photograph for Skilling's team suggested a very different type of work. Instead of dealing with
large material structures, such as pipelines, power plants, and exploration
rigs, there were knowledge workers busy manipulating information—sitting
at desks, answering phones, and consulting each other. A brief description
accompanying the photograph underscored the inherent abstractness of
"marketing products" and "financing alternatives." Through such "innovative" work, the description touted the unit's ability to handle the chaotic
world of the "rapidly changing natural gas industry."[66]

   With spot market prices for natural gas fluctuating, the Gas Bank would
provide a service by offering fixed, long-term prices to customers—industrial
users and local distribution companies. This would bring a sense of stability
and predictability to the natural gas business. Some gas contracts were "in-
terruptible," meaning that the gas pipeline company could, if it needed to,
stop delivery to a buyer. One benefit that Enron Gas Services would provide
would be to offer "firm" contracts with a guaranteed supply of gas. However,
there were a few problems that Skilling's team would have to deal with.

First, the business unit needed to secure supplies of natural gas. Doing so, however, was not necessarily a straightforward proposition. Much like what had happened when the oil glut crashed Houston's economy in the 1980s, gas producers were in trouble because of the low price of natural gas. To make matters worse, in the wake of bankruptcies that spread through Houston in the late 1980s with the collapse of oil prices, natural gas suppliers were finding it difficult to borrow money. While there was an ample supply of the resource in North America, it seemed as though much of it would remain in the ground for the foreseeable future. The solution that Skilling's team devised met this need while also securing a steady stream of gas from financially weak production companies. Enron offered to buy gas from these producers that hadn't yet been extracted from the planet. Calling this arrangement a "volumetric production payment," the Gas Bank offered struggling companies the cash they needed to survive.[67]

Skilling, to be sure, had long held an interest in the world of finance, but in some ways Enron had no choice but to function as a bank. Enron's first two deals typified the approach that the company would use to get natural gas from producers. In the spring of 1991, Enron's new business unit used the volumetric production payment strategy and paid over $44 million to a company named Forest Oil. In return, Enron received an ownership stake in and guaranteed access to around thirty billion cubic feet of natural gas. Soon after this deal, Enron entered into another volumetric production payment agreement with a small, Houston-based oil and gas company called Zilkha Energy. While the size of that deal was not as large as the one Enron had just signed with Forest Oil a bit earlier, Enron still paid $24 million to the other firm for seventeen billion cubic feet of gas. Such deals provided Enron with an obvious benefit—ownership rights to gas that wasn't even out of the ground yet. Not only were such arrangements immediate relief for cash-strapped companies, if these gas producers went bust (certainly a possibility since Enron was doing business with struggling firms), Enron could get the gas itself.[68]

With reliable sources of natural gas secure, and the infrastructure to move the gas around the country as needed, the team Skilling assembled now set out to offer deals that would be attractive to gas buyers. Even though the financing and purchasing of gas for Enron had become a complicated procedure, Skilling wanted to make buying gas from Enron a straightforward process. The firm's employees had already been able to craft derivatives that would be attractive deals for gas buyers. At the end of 1990, Enron had announced a twenty-three-year deal with the New York Power Authority to provide the utility with natural gas at a fixed price for ten years, and a floating price after that. The terms of this agreement mimicked those of an interest rate swap—a derivatives deal built from a series of forward agreements that had previously been used to mitigate risk arising from fluctuating currency rates. The company even began running advertisements warning potential gas buyers about the volatility of the gas market. Much in the same way such financial derivatives in the 1970s offered a degree of stability after the system of fixed exchange rates collapsed, the Gas Bank could give gas purchasers a sense of certainty in the middle of the industry's most turbulent moment.[69]

By the summer of 1991, Enron Gas Services had completed around seventy transactions, more than three-fourths of which were for actually delivering natural gas. In one typical deal, EGS agreed to provide gas to Northwestern Indiana Public Service Company with 5,000 million British Thermal Units (MMBtu) daily—about five billion cubic feet of gas—over a two-year period at a rate of $1.87 per MMBtu. Northern Indiana would submit a schedule for gas delivery on a monthly basis. Although the amount of gas it received on a given day could vary, each month the buyer had to take 90 percent of the daily rate. Eventually, Northern Indiana was responsible for the total contract order. Enron then sent gas to a delivery point where the Natural Gas Pipeline Company of America connected with the Northern Natural Gas Company in Moore County, north of Amarillo in the Texas panhandle. From there, Northern Indiana would take the gas to its end point.[70]

The remaining quarter of the business was made up of derivatives deals, such as a fixed for floating rate swap agreement EGS entered into with the French bank Banque Paribas at the end of 1990. Under this agreement, which was meant to protect Enron from changes in the price of natural gas, the firm and the bank exchanged the difference between a set agreed-on price and the going market rate. The contract itself was unrelentingly abstract. The first two pages were primarily devoted to defining terms such as "calculation bank" (Paribas), "guarantor" (Enron), "notice of execution" (some form of communication between Enron and the bank), "fixed price" ("the amount designated as such in the Notices of Execution"), and even "United States" ("the United States of America, its territories and possessions"). As such language might suggest, the document did not establish anything specific about the swap (these details would be worked out in the notices of execution). However, the agreement set the stage for enormous amounts of information and money to flow between the two companies. Under the terms of this arrangement, the two parties exchanged notices of execution that established the "proposed Effective Date, Termination Date, Fixed Price Payer, Floating Price Payer, Fixed Price, Period End Dates, Quantity Per Settlement Period, Index Price, Cap, Floor and Arrangement Fee." The other party had a day to confirm the terms via its own notice of execution with identical details. Before the agreed-on settlement date, Paribas would notify Enron about the floating price in the agreement. On the settlement date, the two parties made payments that settled any difference between the floating and fixed price. Throughout the year, Enron would send quarterly and annual financial statements to Paribas. These two deals—the first that moved gigantic quantities of natural gas that would change hands in northwest Texas, and the second, that through its dull linguistic density allowed for the transfer of information and money across international borders—were both indications of the ways in which Enron Gas Services was developing.[71]

In early 1992, Enron Gas Services introduced five different branded products for natural gas buyers. Despite their different contractual terms, all five of the "EnFolio Gas Resource Agreements" promised certainty for gas users. "EnFolio SM GasBank RM," for instance, offered customers a steady and reliable source of natural gas for a ten-year term. Another contract in the EnFolio line, "EnFolio SM GasCap," also offered firm delivery of gas (this time for five years) but based the price on a "floating index" and also offered a ceiling on the price of the gas. With these financial contracts, Enron entered into a number of different derivatives deals. Through forward contracts and options with Enron Gas Services, customers could buy gas at a set price. Or, through a swap agreement called GasCap, a customer could buy gas at a fixed price in exchange for a floating price. In some respects, the Gas Bank was a remarkable achievement. With the volumetric production payments and EnFolio agreements, Skilling's business model had both secured gas supplies and created attractive products for customers. But the Gas Bank system had also given rise to a number of thorny issues.[72]

First, the terms of the volumetric production payments meant that cash was flying out of the company's vaults. For instance, though Skilling's team had locked in gas supplies, with the Forest and Zilkha deals, Enron had paid out nearly $70 million. Enron was now the company that had a cash problem. Much in the same way that derivatives suggested marketable contracts to potential gas buyers, securitization offered a solution. The practice of combining assets into a single "security" resembling a paper asset such as a stock or bond, "securitization" had first been used in the early 1970s to pool the revenue from multiple mortgages. Though adopting the practice would let Enron Gas Services work around the cash flow issues that the volumetric production payments created, securitization was not used widely beyond the mortgage-lending industry. Skilling would have to look to investment banking, outside of Houston, in order to find someone. It was to fill this need that Skilling hired an investment banker named Andrew Fastow, who had started his career at Continental Bank in Illinois and had become adept at securitizing assets other than mortgages. At Enron, Fastow was charged with securitizing the volumetric production payments, and he began pooling the payments as assets (in the same way that mortgages were pooled together as a single security) into a "special purpose entity" or SPE.[73]

The technical name belied a relatively simple idea—a company that existed on paper to help another, more tangible company carry out some specific goal. Often established as legally independent corporations, SPEs were especially helpful in quickly realizing money through securitization. Ownership of the assets could be transferred to an SPE, which could then issue a single security to investors. If executed successfully, real cash replaced the potential value of a contract. The first entity, called the "Cactus Fund," pooled $900 million worth of volumetric production payment agreements that were then sold to investors. Despite the convoluted arrangement that created an independent corporation that existed only on paper—and existed to perform only a single operation—SPEs and securitization were the only way Skilling's Gas Bank could work. Without actual cash that was generated in the wider economy flowing through the Cactus Fund and back into the organization, the Gas Bank's success would have been purely theoretical. In bringing cash back to Enron Gas Services through securitization, in other words, Fastow's role and the SPEs he created were central to the business unit Skilling oversaw. Additionally, because the financial details had been moved into the special purpose entity, Enron did not have to record any debt in the process.[74]

Fastow's success with the Cactus Fund was soon followed by another big deal. In the summer of 1993, he created another special purpose entity called the Joint Energy Development Investments Limited Partnership, or JEDI (a deliberate reference to the *Star Wars* movies).[75] However, unlike the Cactus Fund, the JEDI fund was not directly connected to the volumetric production payments that Enron had set up. Rather, this special purpose entity was established with the California Public Employee Retirement System

(CalPERS), the biggest public pension fund in the United States, with both Enron and the pension fund contributing $250 million. The deal provided Enron Gas Services with access to a significant pool of capital for investing in new energy-related projects. With the cash, Enron would be able to expand its pipelines and reserve assets. The partnership established another pattern of financing such side deals at Enron. While CalPERS put cash into the fund, Enron Gas Services contributed stock.[76]

Financialization was taking root at Enron Gas Services in other ways as well. Derivatives deals like the EnFolio agreements were popular with the Gas Bank's customers, but they required Enron to assume risk by offering fixed-price, long-term deals. Indeed, the big selling point for EnFolio had been that the agreements would protect a buyer from price risk—which was now held by Enron Gas Services. Here, more than any other aspect of the Gas Bank, Skilling's long-standing interest in finance came into play. The heart of Skilling's business unit was Enron Risk Management Services. Much like the search for an expert in securitization had led him far from Houston to find Fastow, Skilling recruited Wall Street traders. At Enron Risk Management Services, these traders would set the prices that the company could offer in EnFolio agreements and other contracts with buyers, as well as manage the risk brought to the company with every EnFolio agreement, by entering into a number of derivatives trades. Still, the approach was as foreign to the natural gas industry as it was central to Enron Gas Services. Even as late as 1993, the idea of a derivative was strange enough to most in the company that *Enron Business* ran a brief article explaining derivatives to other Enron employees in a breezy tone that belied the Gas Bank's intricate structure. Though the business model allowed the company to market its products as a way for customers to simplify the process of buying natural gas, that veneer of simplicity rested atop a complex series of financial instruments and processes that juggled cash, risk, and gas.[77]

In another parallel to investment banking, Enron Gas Services and the Gas Bank also introduced mark-to-market accounting, which was used to account for assets that would see their value change over time, to the company.[78] The use of this accounting method meant that assets, such as derivatives contracts, were assessed at a "fair value" based on the current market valuation. As those assets changed, the accounting was supposed to be adjusted. For a natural gas transporter like Enron, the mark-to-market method was entirely foreign, and the company's managers were compelled to put in a special request with the Securities and Exchange Commission explaining the move. Adopting the practice had big implications. Though the method was intended to provide a more accurate way to measure such changing values, the practice also had the potential to turn a balance sheet into a collection of numbers and charts that disfigured accurate financial representations. In practice, a company could record the value of a deal's entire life upfront. The presentation that two financial officers at Enron Gas Services, Jack Tompkins and George Posey, sent to the SEC reflected the pervasiveness of the firm's banking mentality, describing the business unit as more of a bank than anything that had been previously connected to the natural gas industry. Tompkins and Posey argued that the company should be allowed to use mark-to-market accounting because the business unit was "substantially different" from the company's other businesses because its "assets" were financial abstractions, rather than the sturdy and fixed material of gas pipelines.[79] The authors even included a list of financial institutions that were comparable to Enron Gas Services. The message was clear: Enron Gas Services was more like Merrill Lynch or Lehman Brothers than a regular pipeline operation.

In a decision that journalists and filmmakers would later treat as an example of oversight failure and a fateful move that paved the way for the accounting fraud that would proliferate under Andy Fastow's direction in the second half of the 1990s, the SEC did ultimately grant Enron Gas Services permission to use mark-to-market accounting methods. If the journalists who later chronicled Enron's demise were baffled by the SEC's decision, many of the firm's own employees must have been similarly bewildered. Much like the derivatives contracts the business unit had begun using, the accounting practice was foreign enough to the natural gas industry that an explanatory article in *Enron Business* was needed even years later, in 1994. Forebodingly, the article also addressed criticism that the accounting method could allow the company to inflate profits and avoid immediately reporting financial losses. In retrospect, and after men like Fastow began their jail terms, that convoluted schemes like the SPEs and mark-to-market accounting invited criminality seemed clear. But in the early 1990s, the Gas Bank's performance appeared to vindicate Skilling's plan as an intellectual achievement that was closer to a sophisticated baroque orchestral suite than a street hustle.[80]

Despite the tremendous, dynamic complexity at the heart of the business, the Gas Bank's products were also wildly successful. Income from Enron Gas Services grew steadily in the early 1990s, from over $70 million in 1991 to $224 million by 1994.[81] Significantly, income from Enron Gas Services was growing faster than the company's pipeline transportation business, and along with that income, the number of deals was growing, too. As a *BusinessWeek* article about the success of the Gas Bank noted, in a few short years, Skilling's team (by his own count) was offering fifty-seven different types of natural gas contracts to customers. Before long, the company had created the world's largest natural gas derivatives portfolio. The large number of deals was a point of pride for the company, but it was also the result of new competitive pressures that Enron Gas Services was facing. Gas futures were now trading on the New York Mercantile Exchange, and other companies (including rivals such as Coastal Corporation) were entering into the field. In response to such competition, Enron Gas Services began offering even more complicated financial contracts, such as "exotic options," which were options to buy options. In a market where Enron Gas Services had initially secured a competitive advantage by crafting a complex solution to a complicated problem, the only way to maintain that advantage was through an engagement with even further complexity.[82]

The increasing "exoticism" at Enron Gas Services also introduced a distinct problem for the unit. While projects in different parts of the world, such as Teesside and the Cuiabá pipeline project in Bolivia all fit (though sometimes uncomfortably) under the umbrella of sustainable development and a green globalization, describing what was going on at the Gas Bank to the wider business community (let alone the public) was proving to be very difficult.[83] Enron's managers found that, unlike environmentalism, there was no language or compelling visual shorthand for what Skilling had built. Throughout the middle of the decade, Enron's managers struggled to find the words to describe Enron's derivatives business, settling on increasingly vague language imparting feelings and values, rather than defining concrete products and processes.[84] Years later, Skilling could still recall grappling with language. While he disliked words such as "merchant" because they did not "sound quite right," others at the company rejected his preferred term, "intermediation," as "too technical."[85] If, however, words failed to pin down the precise nature of what Skilling had created, in other ways, subtle linguistic shifts revealed an unmistakable drift toward financial services. By the end of 1993, the Gas Bank had a clearly established business model and culture. For the unit, "entrepreneurship" was paramount. As Skilling put it in the pages of *Enron Business*, the Gas Bank's success was derived from the combination of financial products with the ability to actually deliver natural gas.[86]

The banking activities at Enron Gas Services also had implications that transformed the unit's internal structure and set it apart from the company in a number of ways. The strategy had proven enormously successful and, Skilling reasoned, was expandable to other industries, like electricity.[87] Signaling these ambitions, in 1994 Enron Gas Services underwent a name change, to Enron Capital and Trade (ECT). The new name was treated as a momentous event, and an *Enron Business* article announcing the change reported the team involved in coming up with the new moniker took their charge seriously by evaluating the "marketplace" and consulting "dictionaries and thesauruses."[88] Significantly, the word "gas" was removed from the title. Enron Gas Services may have seemed like a good name at first, but Skilling worried about being too closely tied to the material itself, as the company's stock would rise and fall with the price of gas (something Skilling felt was unfair because the company was providing services related to gas). The material commodity that Enron had been dealing in since its inception was removed altogether. In losing a direct reference to the firm's original business, though, the unit acquired a sense of expansiveness. The word "Enron" communicated "the notion of energy," while "Capital" represented finance and "Trade" (according to the article) represented the physical side of the business.[89] Still, even though the last word in the title was meant to signify the physical, material aspects of the unit's operations, the description had more to do with risk management services than physical delivery of natural gas. Within a few years, this preference for vague language would dominate Enron's corporate image. The new name, as imprecise as it was, served as an important marker for an approach to business at Enron that was beginning to supplant the global environmentalism Lay had embraced a few years earlier.

Though Enron Gas Services was focused squarely on the domestic U.S. gas market, the unit's growth was indicative of other business responses to globalization. Not only was work becoming increasingly international; it was becoming more and more abstract. Management professors in the earlier part of the decade were writing furiously to characterize what was happening. Even Peter Drucker, an influential thinker and writer focused on the ideas of the corporation since the 1940s, heralded the coming of a "postcapitalist society." Drucker's earliest understanding of large corporations was that of organizations responsible to multiple groups of stakeholders, including employees, investors, customers, and the communities where they operated. A thinker rooted in the stable political economy of the mid-twentieth century, he had even been critical of the shareholder revolution of the 1980s.

Now, however, Drucker was describing a world where human talent and knowledge mattered more than controlling the levers of capital itself. Much like the environment helped shape the context for globalization, Drucker was convinced that changes to business and work had implications beyond the confines of the corporation. The transformations businesses had to confront were so fundamental and wide reaching, he reasoned, that they were binding the world together. "Western" history and civilization were no longer useful ideas. "There is only world history and world civilization," he wrote in the pages of *Harvard Business Review*. The task confronting business organizations (and, indeed, organizations of all types) was to "integrate" "specialized knowledges into a common task." The implications for the octogenarian business intellectual were profound. Even the way the economy was measured and studied—weighing land, labor, and capital—was no longer adequate. The change that managers would confront in the coming years would be both turbulent and constant. As Drucker saw it, managers would have to move away from actually managing, and he even pointed to Michael Hammer's earlier *Harvard Business Review* article about flattening hierarchies. Success would instead be determined by how quickly firms could react to changes around them.[90]

As terms like "post-capitalist society" and "symbolic analysis" (a term coined by the economist Robert Reich) indicated, a distinct future-oriented language was settling in among management theorists.[91] In 1994, for example, management professors Gary Hamel and C. K. Prahalad published *Competing for the Future*, warning executives and managers that some companies "may be devoting too much energy to preserving the past and not enough to creating the future." Though disruptive, the future these authors described was not a dystopian world out of a science fiction movie. For instance, Hamel and Prahalad were confident that new technologies would "help clean up the earth's environment." Still, the new business climate also meant more pressure for companies. The challenges that confronted managers when books like *In Search of Excellence* appeared in the early 1980s had multiplied and quickened.[92]

Since the middle of the 1980s, at the same time Enron was formally established, Hamel and Prahalad had been writing about the need for corporate strategies that were global in their orientation. Now, almost a decade later, they argued that businesses had to engage in *"global preemption."* Because of this, managers and organizations would need to *"unlearn"* the past. Successful firms would be focused on "future markets." The two writers

counseled that managers needed to challenge "orthodoxy" and compared
business to art.[93]

Though Hamel and Prahalad were somewhat critical of Peters and Waterman, there was a good deal of continuity with the looseness that those
authors had advocated for a decade earlier in *In Search of Excellence*. However, Hamel and Prahalad were extending the analysis that those two earlier
authors provided. A new way of doing business was clearly emerging and
upending older assumptions about managing business organizations as
well as approaches to strategy. In very real terms, Enron Capital and Trade,
the business unit Skilling had built at Enron, mirrored the changes that
these authors were describing.[94]

Management gurus weren't the only people who were preoccupied by the
global economy's changes. By the middle of the 1990s, it was clear to anyone
watching that a more distinct picture of globalization was emerging in both
real and conceptual terms. What had started at the 1990 World Economic
Forum in Houston—the process of making sense of the "post–Cold War order" and addressing global environmental concerns and continued with
tentative steps toward the formal integration of national economies through
treaties like 1993's North American Free Trade Agreement (NAFTA) grew
in scope. By this time, Lay's understanding of the world economy had undergone a substantial evolution. At the start of the decade, the Houston executive worked with business lobbyists to press Bush on a proposed tax credit
aimed at encouraging more domestic manufacturing and production. Offering Enron as an example, Lay wrote to Bush that his company would "earn
the credit by purchasing more efficient equipment to drill for or transport
natural gas" but not "for a new computer system devoted to accounting and
financial as opposed to production purposes."[95] This "targeted investment
tax credit," in other words, was an expression of confidence in American industrial might.[96] The executive's tax plan, though, was at odds with the way
the global economy was evolving, as well as his firm's own strategy. But over
the span of a few years, Lay's thoughts about globalization had caught up
with the dramatic changes that had taken place in the first half of the 1990s.

In late September 1994, Lay wrote to members of Congress in support of
the United States approving the recently concluded Uruguay Round of the
General Agreement on Tariffs and Trade (GATT) negotiations—a pivotal
moment in the history of globalization that resulted in the creation of the
World Trade Organization, which was intended to help manage the rules of
global commerce. In his letter, Lay declared his support for the Uruguay

Round in general terms, suggesting that it would knit the world closer together through "long-term economic and political relationships among nations which are just beginning to understand the value of liberalized trading systems and privatization."[97] The establishment of the WTO as an international institution that would facilitate further international trade registered a growing consensus about how the world economy would best function. Though in the years since the Cold War's end global capitalism had become "common sense" (a set of historically specific and unexamined assumptions), in the mid-1990s such expressly ideological pronouncements were still paired with the era's environmental concerns. In this regard, Lay's letter was no different. To bolster such claims about the potential benefits of this next phase of globalization, Lay specifically pointed to the rapidly "maturing" global market for clean energy.[98]

Though the company's initial response to globalization at the start of the decade turned on widespread national and international concern with global warming and sustainable development, the strategy that had been developed at Enron Capital and Trade was also getting a global makeover. In 1994, the unit created Enron Global Power and Pipelines, which would be headquartered in London. This was a different sort of "globalization" than the green-tinted clean power projects that had formerly typified the company's international presence. The reorganization transferred some employees from Enron International. There were now two different approaches to the global economy at Enron.[99]

Outwardly, though, Enron maintained its environmentally friendly image, and apart from Ken Lay, Rebecca Mark remained Enron's most public face. Still, in spirit—and, more important, in terms of revenue—Enron Capital and Trade was starting to define the entire firm. The next time the company changed its "vision" in 1994, it reflected the internal changes in Enron's culture and operations. The company was, it now declared, "the world's first natural gas major . . . creating energy solutions worldwide." Though the 1994 annual report still mentioned the environmental benefits of natural gas, the green rhetoric was starting to lose ground to more abstract ideas and values—as evidenced by the use of words like "creative," "energy solutions," and, of course, "innovative." The more ambiguous, less grounded language was indicative of a crossroads the company had come to. In the first years of the 1990s, the sense of a globally interconnected world—viscerally felt but dimly understood in earlier years—became more defined and more pronounced. For Enron's managers, this growing global sensibility had huge implications because, particularly in the early 1990s, environmental concerns and energy production occupied a central place in policy and rhetoric. At the same time, continuing shifts in domestic energy policy created new prospects and opportunities for Skilling's business unit inside Enron. Less than a decade after the merger that created Enron, it was clear that the world of work and business was shifting in dramatic ways. These changes had profound effects on how Enron was adjusting its strategy and structure during these years and would soon lead to a new approach to business at the company.[100]

CHAPTER 3

From Natural Gas to Knowledge

During the first four years of the 1990s, both "globalization" as an idea and international environmentalism had emerged as powerful forces that energy companies like Enron would have to confront. Kenneth Lay, for his part, had actively worked to make sure that policy makers and presidential administrations, as well as the broader public, saw Enron as a reliable partner in fighting climate change. However, as the decade wore on, such plans launched in the name of sustainability would lose favor with the company as the financial strategies Jeffrey Skilling had first developed with the Gas Bank began to seem expandable to other industries. These changes, though, were far from view in the early 1990s.

Just as Enron Global Power and Pipelines prepared for Enron Capital and Trade's international expansion, by the middle of the decade, there were also domestic parallels to the massive sustainable development projects in England and India. Both the 1992 Rio Earth Summit and the Energy Policy Act encouraged renewable energy projects in the United States, and in the early 1990s, the federal government began studying the possibility of converting its Cold War–era Nevada atomic bomb test site into a massive solar field. Renaming the location the Nevada Solar Enterprise Zone, the Department of Energy intended the sun-soaked land to serve as a vivid demonstration of solar energy's commercial competitiveness. By 1994, the agency had dedicated a taskforce to studying the project in detail and was encouraging corporations to develop solar projects using the site. For Robert Kelly, who had been involved in the Teesside project and was now leading Enron's emerging technologies unit, such policy actions represented a clear business opportunity. That year, Kelly began contacting members of the Energy Department's Energy Efficiency and Renewable Energy Office about the company's possible participation in the Nevada Solar Enterprise Zone by constructing a

"100-megawatt photovoltaic facility." Enron would then sell the electricity it produced to the Department of Energy.[1]

Department officials, for their part, were receptive to Kelly's offer. At the end of a letter that Deputy Secretary of Energy Bill White wrote to Kelly in early 1995 regarding the taskforce's recommendations, he jotted down a note of encouragement that read: "Bob—I am keeping after this to make something happen and am being briefed on the availability of markets this week." The handwritten note at the end of an already positive letter indicated the friendly relationship Kelly was building with the Department of Energy.[2]

A few years earlier, both Lay and the American Gas Association had referred to gas as a "bridge fuel." Renewable energy production was a logical step, but the firm did not have any existing expertise or assets when it came to solar or wind power. However, rather than build such practices from scratch, the company began expanding through strategic purchases. In order to take advantage of the opportunity Kelly saw in the Nevada Solar Enterprise Zone, Enron purchased a stake in a Maryland-based photovoltaic cell producer, Solarex, which was owned by the oil giant Amoco. The partnership, now named Amoco/Enron Solar, was an ambitious undertaking. Enron's proposal for the Solar Enterprise Zone amounted to the largest solar facility in the United States and would sell power to the American government at the shockingly low price of five and a half cents per kilowatt hour. The size, as it turns out, was a crucial element. The price Enron was aiming for could be achieved only through economies of scale. In moving into renewable energy, in other words, Enron was engaging in more capital-intensive, asset-heavy projects.[3]

Kelly's interest in the Solar Enterprise Zone was emblematic of the ways in which Lay and others at Enron had adjusted both strategy and rhetoric in response to an American public and political sensibility that, by the mid-1990s, had by and large developed deeply held environmental values. But the solar experiment in the blasted Cold War landscape was not the only way Enron's leadership was thinking about the western United States. Closer to the coast, Skilling saw a way to expand the successful trading business he had built with the Gas Bank at the end of the 1980s. But this was not simply a matter of adding a new service or product. Rather, the promise of a new market in the West pushed Enron further from its origins as a gas pipeline operator and raised the stakes for Lay's involvement in both national politics and Houston's affairs. In the middle of the 1990s, strategy restructured so much more than just the company.[4]

As early as 1994, the California Public Utilities Commission was exploring how the state's electricity market could be restructured. For someone like
Skilling, who was convinced that the company had found a winning formula
with the Gas Bank, which could be applied to electricity, the possibility was
exciting. Indeed, the company already had long-term contracts with utilities
around the country. California could be a test case for the company in addition to a market opportunity, and managers such as Skilling were particularly interested in establishing a forward market for electricity.[5]

Before long, these developments began to take shape. In the spring of
1996, electricity futures began trading on the NYMEX. It was a development
that executives at Enron Capital and Trade had been involved in shaping for
several years through Enron's participation in steering committees. Though
the trading itself was happening on an East Coast exchange, the best market
opportunities were in the West. Indeed, the futures contracts themselves
were for delivery at a nuclear power station in New Mexico and at a delivery
point on the border between California and Oregon. As Enron managers realized, a history of cash deals among investor-owned utilities in the West
had created the sort of price volatility that Enron had become expert in managing. If all went well, managers reasoned, a similar futures market might
very well develop on the East Coast the following year. By contrast, the proposed solar field proposal was a mere side thought compared to the broader
opportunity that other measures of the Energy Policy Act created. In fact, the
law had dramatically expanded the potential markets for Enron.[6]

Over the course of the next couple of years, Skilling and Lay would continue to develop a new sense of what Enron's core business should be, setting
the stage for a dramatic change in direction in the last few years of the twentieth century. As the simultaneous rise of Enron International and ECT suggest,
internal corporate identities are rarely stable. The early 1990s may have been
a time of heady optimism, but they also represented a moment of economic
flux. Already, Enron's leadership had responded to the changes ushered in at
the start of the 1990s, but internally, there was also a split. During the first
years of the 1990s, policy makers in the United States began to develop
responses to a world that was increasingly interconnected. The approach was
indeed new and had big implications for energy companies like Enron. However, these policy changes resulted in two distinct lines of business at Enron.

While managers who began their career at the company in international
development, such as Rebecca Mark and Robert Kelly, continued to pursue

large-scale projects, many of which had a "green" sensibility, Skilling's Gas Bank had been a huge success. By the middle of the decade, the company stood at a crossroads. Globalization and ideas surrounding sustainable development might have opened up new opportunities for Enron, but globalization also meant that both money and the highly educated workers Skilling wanted for Enron Capital and Trade could go anywhere in the world. Gradually, these opportunities and pressures displaced the older emphasis on sustainable development. Over the next few years—and very much in concert with discussions in business, government, and investment banking—Enron's management moved toward a vision of an abstract and expansive global free market.

Just as the Federal Energy Regulatory Commission (FERC) pushed the natural gas industry toward a market structure in the 1980s, by the middle of the 1990s, the commission was taking similar steps in wholesale electricity. The Energy Policy Act of 1992 required FERC to explore open access to power transmission lines on a case-by-case basis and established a new category of wholesale electricity generators that were not regulated by the decades'-old Public Utility Holding Company Act (PUHCA). The energy bill, which included language encouraging natural gas power generation, created new opportunities for "wheeling"—the term for a third party's use of open access transmission lines. But for a gas company like Enron, "wheeling" was an impossibility while PUHCA was still in place. The law itself had long been an issue with the company. Lay had advocated for using President Bush's National Energy Strategy to "reform" the New Deal–era law and had even pointed to the Teesside plant as an example of the benefits Americans could enjoy without PUHCA in the way.[7]

Because of the opportunity, Skilling continued to develop a business in anticipation of electricity deregulation at the wholesale (and perhaps even retail) levels. Electric utilities were closely related to Enron's historically core business; there was an undeniable logic to Skilling's plans. However, there was also a big difference between the deregulation of the natural gas industry and electric utilities. Natural gas transportation had been deregulated before Enron developed the idea of the Gas Bank. If Skilling and others at Enron wanted to enter the electric market, they would have to work to remove the regulatory structures that had been in place since the Great Depression. Indeed, the Public Utility Holding Company Act explicitly prohibited corporate combinations of gas pipelines and power utilities. Additionally, pushing for regulatory rollbacks did not present the easy public relations strategy that something like solar energy development did.

Public opinion wasn't necessarily on Enron's side. To the extent they thought about electric utilities at all, the majority of Americans were happy with their power service. In 1994, Texas consumer groups had even allied with utilities in the state to stop a move toward deregulation and an open power market. Enron's managers, on the other hand, viewed the regulatory oversight of the nation's electricity as woefully outmoded. Despite facing such an uphill struggle, privately Lay continued to reach out to his political connections in Texas. If the World Economic Forum had helped ease Lay into Houston's public life as a power player in a way that the state's chroniclers could not have predicted in the mid-1980s, he continued to exercise his power inside the state through personal connections—much like the way the 8F Crowd had operated.[8]

In terms of electricity, by the middle of the 1990s, FERC was taking steps similar to those they had taken a decade earlier with natural gas transportation. In early 1995, the governmental body proposed open access to some of the country's electric transmission systems. Executives at Enron Capital and Trade were hopeful that the nation was poised for greater competition in the wholesale power market.[9]

At the end of April, 1996, FERC issued Order 888, representing a significant step toward a more fluid market for wholesale electricity. For managers at Enron, the parallels must have surely been striking. Much like FERC rulings had fundamentally altered the natural gas business in the 1980s, Order 888 split the production and transmission of electricity and established open access to the transmission lines for over 160 utilities. The way electricity was developing mirrored the company's experience with natural gas just a few years earlier.[10]

However, it was clear that the industry's restructuring would not unfold in the same way that the natural gas business had years earlier. Rather, executives had to keep a close eye on politics at the state level. *Enron Business* periodically featured maps that kept employees abreast of deregulation across the country (Figure 4).

As one Enron executive noted, Enron (as well as its lobbying allies) would have to work on a "state-by-state basis." The "battle," readers learned, was "being fought on several fronts," including both the federal and state levels. Through these articles, employees learned that Enron was in the "thick of the

**Competitive Reform of the Electric Industry is
Currently Being Evaluated in Most of the U.S.**

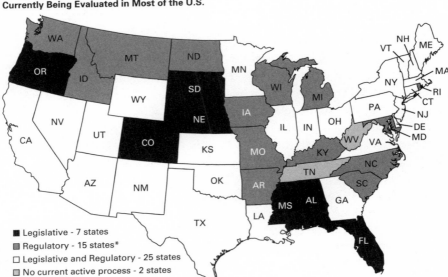

■ Legislative - 7 states
▣ Regulatory - 15 states*
☐ Legislative and Regulatory - 25 states
▨ No current active process - 2 states

*Includes District of Columbia
Source: EEI Retail Wheeling & Restructuring Report, March 1996, and Internal Enron.*

Figure 4. The uneven state of U.S. electricity deregulation in the mid-1990s.

fight" in a "massive public relations and legislative battle" to "bring competition to the U.S. retail market for electricity, one of the last great monopolies." As they would do on other occasions, managers pointed to deregulation
in the airline, trucking, railroad, natural gas, and telecommunications industries to argue for the wisdom of electric deregulation. Such comparisons
looked back to historical precedent, suggesting that deregulation was nothing new. However, when Lay and others began contacting politicians around
the country, their arguments were not rooted in the past, nor in the "new
environmental world order" Lay had heralded shortly after the Earth Summit's conclusion, but under the shadow of a looming global economy. What
is more, the politically savvy executive began making these arguments very
close to home.[11]

Ken Lay, of course, had developed a special relationship with George H.
W. Bush. The two had worked together when Houston played host to a meet-

ing of world leaders trying to make sense of a dramatically changed global landscape after the Cold War. The president's loss to Bill Clinton in the 1992 election, however, did not mean the end of Lay's working relationship with the Bush family. In 1994, not long after his friend George H. W. Bush left the White House, the former president's son George W. Bush won a race for the Texas governorship. In some ways, this was a lucky break, because Enron's leadership was preparing to lobby state governments about wholesale electricity deregulation. But the company's message for governors like Bush was not a local one.

Just as Lay had helped his father prepare Houston for an international stage, Enron's chief executive connected Texas to a new global landscape for the new governor. However, the optimistic rhetoric of a "new environmental world order" was gone. As the two traded friendly letters over the years, the governor teasing the energy executive about his age, Lay would freely offer his own assessment of world affairs. Throughout, Lay presented the globalizing economy in a very different light. In a February 1995 letter to the governor, he warned that "restricting important competitors from the wholesale power market harms the Texas economy by causing higher electric prices, less investment, and fewer jobs." By contrast, Lay continued, "more competition, leading to lower electric rates, would benefit all Texans and help keep Texas business competitive in world markets." Texas, Lay insisted, had to start moving toward deregulation because not doing so could lead to "less investment."[12] In the newly connected world his father had worked hard to foster after the end of the Cold War, money and business would surely flow to the friendliest spaces. If the threat of interstate and international competition was only implied in the February epistle, Lay was more direct about the dangers of failing to adopt his point of view a scant two months later. Writing to Bush, encouraging him to sign a bill into law (S.B. 373), Lay reassured him that the "historic legislation represents a major step towards competition in the electric business and will help keep the regulatory environment in Texas in step with that in the rest of the country." Though Lay promised that like "every other industry, competition will reward innovation and efficiency and keep electric prices low," he also warned the governor that "Texas industry" needed to be "viable in the face of stiff national and international competition."[13] Adopting a familiar role, Lay cast himself not as a power player in search of a favor, but as a knowledgeable and concerned advisor who could help the state navigate an all-but-inevitable globalization. In preparing for this looming global shift, Texas simply had no choice but to deregulate electricity or risk economic ruin. The global sense that emerged with the political up-heaval and environmental urgency at the end of the 1980s was firmly in place, but the character and contour of this new world order was still un-determined. Lay's message to the younger Bush revealed the fluid nature of this new international system, as well as a similarly shifting set of priorities inside Enron.

When it came to electric restructuring, Lay warned the governor of Texas, the Lone Star State could not "afford to wait" because a "delay could diminish our state's ability to compete for domestic and global business." Texas now faced a choice, Lay reasoned. "We will control our energy future and therefore our economic future," he wrote to the younger Bush, "or others will realize the competitive advantages of the new system before we do." This was a far cry from the unified vision of a "new environmental world order" that Lay had used to describe energy and business after the Earth Summit. The global economy Lay described to the younger Bush in these letters was com-prised of distinct regions, countries, states, and even cities connected to one another by worldwide competition. The executive's letters made connections between the state's regulatory framework and rest of the country and, with phrases such as "global business," this reimagined landscape of globalization. Indeed, warning that Texas had to take care of its power future before it got left out in the cold was a strategy that the ultimately fragmented world of global capitalism provided.[14]

States, cities, and, in the developing world, entire nations, felt pressure from different corners to race to deregulate industries and open up markets before other places did. Lay frequently invoked this concept of becoming attractive to money and businesses that were increasingly mobile. Global-ization might have been an incomplete process, but this incompleteness pro-vided Lay and other proponents with a rhetorical advantage. Much in the way that the "green" rhetoric Lay had drawn on earlier had its roots in a lon-ger discourse around sustainable development and widespread concern over the environment, Lay's new arguments were not original, but the source was different. In these letters to the governor that warned of a race to prepare for a changing global economy, Lay's message recalled the futurist analysis of management gurus like Peter Drucker, Tom Peters, and Gary Hamel.[15]

Significantly, Lay's letters echoed what analysts at Wall Street banks had been writing in their reports assessing Enron as an investment. Some ana-lysts covering the natural gas industry had long written approvingly of En-ron's "innovative management," which was "entrepreneurial," primarily in reference to Skilling's success with the Gas Bank.[16] The new description in the firm's annual reports was at least in part an adoption of how professionals in the financial services sector wrote about the company. There would now be a unified message. Wall Street analysts rarely mentioned sustainable development and clean energy projects as reason to invest in the firm. Instead, equity analysts tied their positive assessments of Enron to the deregulation of wholesale electricity and emerging markets outside of the United States.[17] Politics on the state level certainly seemed to validate such predictions, especially in California.

Significantly, trading on the West Coast seemed ready to open up. California Bill 1890 helped establish the state's newly deregulated power system by creating the California Power Exchange (CalPX), which required investor-owned utilities (IOUs) to purchase electricity in a short-term spot market. The parallel with gas deregulation a decade earlier was clear, and with its massive energy needs, California could have also served as a vivid demonstration to other states that an open market for electricity could benefit consumers. Though the market structure was not to be implemented for another two years, the company moved immediately to take advantage, merging with a utility, Portland General Electric (PGE), in 1996 after successfully claiming an exemption from PUHCA. It was a clear sign that regulators and corporate leaders were beginning to see New Deal–era regulations as waning in relevance at the end of the twentieth century. But amid a general sense that globalization had ushered in a fundamentally new economic landscape, the combined company was in some ways a return to the octopus-like utility corporations that had caused so much ire just before the Great Depression.[18]

While the 1985 merger of InterNorth and Houston Natural Gas had created a pipeline system with enormous geographic reach, the company needed similar infrastructure to take advantage of power deregulation on the West Coast. A press packet about the merger boasted that the combined company now possessed "more than 5,900 megawatts of electric generating capacity worldwide and more than 37,000 miles of natural gas pipeline," while a map revealed power lines from Oregon snaking through the western United States, and into California. An *Enron Business* article celebrating the merger even featured a photograph of Ken Lay, Jeff Skilling, and Ken Harrison (of PGE) cutting a cake in the shape of the continental United States with decorative power lines stuck in the frosting (Figure 5). Literally a map waiting to be carved up, the image served as a fitting metaphor for the company's ongoing process of pushing for electric deregulation in the United States.[19]

Figure 5. Jeffrey Skilling, Kenneth Lay, and Ken Harrison celebrate the merger between Enron and Portland General Electric. Photo courtesy of Southwest Collection/Special Collections Library, Texas Tech University, Lubbock, Texas.

The 1985 merger that created Enron in the first place had simply combined two natural gas companies to create a much larger gas pipeline system. Just over a decade later, though, the merger with Portland General Electric indicated how much the firm had changed. Combining with the utility was intended to facilitate the expansion of the financial strategies that Skilling had pioneered with Enron Capital and Trade. Now, Enron barely resembled the company that had been created out of the first merger. Enron grew dramatically over the first ten years of its life. By 1996, the company had eleven thousand employees and was reporting revenues of over $13 billion. But alongside such growth, there had also been a qualitative shift. The "financialization" (as an industry executive had put it in 1993) of natural gas was spreading to other areas that Enron was involved in.[20]

The company's marketing literature also registered this shift, declaring that Enron had established itself as an "entrepreneurial, innovative, and vision-driven company." Rather than presenting the firm as a vertically integrated clean energy company, in a section of the 1995 "Letter to Shareholders" entitled "Unique and Forward Strategy," management predicted that "40 percent" of the company's "projected $1 billion net income in the year 2000" would come from "businesses that did not exist in 1990." Here, the language in the letter reflected the future-oriented turn the decade's management literature had taken.[21]

Electricity deregulation was promising enough that in 1996 the company created a new unit, Enron Energy Services, to sell power directly to end users and potentially even retail customers. The venture would be headed by Lou Pai, who had first worked in the Gas Bank. Increasingly, as markets seemed as if they would replace the regulated New Deal state, Enron's managers had become confident that deregulation would inevitably crack open "the nation's last great monopoly."[22] Steve Kean (head of the company's government affairs team) noted that the question of reform had "shifted from 'if' deregulation will occur to 'when.'"[23] Such confidence, though, would not necessarily translate into a winning public relations campaign. Despite such bullish language in the pages of *Enron Business*, the company's message that deregulation was nigh had all the charm of a Puritan sermon. Still, as Kean argued, the nation was "connected by an electricity grid that knows no state boundaries," and to many at Enron, the superiority of free markets to other forms of economic organization was plain common sense.[24] Lay himself was confident that there wasn't "one cultural, economic or technical barrier that cannot easily be removed with a little teamwork among the stakeholders."[25] Enron's message machine had found a higher purpose.

The PGE merger, as well as the state-level lobbying, was representative of how Enron's managers were concerned with the gradual deregulation of the country's electricity system. What is more, the firm's response to the increasingly market-oriented approach to energy extended the practices that Skilling had pioneered with the Gas Bank. "The electricity industry," Skilling had written to Bush earlier that year, was in the midst of a "competitive revolution" that would "fundamentally change the way that electricity is bought and sold." Skilling even offered to arrange for the governor to tour Enron's electricity trading floor. "We would like to show you how we do business," he wrote in closing. It was an offer Lay would repeat a few months later. The tours (which it seems the governor never took) underscored the connections among the transformation of Houston's economy, the firm's evolving business practices, and the push for electric deregulation. Sitting at computer terminals in the wall-less office that Skilling had demanded when he had first come to Enron, traders were ready for the nation's power grid to be opened up to competition. Indeed, Skilling's new business model depended on it.[26]

Transforming Houston

The markets for Enron's new business may have been primarily on the West Coast, but fully realizing the opportunity meant new pressures at the company's headquarters in Texas. Increasingly, the sort of workers Skilling regarded as essential were presumably drawn to cities like New York and London. If Houston was seen as a town full of "cowboys who appreciated Cezanne," the business would likely suffer. In order for the Gas Bank to succeed, both Lay and Skilling reasoned, Houston would have to change. Recruitment efforts for Enron Capital and Trade (which operated the Gas Bank) at elite colleges revealed the extent to which the company's managers felt that they had to compete with other cities for talent.

Since the World Economic Forum five years earlier, Lay had embraced the role of city booster against the backdrop of a post–Cold War sense of internationalism and globalization. In the years since the World Economic Forum, Lay had remained active in Houston's affairs. While he did not plan anything as grand as another global summit, Lay's smaller gestures were also intended to recast Houston's role when it came to the rest of the world. For instance, the executive had lobbied the elder President Bush to consider Houston as the location for his presidential library. Now, Lay began to incorporate his company's name into these efforts. In late 1995, the Baker Institute at Rice University began hosting an annual conference that was intended to highlight foreign policy issues. As a part of this, Lay helped to establish an Enron Prize for public service. In a ceremony that autumn, Ken Lay presented Colin Powell with the inaugural award. If Houston was becoming an international city, then Enron would have to be a part of that internationalism.[27]

Even when it came to community-based charity work, the impulse to alter Houston according to Enron's needs was an ever-present undercurrent. During his trial, both Lay and his close confidante Cindy Olson (who was head of both community relations and human resources) pointed to the confluence of community work and the company's recruitment strategy. From educational to arts to health organizations, by the mid-1990s, around eighty Houston institutions benefited from the Enron Foundation, which donated over three million dollars in 1994. This commitment to charity in Houston could also be found in the pages of *Enron Business*, particularly the "Enron Envolved" section. Throughout the 1990s, for instance, Enron sponsored a program that invested in and advised black-owned businesses in the city.[28]

During his trial, Lay proclaimed that he had "always believed very strongly that businesses should give back to the communities where they do business, and the individuals working for those businesses should become active in those communities and help make them a better place to live and a better place in which to work."[29] While Lay professed that this desire sprang in part from his personal religious devotion, both he and Olson were also quick to note that such charitable activities could also work with more overt efforts at gentrifying parts of Houston. The partial success of the Houston summit in 1990 had revealed the need for a more sustained effort at preparing Houston for a changing world. As knowledge workers were becoming mobile at the very moment Skilling needed more of them, Houston would have a hard time recasting itself as a center for such work if the legacies of uneven development and racial disenfranchisement persisted. Even beyond the imbalance of social justice that the 8F Crowd had bequeathed Houston, Lay faced a problem that would have been more glaring to a twenty-two-year-old with a finance degree: Houston could be boring.

Houston elites had long worried that the area's economy needed to develop in a way that would loosen the region's dependence on the supply, demand,

and price of oil. Enron's plans to capitalize on wholesale electricity deregulation made the future of the city a top concern for the company's managers. A 1994 advertisement that ran in Rice University's student paper, for
example, declared that the business Skilling had introduced proved "that
life and career opportunities exist beyond Wall Street" for young, educated
people about to enter the workforce. In this advertisement, Enron tried to
pitch itself as a sort of Western Wall Street. The company's "Analyst Program" (itself an attempt to model investment banking recruitment practices)
would provide "top candidates with the opportunities of Wall Street and the
affordability and lifestyle of the West."[30] The language that the advertisement used reflected the ways in which Skilling was modeling Enron's organizational structures after Wall Street, as well as how important remaking
Houston had become to the firm's managers. Indeed, recruitment advertisements that ran in Rice's student paper were, in part, attempts to stop potential employees from leaving the city after graduating; but such advertisements
would not be enough.

During the late 1990s, the firm's management team worked hard to foster an exciting corporate culture. All-employee barbecues with live music in
a park across the street was just one way Enron's leadership tried to keep their
talent pool entertained. Specific milestones would be marked by ostentatious
celebrations. When Enron's stock hit a certain number, for example, the
company had people literally handing out cash to employees as they entered
the building. Such displays—at once giddy and gaudy—would have been unthinkable in the staid and conservative corporate culture in other Houston
energy companies. Alongside such official displays of celebration, the informal aspects of Enron's culture had become wild and hedonistic. As would
later become integral parts of how Enron's story was told, some employees
indulged in all manner of sexual excess. Executive excursions to strip clubs
were hardly unique to Enron, of course. By the 1990s, a large section of
the strip club industry had undertaken a substantial image makeover in a
deliberate bid to make such places attractive to male executives. Still, some of
the rowdy, money-flushed men at the Houston company were not content to
be mere patrons of "gentlemen's clubs." It was hardly a secret among those who
worked there that the head of Enron Energy Services, Lou Pai, and some of
the others following him out to clubs would bring strippers back to the company's offices at night. Such stories were one reason that Enron would later
be remembered as an oversexed environment. Extramarital affairs among
the company's leadership, including Rebecca Mark, John Wing, and Ken Rice,

proliferated. Yet a bacchanalian corporate culture did not amount to an adequate response to the competitive pressures the city was facing.[31]

If Enron was going to attract the sort of financial talent that Skilling clearly thought of as essential to Enron's success, then the city would have to become a more attractive place to live to an increasingly global, mobile workforce. The compression of time and space that had been introduced through newer communications technologies, as well as new forms of commerce (such as derivatives trading) had eroded some of the regional advantages that some cities had previously enjoyed. Toward the end of the twentieth century, as investment capital and certain groups of people became freer to move around the world, cities found themselves pitted against one another in an "interurban" competition to collect and keep both money and people.[32]

The unpredictable effects of a more connected global economy had already hurt Houston in the 1980s with the oil glut. When the city did recover at the start of the 1990s, it did so with a more diverse economy. Still, the city's downtown did not reflect the area's transformation. In a process that ran parallel to Enron's preparation for wholesale electricity deregulation, there were multiple projects under way to revitalize downtown through building more residential and entertainment spaces. In 1995, a development company announced plans to convert the Albert Thomas Convention Center, which had been left vacant since 1987, into a space for restaurants and nightclubs. The proposed new plans included numerous nightclubs featuring different musical styles (including, of course, country). By the end of the summer of 1996, the project was completed. Named Bayou Place, the 150,000-square-foot development was the biggest "entertainment facility" in Texas. Bayou Place was surely a welcome sign that downtown was rebounding, but this trend was shaky at best, and such advances could just as easily be reversed.[33]

When city officials balked at the idea of issuing bonds to build a new stadium, Houston's football team, the Oilers, was suddenly a flight risk. The fight to keep the NFL team had grown ugly, with the team and the city going to court in an attempt to stop what seemed to be an inevitable lawsuit from the city to keep the team in town. But the logic of increased competition brought other cities into this process. By contrast, politicians in Nashville, Tennessee, issued bonds to finance a new stadium for the team in the hopes they would relocate. Worse, the potential loss of a major sports franchise was not limited to football. Just as the Oilers seemed more likely to leave Texas, the Astros, the city's Major League Baseball team, announced that they, too, could soon leave the city. However, the city's politicians were more determined

to keep the Astros in town. The city officials' predicament worsened when
the Oilers finally announced that they would indeed leave town for Nashville. Losing the Astros threatened to deal a huge blow to the city.[34]

Since 1965, the Astrodome had symbolized Houston's midcentury
petroleum-fueled prosperity. Bayou Place was surely a boost to Enron's recruitment efforts. Still, if the ads the company was running in Rice's student
newspaper were highlighting a pleasant Houston lifestyle that couldn't be
found in eastern cities, losing another professional sports team was not going
to help. It was with these pressures facing Houston that Lay again took an
active and public role in the city's affairs. Before long, Enron's CEO found
himself allied with other prominent Houstonians in proposing a new ballpark as an incentive for the team to remain in town. If Lay ever came close
to emulating the way the 8F Crowd asserted control over the city's affairs, it
was his very public role in trying to build a downtown baseball field for the
Houston Astros.[35] Yet his approach and his reasoning for keeping the Astros
in town were entirely different from the tack the 8F Crowd (who had been
used to working behind closed doors) would have taken. Much as it was when
the city hosted the World Economic Forum at the beginning of the decade,
Lay's role in getting a baseball stadium built was a public one. In late August
1996, the *Houston Chronicle* began reporting on efforts to bring the ballpark
to downtown, often featuring Lay promising that a new stadium in the city's
core "could do some significant things in helping revitalize downtown."[36] Lay's
interest in a downtown ballpark, rooted in the impulse to transform the
city into a cosmopolitan metropolis, was also part of a broader trend.[37]

Despite its unique history with the oil bust, Houston was not the only city
to hatch such a scheme. In the mid-1990s, ballparks were seen as a key to
downtown revitalization. Similar projects had been launched in Baltimore,
Cleveland, Pittsburgh, Detroit, and Philadelphia. In fact, the firm that designed many of these stadiums, HOK Sport, would also design Houston's
ballpark.[38] Though the ballpark faced an uphill battle in terms of public support (by mid-September one poll indicated that only 38 percent of the city's
residents supported it), the paper's editorial board officially came out in support of a ballot proposition for bonds to help finance the stadium. "Where
new downtown stadiums have been built to complement downtown development and entertainment concepts," the *Chronicle's* editors wrote, "the
result has been increased and steady ballpark attendance, a revitalization
of the area and hundreds of new business opportunities and successes for
those communities."[39]

Lay himself continued to publicly argue that the "the fourth-largest city in the country," should have "world-class professional athletics, just like it has world-class ballet and symphony and museums of fine arts and all the other things that make this a great city."[40] Significantly, the reason Lay provided was the need to reframe Houston as a "world-class" city. Indeed, the fates of the city and the corporation now seemed intertwined with one another. Without such "world-class" status, Skilling would have a hard time bringing more financial professionals to Enron Capital and Trade. Much as he had done in 1990 as a cochair of the host committee for the World Economic Forum, Lay was offering a vision of Houston that was fundamentally different from what it had been in the mid-twentieth century.

To the local media, however, it seemed as if Lay and his allies were operating in a distinctly Houstonian tradition. Lay, the *Houston Chronicle* noted, made the declaration of elevating the city to "world-class" status "after he met for lunch at the River Oaks Country Club on Tuesday with more than 15 high-ranking officials of large Houston companies."[41] One *Chronicle* reporter mused that the idea to build a downtown ballpark had finally picked up speed because "the Big Cigars downtown were all at their summer places in Martha's Vineyard until recently. Or maybe their wives made them go along on a shopping trip—to Milan, Rome and Paris. Whatever, we're glad they're back and talking ballpark numbers."[42] Yet in alluding to the days when the 8F Crowd met at the Lamar Hotel and hashed out the city's future over drinks, journalists failed to recognize Lay's aim of resituating Houston's relationship to an increasingly integrated world market.

Political power in Houston had also shifted since the 8F era. In their efforts to pass a bond that stood very little chance of being approved by voters, Lay and others met with Howard Jefferson, who was then the president of the city's NAACP chapter, and other African American leaders in Houston, as well as representatives from the League of United Latin American Citizens (LULAC) and the Urban League. Talks began with (in Jefferson's words) "the mayor, city council, the owner," and the "big-time city fathers who run this city," a group which now included Lay. As the meeting began to drag on for ninety minutes, Jefferson finally told the city fathers, "Put thirty percent minority participation on the table, we will pass it. Failure to do that, we will kill it." To Lay and others, the deal seemed to be a fair one, and in a signed agreement, they pledged that 30 percent of the contracts for construction and stadium concessions would go to minority businesses. Through the deal that Lay and Jefferson struck, Houston's history of racial disenfranchisement, city

politics, national deregulation, and global economic restructuring collided.
The bond ultimately passed, albeit by the slimmest of margins. This was good
news for Enron. Major League Baseball would stay in Houston and make recruiting easier.[43]

To be sure, at the end of 1996, Houstonians were feeling positive about
how much their city had rebounded from the 1980s. Downtown seemed to
be changing in exciting ways, and the proposed ballpark that Lay pushed for
was a part of this revival. Already, the city had helped refurbish the home of
the Houston Rockets. The *Houston Business Journal*, for instance, included
the Astros' future home along with projects like the renovated Rice Hotel
(which had been empty since the late 1970s) and Bayou Place when cata-
loging the particulars of the area's revitalization.[44]

Lay was clearly bolstered by such public support. As the head of the Houston Sports Facility Partnership, which had been created to realize the stadium,
he disdainfully characterized the project's critics as "the usual suspicious
people nervous about business in general."[45] The statement itself was unusually harsh coming from someone who was otherwise deliberately crafting a
much more thoughtful public image. Lay's dismissive comment also reflected
a growing insistence in many quarters that business was generally aligned
with the public good. The U.S. economy appeared to be in the middle of
one of the greatest economic booms in its history, and such anticorporate
voices were increasingly marginalized. In Texas, at any rate, some Houstonians were optimistic about the renewal this public-private partnership
seemed to be fostering.

Writers for the *Houston Chronicle* appeared to think the ballpark was a
sign that augured well for downtown. As one journalist wrote in an article
for the paper's Sunday magazine, "Houston's decade-long-suffering downtown appears fully poised to rebound from the oil bust."[46] If the ballpark's
new location and proposed design symbolized a break from midcentury
Houston's sprawling suburban landscape, it also promised to complete the
transition away from an oil economy that many Houstonians remembered as
having devastated the city in the 1980s. Downtown Houston was "on the precipice of success" but still needed work "before it enjoy[ed] a retail and entertainment revival that [would] give it the vitality many Houstonians want[ed]
to show the rest of the world."[47]

Crucially, such articles also connected the neighborhood's revitalization
to the sorts of businesses that Skilling was setting up inside 1400 Smith Street
at the edge of downtown. In an "era of deregulated energy," a revitalized

downtown would "serve as the world's energy trading capital." The baseball park and energy trading activity (such as the derivatives contracts being negotiated and drawn up by the employees at Enron Capital and Trade) were promising signs that the city was moving past "the not-so-distant days when some experts predicted downtown would never add another gleaming tower to its skyline." Much in the way that Skilling was removing the word "gas" from the business unit he had started in 1990, new construction projects underway in downtown Houston were, for *Houston Chronicle* writers, a welcome turn away from "the days of $40 a barrel oil." In a reflection of his increasingly public role, articles about downtown included statements from Enron's CEO about the needed to "attract top-notch workers and big business."[48]

"We are the fourth-largest city in the United States; we are increasingly very much an international city," Lay declared in the pages of the *Houston Chronicle*. "We are being compared with New York City and San Francisco and Los Angeles, and London and Paris and Hong Kong. As the world becomes more global, people become a lot more differentiating about the cities they want to go to."[49] Lay's comparison provided a link to his initial step onto Houston's stage six years earlier in 1990. That year, when the Enron executive had helped the city host the World Economic Forum, a sense of a rapidly integrating and globalizing world had been a backdrop to the entire event. Now, six years later, the quick and competitive nature of an integrated global economy was becoming clearer—and both the city and the firm had to adapt. Houston's old Union Station ended up being the site for the new stadium. It was a fitting location. Earlier in the twentieth century, the city's chamber of commerce had once advertised Houston as a place where "seventeen railroads meet the sea." And to be sure, after ground had broken on the project in October, thousands of artifacts (some dating to 1836, when the Allen brothers decided the region might grow to be a thriving commercial center) were removed from the site, and the future Enron Field became for a brief time the largest urban architectural dig ever in Texas. The city's past was literally being upended to prepare it for globalization.[50]

As if the sight of cranes and earthmovers downtown was not dramatic enough, the language in Enron's corporate literature had become just as grandiose as the building project now underway. Rather than adapting corporate image and rhetoric to the prevailing cultural and political currents, Enron's managers were now pushing a new emboldened corporate sensibility. In almost every visible expression from the company, the new role of the corporation was plain. Companies like Enron no longer had to acquiesce to groups of stakeholders or even the almighty shareholder. Rather, corporations like Enron cast themselves as forward-looking organizations charting a new path in a world that had become faster and more dynamic than before.

Enron's leadership had also begun to talk about the implications of a rapidly integrating international economy to investors. This sense of expanding global markets was evident in the 1996 annual report. While Enron's past annual reports had been relatively dry documents, the letter to shareholders in the 1996 edition offered a dramatic assessment of both domestic and international affairs. After a few perfunctory paragraphs, the letter read: "*In North America, the movement to deregulate the gas and electric utilities has begun. Deregulation is coming, inevitably and day by day.*" From this point forward, the document's author predicted that deregulation would be an ultimately benevolent force of creative destruction. The author wrote that "monopolies will be broken up—new markets will be liberated—and consumers will be able to reap benefits so big that they will actually improve the quality of life of individuals here and around the globe." The statement was a significant attempt to unite all the firm's operations under a single philosophical umbrella. Deregulation was "the force of the future," and, by extension, Enron was going to help usher in this future. Martial overtones could be found in statements such as: "*In the U.S. we are moving forward in a state by state advance* to support deregulation and quicken its pace." In addition to the combination of aggressive language and the more typical rhetoric of free markets, the last two paragraphs revealed the corporation's global view and ambition. Toward the letter's end, its author declared, "*In the industrial nations we continue to seize opportunities,*" while announcing in the subsequent paragraph, "*In the developing world we continue to move as markets open— and we continue to open them.*"[51]

Lay, Skilling, and others inside Enron, of course, had long held the view that free and open markets were, universally, the best systems for running industries, and by 1997 the timing seemed right for a more forceful advocacy for such markets. The optimistic rhetoric occasioned by the end of the Cold War now seemed wholly justified. Set against globalization's imagined landscape of countries throughout the world dismantling their own regulatory frameworks and merging into a seamless system that offered citizens of all nations personal freedom and prosperity, the company's aggressive advocacy for deregulation in the United States would not seem as radical to policy makers and a larger public as they would have at an earlier date. Even having a Democrat in the White House did not inspire fear among businessmen like Lay. While he had been active in the Republican Party during the 1992 presidential election, it scarcely mattered that Clinton handily defeated Dole four years later. During the first half of the 1990s, any ideological struggle or philosophical debate over economics had been settled.[52]

Still, the letter's vision of free markets uniformly blanketing the globe was a fantasy. Every geographical location had its own historical legacy and legal framework in place. As a result, there were many different shades of regulation or deregulation around the world. The contradiction mirrored the split at the heart of the Gas Bank. Much in the way an intricate, complicated series of financial procedures churned beneath the smooth surface of the En-Folio agreements offering an easy way to buy natural gas, a messy cultural and political process hovered above the firm's new vision of a world united by deregulated markets. If executives like Lay and Skilling saw their ideal world as one that was united through a free market that operated identically in all parts of the planet, this ideal would have to be pursued through an intense engagement with local politics and culture around the country. States and cities would have to be courted on an individual basis.[53]

Much in the way Lay had presented deregulation in Texas to Bush as a defensive move to prepare for intensified global competition, an implicit threat of economic disruption lurked just beneath the sunny lines about freedom and choice. Indeed, Skilling's own success had only brought more competition. In pursuit of the utopian, natural state of a world united by a single unregulated and free market, the company had to grudgingly acknowledge (and exploit) geographic difference—a contradiction that was most visible in Enron's efforts in the 1990s at electricity deregulation in the United States. To be sure, the mid-1990s at Enron were marked by what in retrospect was an unwarranted swagger and the start of a fraud that would steadily erode the ground underneath the firm. Yet it was also a time when the firm's managers recognized that they had few options beyond encouraging the creation of hypercompetitive markets in new industries and spaces, if only so that the company could briefly enjoy the benefits before frenetic competition inevitably arrived. What is more, "buy" recommendations from Wall Street analysts often assumed steady progress in liberalizing markets around the world and the further deregulation of electricity at home. In real, concrete ways, Enron's success depended on free markets.

No wonder, then, the 1996 letter to shareholders had the undertones of a military campaign. Enron might have been a gas company, but a concern over the state of that industry and Enron's place within it was not much in evidence. Enron's 1996 letter to shareholders was all about space. Luckily for the company's managers though, the letter was not just some bellicose howl into the void. Much in the way Enron's older "green" image mirrored a broader turn toward the environment, the letter's language described a consensus view of the world economy.

For instance, a 1996 report from the International Leadership Taskforce that Lay cochaired as part of the President's Council on Sustainable Development emphasized a global economy that seemed to be defined by competition. "American firms and workers," the report noted, "compete in a global economy shaped by global trends." Because of this, the United States had to assume a leadership role in the world. Summoning an older notion of a city on a hill, the report declared that "the model of American democracy and prosperity has shaped the hopes of many millions of people." Still, this perennial theme in American public discourse was couched in a document that unmistakably looked to the future. As a part of the taskforce's 1996 recommendations, the group championed "open access for, and participation of, nongovernmental organizations and private industry in international agreements and decision-making processes." The "grand new order" that Bush had predicted after the end of the Cold War seemed to have emerged. To be sure, the taskforce was first and foremost concerned with sustainable development and environmental protection. But the document unequivocally extended the logic and architecture of globalization that had a vast market in the center.[54]

Significantly, the 1996 taskforce recommendations also vigorously advocated for "global trading systems that mutually reinforce environmental protection and other social development goals." Indeed, the increasing globalization of markets around the world was presented in this document as an unambiguously positive development. The trade agreements the United States was undertaking, such as NAFTA, that were "designed to reduce trade barriers and improve equitable access to global markets" could do much for "greater global stability." To be sure, the report was clear that there was still a reconciliation needed between "trade and environmental objectives in an increasingly integrated world economy." However, the private sector would play a crucial role in this effort.[55]

Much like Lay's message for Bush earlier in the decade, the taskforce's recommendations did not rise to the level of a new environmental regulatory regime. Action 5, for example, recommended that the private sector "continue to move toward voluntarily adopting consistent goals that are protective of human health and the environment in its operations around the world." Similarly, Action 6 read, "All sectors can promote voluntary actions to build commitments and incentives for resource efficiency, stewardship, information sharing, and collaborative decision-making processes." Business was not a force to be restrained, but a resource to be tapped, and companies like Enron were reliable partners with government.[56]

It was a question, to be sure, of emphasis, but globalization was turning in Skilling's direction. It was markets, not sustainable development, that seemed to auger well for Enron's international businesses. In this regard, 1997 promised to be a pivotal year in terms of a global environmental effort. Not only would there be a follow up to the 1997 Earth Summit that March, but that December, a larger meeting, which would include representatives from both developed and developing countries, was set to take place in Kyoto, Japan. The outcome of that meeting, the Kyoto Protocol, was another development that Lay and his colleagues welcomed. Ever since the Clean Air Act had established a "cap and trade" system, Enron, with its trading expertise, had been a major buyer of emissions credits for industrial pollutants, like sulfur dioxide. Now, the Kyoto Protocol promised to establish an international system that mimicked the Clean Air Act's market-based solutions. Undeniably, though, the logic of a market-oriented vision of globalization had become dominant. Where the balance between the environment and trade seemed subtly tipped in the direction of the latter, Enron's own internal communications revealed a decisive shift.[57]

The change was almost immediately recognizable in the 1997 annual report. While the 1996 letter had declared the inevitable deregulation of industries and liberalization of markets, the new letter revealed a company that had been transformed in a section entitled "Who We Are." "We begin with a fundamental belief in the inherent wisdom of open markets," the letter read. "We are innovative. We are all about creating energy. We operate safely and with a concern for the environment."[58] In many ways, this statement offered a clear indication of the direction Enron was taking. The environmental rhetoric was still there. Indeed, the report's cover featured a photograph of lush, green leaves. However, it had taken a back seat to a political-economic investment in "open markets." The term "innovative," a deliberately highlighted word that the company and Wall Street analysts had always used, now began to form the core of the company's identity. Enron's management and marketing had jettisoned concrete descriptions of its business and instead emphasized a set of cultural, political, and economic values.

If, though, Enron's strategy was increasingly dependent on anticipating regulatory reform, the environmental concerns that permeated Enron's public image earlier in the decade, as well as popular understandings of globalization, continued to be a part of the conversation. Now the head of the firm's renewable energy efforts, Bob Kelly branched out into power projects beyond natural gas. In 1997, he became the head of Enron Renewable Energy Corporation (EREC), a subsidiary devoted exclusively to renewable energy.

The Houston company was hardly alone in its interest in renewable energy. EREC's creation mirrored steps that other large energy companies took in the late 1990s. A Department of Energy publication even mentioned that EREC's organization was just one of a number of welcome developments when it came to renewable sources of energy. That same year, British Petroleum, another energy company that was working hard to establish an environmentally friendly image, announced that it was going to increase its own solar power efforts, and Royal Dutch/Shell also pledged to spend more on renewable energy. Still, Enron's efforts were notable. In addition to the company's solar power partnership with Amoco, EREC acquired two wind turbine manufacturers, the German firm Tacke Windtechnik GmbH, and Zond, a California firm. Compared to the gas pipeline system that still formed the backbone of Enron's business, with fourteen wind farms, Zond was relatively small. After purchasing the California firm, though, Enron controlled over 30 percent of the country's renewable energy generation.[59]

In buying Zond, Enron also gained a stake in an enormously ambitious endeavor called the Northern States Power Project. In exchange for being able to store nuclear waste in outside containers in one of its nuclear power plants, Northern States Power Company (which operated in Minnesota, the Dakotas, and Wisconsin) agreed to building a large-scale wind farm. The project immediately put Enron at the center of the push for renewable sources of energy in the mid-1990s. Once Zond had become an Enron company, the project continued, with Enron's name now connected to it. The plan called for building a 107-megawatt wind power facility in Minnesota, making it the world's largest wind power project. In fact, the Northern States project was one of EREC's main goals for 1997 and a "critical project" for the wind group.[60] The scale of the project was indeed impressive. The wind turbines on Buffalo Ridge, in Minnesota's southwestern corner, stretched for fourteen miles. From this point, Enron Renewable Energy Corporation continued to add onto the project. In 1998, Enron Wind, as the subsidiary now running the project was branded, completed and inaugurated the Lake Benton I Wind

Power Generation Facility (also in Minnesota), which was intended to supply wind-generated energy for Northern States Power. Impressively, the project was the largest wind facility in the world.[61]

As with the environmentally inflected work the company undertook in the 1990s, Clinton's Energy Department was actively involved in encouraging the Northern States Power Project. The department, which was now headed by William "Bill" Richardson, even released a statement in support of Enron's efforts. Similarly, the assistant secretary of energy efficiency and renewable energy, Dan Reicher, attended the wind farm's dedication, regarding it as a "large-scale test of the wind resource in the Upper Midwest."[62] The department even claimed some credit in playing a "key role in supporting Enron Wind Corp. as they have become the current premiere wind turbine company in the United States."[63] To be sure, the Nevada solar field and the Minnesota wind farm were massive projects and—in the case of Minnesota—a dramatic transformation of the area's landscape. The press release indicated the degree to which Enron still maintained a considerable interest in environmentally sensitive lines of business.

Even if U.S. businesses were no longer scrambling to adopt the mantle of environmentalism with the same urgency that they had at the start of the decade, the American public remained concerned with environmental stewardship. EREC's domestic projects provided visible evidence of the company's sensitivity to cultural trends. Sustainable development projects outside of the United States, however, still presented a greater opportunity as countries continued to liberalize their economies. In fact, EREC extended the connection between Enron's interest in international development and clean sources of energy. Much in the way Enron's strategy in the early 1990s linked clean energy and international development, many of the projects that Kelly's group undertook in the second half of the decade were based abroad. By 1997, EREC's managers saw opportunities in far-flung places like China, Nepal, and (despite the trouble Enron's large power plant in Dabhol had run into) India.

In some ways, these renewable energy projects were parallels of a huge push from Kelly's old colleague in Enron International. Much like Lay, Rebecca Mark had become a vocal proponent of globalization and would just a few years later launch her own audacious project. In 1998, Enron created a water company called Azurix by acquiring an English utility Wessex Water (much in the way that Enron's initial venture into sustainable development began in England with Teesside).[64] However, Azurix also indicated how globalization's visibility and the decade's optimism were shaping management discourse. Speaking with a group of business school students at Baylor University not long after Enron's purchase of Wessex Water, Mark told the students, "Obviously, the world is not quite what it used to be, and those who believe that history will be a predictor of the future are apt to end up being blocked off" because "over the past decade, some truly significant strides have been taken" that "have changed just about everything we do, the way we relate, and the way we understand our world."[65] The statements reflected a dismissal of past experience that had become pervasive in the business world. Mark's insistence that deep industry experience and historical precedent did not matter reflected the same sense that the rules had fundamentally changed and that Skilling's success with the Gas Bank seemed to justify.

Indeed, Mark was not the first (and, in the way she prefigured similar pronouncements from figures like Jeff Skilling, nor the last at Enron) to make such statements. In fact, one of the messages of 1982's *In Search of Excellence* had been that the historical experience of American dominance after World War II could no longer be taken for granted. Indeed, after the dismal experience of the 1970s, it was business discourse and the shareholder revolution that had tossed out historical precedent (even if some corporate raiders insisted that they were agents of a return to basics anticonglomerate philosophy). However, discourse in the 1980s was still one of crisis—a feeling that by the mid-1990s had become an affirmative statement of a new age in global trade opening up. American corporations seemed to be doing better, and Mark's comments to the Baylor students reflected this optimism. The reasoning behind Azurix, though, had less to do with conserving a scarce resource than quickly seizing on the privatization of what had once been state assets. EREC, then, was still a unit that did not entirely line up with the firm's overall strategy.[66]

In other words, Kelly's plans were out of step with the rest of the company's direction. In some ways, the plans that EREC's team had for Enron was a high-water mark for the company's older environmental focus and image. Likewise, in some ways both EREC and Azurix were the last gasps of the older, vertically integrated organization that Enron had once been. Much like the environmental image that the company had been building for years, most of EREC's proposed plans involved large-scale, capital-intensive projects at the exact moment when such ideas were losing favor with influential managers like Jeff Skilling. The projects that EREC's management developed during these years mostly pointed in an entirely different direction for the company as a whole. While Skilling's unit was enjoying enormous success by selling financial products associated with the company's ability to move natural gas around the country, Kelly's presentations to Enron's board of directors emphasized large-scale, physical operations that were expensive and predicated on a long-term profit outlook, not short-term gains. Enron as a whole was morphing into something very different than it had been in 1985. By their very nature, renewable energy projects carry a heavy emphasis on the material world. The problem such ventures seek to address is how to extract energy from the natural environment without leaving it in shambles. Physical processes have to be addressed—what to build and where to build. However, Kelly also saw a role for EREC as Skilling began to prepare for wholesale electricity deregulation on the West Coast.

On February 2, 1997, Robert Kelly updated Enron's board of directors on Enron Renewable Energy Corporation's various activities. In an overview of the subsidiary's progress, Kelly reported on the company's wind and solar activities, which, in addition to Nevada, included activities in places like Hawaii and Rajasthan, near India. Kelly's presentation also called attention to the potential for "Green Power" in both the United States and Great Britain. However, more than anything else, the group was focused on looming deregulation in California. Throughout his presentation, Kelly framed the growing demand for clean energy among Californians as an opportunity for the company.

California's Bill 1890 called for "immediate direct access for customers who consume 50% renewables." There was, in other words, a substantial opening for a renewable energy company in California. In fact, EREC was already working to have wind-generated power ready to sell by the first of the year. Much like Lay and Skilling regarded energy deregulation in California as a way to demonstrate to the country the benefits of the free market, Kelly saw the state as only the first move in a nationwide push for marketing energy that the public would view as environmentally sound. Enron Renewable Energy Corporation was not the only company seeking to capitalize on the expectation of clean energy, but in his presentation Kelly highlighted what he regarded as a distinct advantage in "green power." EREC was ultimately a part of a much larger company and could draw on those resources. The scheme that Kelly presented to the board mobilized and connected significant portions of Enron's overall corporate structure. EREC would be in charge of generating renewable energy—wind and solar power—which could then be bundled, priced, and combined with other sources of kilowatt hours through Enron Capital and Trade, the business unit Skilling had created at the start of the decade. From there, the company's retail arm, Enron Energy Services, would be responsible for marketing renewable energy. What is more, Kelly also envisioned an advertising campaign for the environmentally sound sources of energy. Enron's brand in California would trade heavily on the promise of clean energy.[67]

Throughout the year, Kelly continued to stress the importance of California to the company's environmental efforts. Indeed, the tone that Kelly adopted became more urgent when he presented to the board of directors in May. "Enron Needs to Move Quickly to Capitalize on the Market in California . . . and to Be a First Mover Nationwide in Green Power," read one particularly insistent Power Point slide.[68] As the presentation noted, immediately after deregulation, California would have a $20 billion market for renewable energy that would only continue to grow. Enron's public relations strategy ahead of deregulation in California also highlighted environmental stewardship. For example, a 1997 press release announcing a partnership between NCPA (the Northern California Power Agency) and the company quoted a new state law calling for energy that would maintain "California's commitment to developing diverse, environmentally sensitive electricity sources."[69]

Importantly, Kelly also highlighted the cultural dimension to using clean energy in California. In April 1997, EREC commissioned a Gallup poll to gain insight into Californian attitudes toward clean energy. Much like the "feedback loops" that corporations had used for years to help them determine consumer desires, the poll's questions asked respondents in California what they regarded as "renewable, clean energy." The results were good news for the firm—Californians overwhelmingly regarded solar and wind power as renewable energy. A thin majority (51 percent) even regarded natural gas as clean energy.[70]

For Kelly, the implications for the company were clear. Much as it helped Lay position the corporation at the start of the decade, a culture of environmental concern in the state meant opportunities for Enron. One slide asserted, "Electric Power Consumers in California Are Increasingly Concerned About the Pollution Resulting from Electric Power Production," and "California Consumers Are Disposed to Buying Green Power." In fact, Kelly's presentation emphasized that Californians would be willing to pay a premium for "Green Power."[71]

Kelly's presentation, though, was more than just a description of EREC's activities and the opportunity that California represented. There were specific steps Kelly had in mind for capitalizing on this opportunity. Kelly was ultimately seeking $31 million for what the group was calling the "Green Project"—a fifty-megawatt wind facility—the first step in an integrated strategy. Adopting the phrase "Green Electrons," EREC's management imagined a marketing campaign that would highlight Enron's ability to produce power without "local pollutants" or "greenhouse gases." Kelly wanted to trademark the term and start running advertisements in the second half of 1997, ahead of deregulation, to "Push the Green Electron Image for Enron Corp." Though he was chiefly concerned with marketing in California, Kelly was also convinced renewable energy was destined to play a large role in Enron's future, and he pointed to a number of global energy trends, including "concern about the global environment" and "energy independence." While his presentation recalled the environmentalism and sustainable development that Lay had emphasized in the first part of the 1990s, by 1997 green globalization was no longer central to Enron's strategy. The business press was on the cusp of declaring a "new economy" that was centered on new technologies, and many companies were keen to become a part of this broader narrative. Enron, Kelly argued, could become a part of this "new economy" through marketing green energy.[72]

In May, Kelly asserted that EREC would be "an excellent IPO candidate" because the company's wind operations had a high potential for growth and the company's solar collaboration with Amoco was "High-Tech" in nature. Indeed, the unit aspired to be the "Microsoft of the Energy Business" with a stock that "Should Command High-Tech Growth Multiples on the High End of the Range." The way Kelly framed a potential stock offering for EREC—as Enron's opportunity to have a dotcom-esque stock price—was indicative of the overall business environment Enron was facing toward the end of the 1990s.[73]

In comparing EREC to Microsoft and emphasizing the high-tech nature of some of the business unit's operations, he was, in effect, downplaying the inherent materiality at the base of the company's business, and offering the board of directors and management team a way to position Enron as a high-tech company that was in step with the times. That Kelly would pitch a stock offering for EREC via comparisons to technology businesses was indicative of how the gravity of the U.S. economy was shifting. In the long arc of a historic bull market that began in 1982, 1996 represented a turning point when technology stocks began to take off. In 1995, Netscape, an Internet company, had become the largest initial public stock offering in the world. Over the first few years of the 1990s, management theorists like Peter Drucker and Gary Hamel had encouraged business leaders to think about the future. With the rise of Silicon Valley, that future seemed to be taking shape on the West Coast. Northern California's signature industry had clearly grabbed managers' attention in Houston.

Kelly's presentation was a far cry from the solar field proposal that was just a few years older or even the more recent wind farms in the Upper Midwest. In that short time, priorities and strategy at the company had shifted. The "green" California strategy and the emphasis on its prospects for a stock offering were more fully in line with a vision for the company that Skilling had developed. It also hinted at the priorities investment banking analysts had set for the company. Equity analysts had never fully embraced the company's emphasis on sustainable development and clean energy. Rather, Wall Street had long pinned the company's fortunes to deregulation at home and abroad. And in this regard, there was a great deal of continuity between Enron's leadership and Wall Street. Lay, of course, had always embraced the idea of free markets, and Skilling had developed a strategy for the Gas Bank that provided services for deregulated markets. Still, markets had always been talked about in secondary terms to issues, most notably sustainable development and clean energy. Yet by the middle of the decade, the company's annual reports increasingly reflected the more abstract emphasis on innovation and more deregulation and globalization that had long been a feature of analyst reports. Even Ken Lay, who had shrewdly wrapped his public remarks in terms of sustainable development and balancing business interests with environmental priorities, began to change his tune.

Now, he was a vocal proponent of trade policy reform that was not necessarily connected to clean energy. For example, *Enron Business* ran a story on the World Trade Organization's 1999 Seattle meeting where amid the loud and angry cries of an emerging antiglobalization protest movement, Lay described his "vision" of a "global economic future in which companies like Enron" would "compete in a 'transparent' free marketplace of goods, services and ideas, promising significant benefits to billions of people around the globe."[74] Lay now considered his company to be part of a "global trade agenda," and the firm's managers would have to become increasingly involved in a political-economic project of policy reform.[75] Lay himself, it appeared, never

missed an opportunity to promote this "global trade agenda." In a 1997 letter to Texas governor George W. Bush, the CEO wrote that he and his wife
"attend the World Economic Forum most years" and even sent Bush an article by the *New York Times* columnist Thomas Friedman about globalization.[76] Though Lay recommended the article as an "excellent overview of most
of the major issues concerning international financial markets and trade,"
he warned his friend that the piece also included "some of Friedman's own
biases toward particular safety nets."[77] The Houston executive, it seemed,
favored a purer globalization.

But to realize this vision required action. To that end, "grass-roots support from Enron employees" in "dealing with Congress on trade matters,"
would be needed to overcome the "subtle and overt" obstacles restricting the
"free flow of services between providers like Enron and the nations that need
and want them."[78]

That same month, Lay sent a letter to each member of Congress supporting a host of international issues such as funding OPIC (the Overseas Private Investment Corporation) and the Ex-Im (Export-Import) Bank (both of
which had benefited the company for years), as well as normalizing trade relations with China because the company believed "engagement in China, both
commercial and diplomatic, is the most effective way for the U.S. to promote
continued growth towards democratic ideals and free-market principles
in China."[79] Interestingly, though Lay opened his letter by describing Enron as
a "leading global energy company," he also wrote that the company looked
"forward to working with [Congress] on domestic legislative issues important to Enron, including electricity restructuring, water issues, Commodities
Future Trading Commission (CFTC) reauthorization, bankruptcy reform,
trade and tax policy."[80] Similarly, in 1999, when *Enron Business* listed the
government affairs group's accomplishments, it included the "accelerated
opening of the Pennsylvania market" and "significant progress of deregulation legislation in Texas, Ohio, Maryland, New Jersey and Nevada" alongside
the "lifting of sanctions against India and Pakistan" and the "re-authorization
of the U.S. Export-Import Bank, the Overseas Private Investment Corp.,
and the Trade and Development Agency."[81] The connection between the
company's domestic and international priorities was significant. In these
statements, Lay and *Enron Business* writers implied an ideal, economically
unified world that allowed capital and trade to flow across wide spaces without hindrance.[82] If environmental stewardship had started off as a centerpiece
of crafting the post–Cold War world, by the end of the twentieth century,

concerns over sustainable development had gradually been marginalized in favor of promoting a world market.

These years had also transformed Enron's strategy and structure in ways that reflected this broader shift. As FERC began to implement sections of the 1992 Energy Policy Act, and as states, particularly California, began to explore the ideas of electricity deregulation, Skilling and others at Enron Capital and Trade, which was becoming a more significant part of the firm's strategy, recognized a distinct advantage. What is more, this shift meant that Lay and others at the firm had become more invested in regulatory rollback on a variety of geographic scales. Just as important, Enron Capital and Trade's growing role led the company's managers to become intimately involved in transforming Houston's downtown. In some ways, these were gradual and subtle changes. By contrast, beginning in 1997, Enron's managers also devised a new and stunning corporate image. From that point forward, new ways of talking about and representing the company percolated both inside and outside of the firm's walls, ultimately leading to unintended and dramatic consequences.

CHAPTER 4

Selling Instability

The names of so many of them—Nighthawk, Osprey, Rawhide, Whitewing, Chewco—were downright goofy. And if they hadn't in the end ruined so many, the names of these special purpose entities, legally independent corporations that existed for the exclusive purpose of doing business with Enron, might all be laughed off. The flippancy with which these complex financial arrangements were named belied a wider sense of invincibility at the company. Enron's managers would soon be heralded as brilliant strategists. The company's next marketing campaign would have the wild feel of a visionary's fevered declarations, and amid all the adulation many failed to notice the growing problems with the goofy names.

Jeffrey Skilling had originally hired Andy Fastow to securitize the volumetric production payments the Gas Bank needed in order to function. Since then, the banker from Illinois had led JEDI, Enron's investment partnership with California's pension system (CalPERS). But despite these career successes, Fastow was restless, and in 1997, he (and others at Enron) wanted CalPERS to invest in a second JEDI fund. Pension managers on the West Coast, though, asked to cash out of the first investment fund. In order to pay CalPERS $383 million, Fastow created a special purpose entity named Chewco (like JEDI, a deliberate reference to *Star Wars*). But if that bargain seemed clear enough, the details were murky. Like all SPEs, Chewco was required by law to have at least 3 percent of its equity come from a source other than Enron. This rule was a sticking point. Unlike the company's first SPE, the Cactus Fund, there was little corporate appetite for investing in Chewco. But Fastow had originally been hired because of his novel approach to securitization. Finding the 3 percent should not have been a problem—and indeed it wasn't.

Because Fastow was unable to find an outside investor for Chewco, Michael Kopper, who worked with Fastow at Enron, became the source of the required outside equity—mostly through funds provided by Barclays Bank. While the arrangement at first skirted the lines of legality, the bank required Chewco to hold over $6 million to secure the Barclays financing (which was itself directed through Kopper). Because of the guarantee, there was no meaningful outside equity stake in Chewco.[1] Barclays had really made a loan, not an investment. Despite the convoluted financing, JEDI II, the new fund, was off and running. In the way that Enron's story is usually retold, Chewco's creation is a pivotal moment. The complicated arrangements of SPEs that soon followed JEDI II were connected to Enron through loan guarantees, derivative arrangements, hidden investors, and shares of Enron's stock (which was on the rise) and have become central features of most Enron narratives. Despite the enormous complexity of Fastow's schemes, the SPEs were irresistible for writers. Some of them, after all, were named after *Star Wars* characters.

Perhaps such inspiration for the names was fitting. In her own memoir, the whistle-blower Sherron Watkins remembered Fastow as a grown man with the temper and impulse control of a toddler. Though he was known as a prankster, he could also be prone to fits of anger. Watkins would also remember him as possessing an unnerving ambition that ultimately overshadowed the more attractive and playful aspects of his personality. At any rate, they served as vivid demonstrations of the basic ethical drift inside the company. They were also almost perfect instruments for delivering the grand irony at the heart of most Enron stories—the company was a failure. For example, over the course of several years an SPE called Whitewing bought assets from Enron and invested in Enron Energy Services, which was faltering. It was an early example of the "balance sheet management" that the company eventually relied on merely to operate. However, some of the more outlandish abuses of the SPEs would not appear until the last couple of years of the twentieth century. Later, so many would marvel that every gatekeeper along the way— lawyers, accountants, bankers, board members, and journalists—managed to ignore such plain fraud. But the clarity one gains looking back after the conclusion was not possible amid the optimistic and future-oriented business culture of the very late twentieth century. Much like their contemporaries, Enron's managers were enchanted, empowered, and ultimately ruined by the euphoric language and imagery of the "new economy."[2]

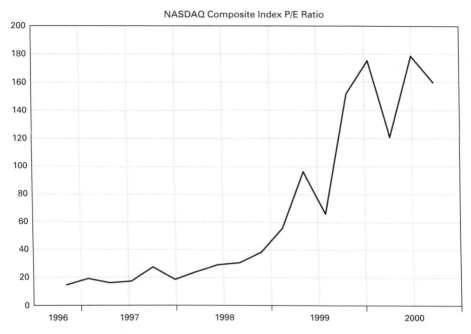

Figure 6. NASDAQ price-to-earnings (P/E) ratio, September 1996–December 2000.

By the middle of the 1990s, a widespread enthusiasm for the transformative promise of new information technologies fueled a sharp rise in the stock
market. In a dramatic vote of confidence in American business, the price-
to-earnings ratio (which measured the relationship between the price of a
stock and a company's income) for the technology-heavy NASDAQ composite
index began a steep climb upward in 1996 (Figure 6). The rise of technology
stocks was not simply a business story. A "new era" seemed to have dawned.[3]

Business reporters in the 1980s had written under the cloud of an uncertain future for American corporations, but economic flux was now seen as
undeniably positive. Business news was, by the mid-1990s, centered around
being the first to report a corporate merger—the sort of news item that was
directly related to the stock market. This shift happened at a time when more
people became invested in the stock market through retirement accounts. In
fact, some business journalists saw the move as the democratization of the
stock market. There were, to be sure, a few onlookers who worried about a

stock mania that had set in, but for the most part the prevailing mood was optimistic. As a result, the shareholder pressure that corporate leaders felt so viscerally in the 1980s intensified. As more national attention focused on stock performance, companies were under pressure to keep their own share prices aloft, and stories began to matter a great deal. Stocks tended to do better when narratives about business were positive. The NASDAQ's high price-to-earning (P/E) ratio, for instance, was a reflection of how stories being told by and about U.S. corporations were bolstering confidence in the economy. Americans were literally buying the story of a new economic age. The effects of these positive stories reverberated beyond stock tickers.[4]

This sense of newness was so complete that it erased older business and economic assumptions. Fears of American industrial decline became distant memories. Epochal change had been a mainstay of management discourse since the 1980s, but the tone was different now. While managers reading 1982's *In Search of Excellence* had been encouraged to experiment with organizational structure as a way to reinvigorate American businesses competing with Japanese firms, by the late 1990s business professionals were being told to experiment in the name of an expansive freedom. "Creative destruction" was not something to shrink from. American business writers were still Darwinian in their thinking, but they were no longer gloomy.

Like many corporate leaders, some of Enron's top managers had internalized this sunny futurism. Much like his rival Rebecca Mark had told students at Baylor that history was no longer a reliable guide to business planning, Skilling would promote the idea of a new economic epoch throughout the second half of the 1990s. His own experience with the Gas Bank seemed to vindicate such a sensibility, but communicating the ways in which the company was changing continued to be a challenge. In the past, Skilling had drawn on East Coast banks to provide analogies for the business he had created. Now, however, the West Coast would be the source of inspiration. At the same time the company was pursuing electricity deregulation in California, the new businesses sprouting up in the northern part of that state would provide Skilling with the language that Enron lacked. In addition to their shared business sensibilities, the respective lexicons of both Silicon Valley and Wall Street arrived in Houston.

The technology companies fueling the post-1996 stock boom were the products of Silicon Valley, far from Enron's offices on Smith Street in Houston or the gas fields in places like Big Piney, Wyoming. Alongside the new technologies northern California firms were creating, the "new economy" was also a cultural project that offered a new vision of work and life through cultural outlets including management consultants, business schools, books, and magazines such as *Fast Company*, *Wired*, and *Business 2.0*. Though the "new economy" sensibility had been building since the 1970s, by the mid-1990s, through these outlets, the new economy's chroniclers and champions developed a distinct visual and rhetorical style. Before long, Enron's managers became participants in the "new economy's" cultural project.[5]

As journalists, copywriters, and graphic designers in northern California crafted a ready stock of tropes, images, and metaphors, Enron's managers adopted them as their own. In particular, Silicon Valley's rhetorical emphasis on "the entrepreneur" and "knowledge work" aligned closely with the ways in which Skilling was reshaping Enron's strategy and structure. In the firm's London office, for example, an employee named Louise Kitchen was leading a team working to develop an online trading platform. But while Kitchen's team worked quietly on this project, Silicon Valley's influence on the Houston company became otherwise hard to miss.[6]

In the first few months of 1998, the company's share price dropped below twenty dollars, its lowest point since 1992. With the freneticism of the new economy playing out in the stock market, corporate image and narrative had become all the more important. Soon, the language in Enron's marketing literature began to resemble the rhetorical style of "new economy" writers. Enron's "new economy" image signaled an organizational pivot toward business strategies that resembled the Gas Bank and publicly aligned the firm with technology start-ups with soaring stock prices.[7]

Kevin Kelly, *Wired* magazine's editor in chief, might as well have had the Houston company in mind while at his writing desk. In his book *New Rules for the New Economy*, the Californian declared that "intangible things" would "soon command the world of the hard—the world of reality, of atoms, of objects, of steel and oil." Though primarily concerned with computer code and small slivers of silicon, the magazine editor wrote that these "new rules" held for other "wispy entities" including "information, relationships, copyright, entertainment, securities, and derivatives." For Kelly, the triumph of "wispy entities" had weighty implications. "Networks," the author proclaimed, had become "the central metaphor around which our thinking and economy are organized." Perhaps the wispiest of anything the new economy produced, in 1997, the company had begun trading derivatives contracts to hedge against changes in the weather that might hurt businesses (such as gas heating companies).[8]

The Silicon Valley writer also shared a political sensibility with the Houstonians. Much in the way Kenneth Lay and Skilling were becoming increasingly vocal about the benefits of free markets, Kelly reasoned that the "network of objects" could "govern itself."[9] Besides, he argued, the "best systems" had a "living quality of few rules and near chaos."[10] A decade and a half after Tom Peters had championed the idea of "chaos" in an organization, Silicon Valley boosters had reworked management writing to assume a much larger cultural and historical significance. Even before the tech boom, Skilling had taken to heart the management literature of the 1980s. Now, Skilling had a way to push this vision outside of the firm's walls.[11]

Apart from the connection between narratives and the stock market, Ken Lay acknowledged the importance of stories in his contribution to the 1998 management book *Straight from the CEO*. Because of deregulation in wholesale electricity, Lay noted that energy companies would have to directly engage consumers through "branding and aggressive advertising."[12] Yet this would be no easy task. "Given the invisibility of both methane and electrons," he counseled, "a company's most important marketing edge will be the public's goodwill."[13] Lay wanted Enron to have the recognition that companies such as IBM and AT&T enjoyed.[14] The company's managers intended to be far more active in shaping Enron's corporate image. By 1997, the company had started this process of overhauling Enron's official identity. Early that year, the company swapped its clunky, old logo (that vaguely resembled cranks turning) for a colorful design that turned out to be one of the last logos created by the famous graphic designer Paul Rand (Figure 7).[15]

Elegant in its simplicity, Rand's design captured the emerging spirit and business strategy at Enron. The logo's distinctive forty-five-degree slant, he asserted, would suggest "a promise of meaning."[16] Similarly, the different colors in the logo would "reinforce the idea of a pipeline" but would not "preclude other ideas."[17] The design's flexibility perfectly suited the company's rapid evolution beyond natural gas. Marketing executives in Texas were thrilled (Figure 8). "All of us at Enron," the company's senior vice president of corporate marketing and resources wrote to Rand, "are quite proud of the 'Big E!' "[18]

This new corporate identity was not just superficial. Though he admitted to initially being skeptical of the Internet, Skilling must have felt a shock of recognition when new economy business magazines began trumpeting the triumph of the " 'Net." Complex networks created opportunities to exploit. As long as a firm had the legal ability to exercise a previously superfluous

Figure 7. Paul Rand's Enron logo was on display outside Enron Tower in downtown Houston. Photo by Orla Schantz.

Figure 8. Kenneth Lay and Jeffrey Skilling with a mascot featuring the new logo. Photo courtesy of Southwest Collection/Special Collections Library, Texas Tech University, Lubbock, Texas.

option when the opportunity arose, complexity itself became a competitive advantage. As the "new economy" picked up steam, Skilling became increasingly enamored of what he saw as its potential. The vocabulary of Silicon Valley quickly slipped into Skilling's own use of language. While describing Enron's gas pipelines for a business school class at the University of Virginia in 1998, Skilling drew on Silicon Valley principles such as Sarnoff's Law and Metcalfe's Law that posited an exponential growth in value in a two-way network. By dubbing such concepts "laws," the more impressionistic and descriptive management literature that had appeared during the 1980s now acquired the certainty of indisputable economic fact.[19]

Houston may have been a long way from Silicon Valley, but Skilling and others at Enron had suddenly been given a solution to the long-standing problems in describing Enron's newer business models. As the visual and rhetorical convention of the "network" began to circulate beyond northern California, Skilling, and Enron's marketing department no longer had to worry about tortured and awkward phrases in descriptions of Enron's services. By self-consciously adopting the ethos of Silicon Valley, the company's pipes and power lines could be rendered as "networks" in both image and word. The covers of the company's last three annual reports (1998–2000) reflected the new style, as photographs of young knowledge workers on the phone or standing in front of computers almost entirely replaced those of power plants or pipelines comfortably nestled among rolling green fields and pastures.

For example, the 1999 cover featured four people in a blank space, standing inside a box with smooth white edges. The rest of the page featured several arcing, elliptical lines. This visual motif, meant to symbolize the company's "networks" connecting people and things across space and time, was persistent throughout the report. The move itself was striking. The predominant visual imagery Enron was now using mostly consisted of metaphors (when nodding toward representation) or entirely abstract, nonrepresentational design.

The change was equally dramatic in the company's rhetoric. In linguistic echoes of the new graphic design, the 1999 and 2000 annual reports repeatedly emphasized the importance of "networks," "innovation" and "creativity." Here, the authors directly drew on the stock of metaphors and "rhetorical flourishes" that could be found throughout what theorist Nigel Thrift calls the "cultural circuit" of the "new economy" that, much like the management literature of the 1980s, both described and celebrated a more chaotic world.

Rather than highlight clean-burning power plants or environmentally sensitive pipeline construction as it had in the past, the company's marketing literature now emphasized values such as innovation and creativity. Paradoxically, this shift exacerbated some of the problems of language and representation that had dogged the company since the creation of the Gas Bank.[20]

In a sharp contrast to the earlier letters to shareholders in the company's annual reports, the 1999 letter's tone became declarative and confrontational. After a few vague paragraphs about the nature of "networks," the document launched into wild statements about a "new economy," proclaiming: "the rules have changed dramatically. What you own is not as important as what you know. Hard-wired businesses, such as energy and communications, have turned into knowledge-based industries that place a premium on creativity." Though it had been a concern in the past, Enron's top executives now embraced the inadequacy of language in describing what the company had become. As the 1999 letter to shareholders declared: "Enron is moving so fast that sometimes others have trouble defining us. But we know who we are. We are clearly a knowledge-based company." The corporation, it seems, was beyond meaning.[21]

By 2001 Enron's literature no longer described the firm as a "vertically integrated clean energy company," but rather an assemblage of "flexible networks" that could "deliver physical products at predictable prices."[22] "With our networks," the company's 2000 annual report declared, "we can significantly expand our existing businesses while extending our services to new markets with enormous potential for growth."[23] The letter made clear the corporation's transformation, declaring that Enron was no longer "an asset-based pipeline and power generating company," but rather "a marketing and logistics company whose biggest assets are its well-established business approach and its innovative people."[24] With such statements, Enron seemed to be the fulfillment of new economy predictions that "intangible things" would control "the world of the hard."[25]

Internally, the vocabulary was shifting, too. In 2000, managers renamed the pipeline division "Enron Transportation Services" to reflect "a cultural shift to add more innovative customer services to our efficient pipeline approach." Here, the linguistic substitutions emphasized nebulous ideals ("innovative customer services") over specific material processes. Instead, the business unit would be "faster" and become "more competitive." In both their internal communications and external marketing efforts, Enron's managers increasingly celebrated a world that was both immaterial and unstable. Such new language swept away the last vestiges of the material world. Enron's pipeline business would now "be driven by customer needs and market demands, rather than the dictates of energy regulators."[26]

But this corporate metamorphosis was not without casualties. Though Enron's top managers were supportive of the United Nations' 1997 Kyoto Protocol on global warming because it presented a greater opportunity to trade carbon emissions, as the firm downplayed its physical assets, its emphasis on ecologically sound energy sources also disappeared. The connection between energy and the environment was rooted in the material challenges of generating fuel and power without scarring the land or spoiling the planet's water and air. The language of the new economy and finance, with all the emphasis on fluidity and creativity, simply could not accommodate something so tangible and earthy as clean air or fresh water.

Nor were these changes limited to the firm's domestic businesses. Overseas investments in capital-intensive projects were now losing favor inside the company. Skilling, in particular, was uninterested in such projects because large-scale capital investments simply did not earn enough of a return.[27] Projects like Teesside and Dabhol were too fixed in place and did not provide the sort of flexibility Skilling now regarded as crucial to the firm's business. Though an "acrimonious" debate among the company's managers had been going on since the middle of the 1990s, Enron's struggling water business was a final confirmation that the new direction for the company was the right one. What Skilling would later call "the last hurrah of the asset-based philosophy," was a clarifying episode.[28] Rebecca Mark left both Enron's board and Azurix in the middle of 2000.[29]

Still, even if it was implied more than it was implemented, being a "global" company was a crucial marker for corporations at the end of the twentieth century.[30] Now, however, the axis of Enron's global operations rotated away from the developing world and toward trading desks in England and Europe.[31] Reflecting this shift, in 2000, the firm launched "Project Summer," an attempt to sell off the company's non-European businesses abroad.[32] Not only would this free up capital (and allow the firm some breathing room to reduce its dividend), but it would also redirect Enron's investments toward prospects with higher returns. Europe was particularly fertile ground for expanding Enron Energy Services, which was reorganized into four different segments: EES–North America, EES–Europe, Global Energy Services, and EES New Ventures.[33] When the annual report's letter to shareholders in 2000 trumpeted the company's "networks," there was a distinct sense that these were global networks. Enron was no longer a potential symbol of sustainable development. In his popular account of globalization *The Lexus and the Olive Tree*, Thomas Friedman even used an Enron pipeline project in South America as an example of new pressures on the environment that came with international development. What excited the journalist about Enron was the ways the Houston company was beginning to resemble a Silicon Valley firm.[34]

At least one new business, Enron Online, had been a huge success. By the end of the first year of its operations (1999), Enron's marketing literature claimed, over half a million transactions had taken place via the online system, and it had become "the world's largest web-based eCommerce system."[35] By the middle of 2000, about half of the company's business was taking place over the system.[36] In many ways, the platform was the culmination of the business model that Skilling had first developed at the start of the decade, but it was also an opportunity to move far beyond the natural gas industry. Enron Online was the entry point through which the company launched trading businesses for a number of commodities. Clickpaper.com, for instance, would allow the company to trade forest products.[37] The new economy's nomenclature also spread to other business units at Enron. Even Enron Energy Services, through a partnership with IBM and AmericaOnline, created a unit called the New Power Company, which quickly went public in anticipation of increased power deregulation in the United States.[38] The evolution of Enron's advertising campaign reflected these internal changes.

The company's 1997 print advertisements had reflected an older aesthetic. One advertisement emphasized a commitment to neighborliness when the company began offering electricity services in Peterborough, a small town in New Hampshire. Underneath a folksy image of a farmer standing in front of a red barn, the advertisement's copy began: "In a state whose motto is Live Free or Die, people didn't like paying some of the highest energy rates in America. So they all got together and went shopping for a new energy company." The state's Revolutionary motto was now about bargain hunting. "One day soon," the advertisement read, "those voices could span a nation."[39] Other advertisements presented similar stories about how the company had provided heating for a zoo in Nebraska and schools in Ohio. This unassuming tone did not last too long. By 2000, the firm's marketing campaign (which had expanded) mirrored the new economy futurism in its annual reports, as well as the problem of describing the company. An article in *Enron Business* on the new campaign opened with the problem of representation, asking: "How do you describe a company like Enron?"[40] It had not been an easy task. The company's ad agency interviewed "Enron's leading thinkers" about the company, a phrase that indicated the company's move toward operating in "brain-intensive businesses" and "intellectual capital."[41] The campaign's eventual title and motif reflected this emphasis. Titled "Ask Why?" the message of the campaign was meant to be "as different and challenging as Enron itself"—which was an understatement.[42] Several years earlier, Paul Rand had suggested that "identity and product are one" in explaining how the new logo he designed could be used in conjunction with photographs of the company's power plants.[43] Though it was only one of several points the late designer had made about his work for Enron, the statement had been prophetic.

The commercials' aesthetic collapsed various thematic strains together to come up with an exciting (if confusing) representation of specific ideological values. Throughout the advertising campaign, declarations that older ideas sometimes had to be "jettisoned" positioned the company as forward thinking. As the *Enron Business* article explained, the commercials were meant to "communicate the spirit of Enron, the drive that distinguishes it from every other energy company, indeed almost any other company in existence."[44]

In one commercial, a figure in a metal business suit wandered different parts of the world. The man, obviously encumbered by the suit (vaguely recalling the Tin Man in *The Wizard of Oz*), slowly moved through a series of spaces, such as busy street corners in cities like New York. The quick, frenetic movement around him offered a striking contrast to his slow, awkward gait. Periodically, an audible phrase would break away from a din of background chatter. As one voice (before cutting over to a close up of an older man with a serious visage) intoned: "We inherit some ideas that are unnecessary. We have to jettison that excess baggage in order to make progress."[45] After a few more seconds another voice declared, "People who have really creative ideas are people who keep asking 'why?'" as the man in the stiff metal suit lumbered through other global, fast-paced environments.[46] The final shot was a black screen with the words "ask why?" below the Enron logo. The *Enron Business* article explained to employees that the "the man in metal serves as a metaphor for the conventional constraints that block change."[47]

The script of one of the commercials proclaimed that "why" was "the word of the nonconformist." Throughout, the television spot cut among a series of unrelated images, such as a space shuttle taking off, a statue of Gandhi, a photograph of Abraham Lincoln, a civil rights march, clips from other Enron commercials, and the Dutch insurance company Nationale-Nederlanden's office in Prague, which had been designed by the architect Frank Gehry and built in the mid-1990s as the pressures of globalization were remaking urban space around the world.[48]

These television commercials had moved far beyond the affable feel of the print campaign a few years earlier. The 2000 advertising campaign was intended, above all, to promote "Enron's restless dissatisfaction with the status quo and its ability to quickly grasp how most things can always be improved."[49] Ultimately, the company's hope was that the commercials' tagline, "ask why," would "become the rallying cry of a new generation of business."[50] The television spots, which began running in February on the business news channels and during the nightly broadcast news, were aimed at "elected and appointed officials who set policy and regulations affecting Enron business worldwide" in addition to potential corporate customers.[51] The "ask why" campaign, in other words, was inherently political.

Though authoring a "rallying cry" for business was an ambitious goal, in some ways Enron was a natural choice to be an iconic new economy firm. Throughout the late 1990s, *Fortune* remained one of Enron's biggest supporters, repeatedly pointing to (and approving of) the company's "innovative" culture and strategy. While Enron's promotional literature and Wall Street analysts had used the word "innovative" for years, the company loudly championed the idea along with the new economy's appearance. By 1997, even Rich Kinder warned that good ideas could, "like a lighted match," be "blown out by the cold winds of rigid management."[52] Such quotations offered direct reflections of what one historian calls the "antimanagerial" rhetoric of the new economy.[53] Along with this new approach to management, an article in *Fortune* attributed Enron's success to ignoring "the geniuses in Washington" and "creating spot markets in gas."[54] Such articles offered a perfect summation of the new spirit of business that Enron championed in its television commercials. An absence of government oversight (the "geniuses" remark was dripping in sarcasm), as well as a staff of smart, young symbolic analysts who were given free reign, were uniformly positive developments. As evidence of the company's success, business journalists and others pointed to the company's rising stock price (Figure 9).[55]

Even though in some ways 1997 was not a good year for the company (Enron reported over half a billion dollars in losses in the second quarter of 1997, and even as late as 2000 some of the "Ask Why" spots raised the

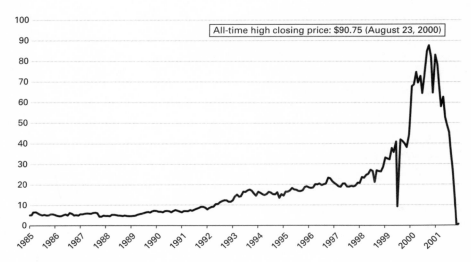

Figure 9. Enron's changing stock price.

anxious specter of unhappy equity analysts), a writer for *Fortune* declared that there were "good reasons to take post-1997 Enron seriously" because of a commitment to "innovation" in creating "new businesses such as electricity trading, in which kilowatts are bought and sold like pork bellies."[56]

There was, though, a distinct irony in these expert assessments that Enron's management was now on the right track. After all, it was the creation of Chewco and JEDI II that same year that marked the firm's slip into a fraud that only grew more elaborate over the next few years. Still, this was far from the view of business journalists covering the company. The turbulent transition out of the early 1990s, in which the world had to first contend with the end of the Cold War and the growing realization of planetary threats to the environment, had given over to a smoother and much more optimistic sensibility. Enron's transformation under Skilling's leadership was becoming a prominent example of such business-driven utopianism.

That Enron was more like a Silicon Valley dotcom than a Texas pipeline company was the prevailing attitude in the business press. *BusinessWeek*, for example, began including the company in "E.Biz" inserts in 2000 and 2001. One such 2001 article featured a photograph of Jeff Skilling in a golf shirt and jeans that was a far cry from the formal suit he had preferred in earlier years. Though such images echoed California business celebrities like Steve

Jobs, Skilling had preserved some details from the Southwest. By 2001, when Skilling was finally named CEO, he had also cultivated a rugged image, preferring his Land Rover Defender 90 to his Mercedes, and leading a small clique of Enron men on trips to Cabo that resembled Mountain Dew commercials. Despite his upbringing in Illinois, he had adopted a Texan's swagger. When asked by *Enron Business* about any advice he could offer to employees, he answered, "If you've got no cattle, don't wear a big hat."[57] Still, even if Skilling had dusted off an old cowboy-ism, to the press, Enron seemed far more forward looking.[58]

In language that mimicked Enron's self-presentation, the article's title, "From Sleepy Utility to Online Turbotrader," suggested rapid movement and flux, while the author described Skilling as "restless."[59] Business journalists, however, were not the only voices declaring Enron's culture and business as "perfectly suited to the Internet Age."[60] In 2000, *Time* magazine described Enron as "a company that thrives on entrepreneurial defiance of convention" and characterized the Gas Bank as a stunning example of "business judo."[61] Enron was pushing ahead while "so many old-economy companies" appeared "helpless against the dizzying pace and technology of the digital age."[62]

In short, the rebranding worked. By 2000, the company had become far more associated with the "new economy," and it was a point of pride for executives when the Motley Fool, an investment website, added the company to its "Now 50" index. The continued *Fortune* coverage revealed how complete Enron's image had changed. In an article that later rankled the liberal writer and cultural critic Thomas Frank (for comparing Enron to Elvis), one journalist described the company's stock performance as "Nasdaq-like." Indeed, the stock price would pass ninety dollars a share toward the end of that year. As these articles suggest, by the end of the century, Enron had succeeded in transforming its corporate image, at least in the business press. No longer a natural gas pipeline company, business journalists now referred to Enron as an "agent of change" helping to usher in deregulation and free markets.[63]

The firm was also becoming a case study in the decade's management literature. In particular, Gary Hamel's end-of-the-century management tract, *Leading the Revolution*, devoted considerable space to the company. Much like his books from earlier in the decade, Hamel continued to advocate for an approach to business centered on tossing off the shackles of the past. Hamel had long criticized business school education in the 1980s, seeing it as too narrowly focused on industry boundaries. In the introduction of his book, Hamel recounted how his dissatisfaction with such thinking had led him to Silicon Valley, where he would be surrounded by dotcoms that were refreshingly "devoid of tradition." The future, all full with furious competition, had arrived. "Incrementalism," Hamel wildly declared, was at its end. It would be the few companies dedicated to "radical innovation" and "creating revolutions" that would find success. Stylistically, Hamel's book, even in its layout, built off of the dynamic and frenetic graphic design that characterized many popular management books in the late 1990s. Pull quotes in large fonts suggested a digital world, or zipped across the page at steep angles to represent the dynamic economy Hamel was describing. Like many management books from the era, the graphic design also leaned heavily on stock footage in order to metaphorically reference Hamel's business principles. In the section on Enron, for example, one page included an old black and white photograph of two men playing a game of tennis on the wings of a biplane as it flew through the air.[64]

Echoing the company's own marketing literature, Hamel praised Enron as a place full of "activists." In the chapter "Gray-Haired Revolutionaries," the author credited Ken Lay and Jeff Skilling with transforming natural gas into a highly efficient market, and changing "electric power grids from stodgy old-boys' clubs into flexible energy markets." But Lay's true genius, Hamel insisted, was in creating an organization where "thousands of people see themselves as potential revolutionaries." Echoing the story he liked to tell about his first days with the Gas Bank, in the pages of Hamel's book Skilling recounted that by the time he learned about Enron Online they had "already started ripping apart the building."[65]

These stories were perfect examples of the "revolutionary" organization Lay and Skilling had created. Enron's organization, Ken Rice told the author, was like a "nuclear reactor" where the company's "cowboys" (like the boot-wearing Rice) bounced ideas off each other. This business nuclear reactor was like a "cauldron" that would allow "Enron's innovative energies" to "circulate." Through this creative process, Enron's managers had arrived at a profound insight: there was no such thing as a business or industry, Rice declared, that couldn't *be structured in a fundamentally different way to create new value.*" Hamel reasoned that Enron's success would come from market-like internal structures. Enron had, he argued, a "vibrant internal market" for new ideas and an "open market for talent." Hamel's writing, of course, was particularly hyperbolic, but not far removed from the wider, market-based metaphors that had become so dominant at Enron and the larger business community.[66]

Houston at the Millennium

Enron's influence also seemed to resonate beyond business books and magazines. When Enron Capital and Trade had begun advertising its analyst program in the mid-1990s, the company tried to frame Houston as a Wall Street in the West—an idea that would seem apt later in the decade. By the end of the 1990s, the city's downtown was also becoming a new center for energy trading. Even Pacific Gas and Electric in California opened an office in Houston because of electricity deregulation on the West Coast. New companies and older firms were opening trading floors in downtown Houston. Likewise, Coastal Corporation, which had launched a takeover bid in the 1980s when Lay's company was considered weak, took a cue from Enron Capital and Trade by forming a partnership called Engage Energy. The new world of energy in downtown Houston seemed more akin to Wall Street in lower Manhattan or commodities trading in Chicago than the old Energy Corridor along a stretch of I-10 west of downtown. Skilling had indeed been prescient when he positioned Enron Gas Services to expand into electricity trading. Now, Skilling told the *Houston Business Journal* that Enron intended to grab as much of the market as they could and as quickly as possible. The journal, for its part, praised Skilling's foresight and genius in anticipating the market, and the changes it had brought to the city.[67]

Similarly, additions to Enron's own headquarters responded to the new types of business in Energy Alley downtown. In 1999, work began on a second building on an empty lot that Enron had purchased during the days of cheap real estate as Houston recovered from the oil glut. "In addition to the tower," an *Enron Business* article informed employees, "a seven-story base that spans a full city block will house four state-of-the-art trading floors with technical capacity that will rival the New York Stock Exchange."[68] If, as the historian Stuart Leslie contends, a building's "façade announces the corporation's civic aspirations," then the additions to Enron's headquarters suggested a new role for Houston in a global economy.[69] The building itself was meant to be massive. This was fitting because Lay was quoted in the article as saying Enron's Houston-based workforce would "swell by 20 to 30 percent" by 2001.[70]

When the new building, named Enron Center, was finished, a circular, space-age walkway above the street provided a connection to the original building (Figure 10). Though such walkways had long been a feature of that neighborhood, the aesthetic sensibility of the walkway that connected Enron Tower with the newer Enron Center seemed a deliberate attempt to refashion the downtown for a more globalized city and economy. While Houston had sometimes been called "Space City" because of NASA's presence, and though the circular walkway recalled a midcentury design style that could even be found in the Astrodome, both Enron Center and the walkway attempted to locate high technology and knowledge work with other energy companies in the city's center, and not on the outskirts (with the old stadium).

Enron Center also hinted at the ways in which a business revolution on the West Coast was influencing Enron. Though the structures were downtown, by providing employees with a gym, daycare, and restaurants, the company hoped to build the "premier urban office campus," indicating the degree to which Silicon Valley workplace philosophies had arrived in Houston.[71] With the blend of Wall Street trading desks and West Coast computer programming campuses on Smith Street, the company had managed to craft the beginnings of the Western Wall Street its old recruitment advertisements had promised. Enron's influence was evident throughout other parts of downtown.

In 2000, just three years after earthmovers and trucks had begun work on the ground where trains had connected the city to a wider world, the Astros played their first game in a new ballpark that bore the name Enron Field—a game that both former president George H. W. Bush and his son George W. Bush attended (Figure 11).[72] Elements like a "full-sized, detailed, vintage locomotive" referenced both the stadium's location and "Houston's most important industry" in the early part of the century.[73] Providing "just the boost downtown Houston needed," the ballpark, *Enron Business* declared, had "ignited the imagination of Houstonians" by recalling the "days when baseball was played on intimate fields, not mammoth multi-sport arenas."[74] What is more, the company's magazine proclaimed, Enron Field had served as a model that inspired "developers to recreate the glory of downtown on a human scale. Modern condominiums hide behind historic facades. New dwellings echo the style of years ago. Construction is designed to invite both the resident and visitor to linger and unwind."[75] However, such a nostalgic sensibility was selective. The ballpark anchored a downtown revitalization that was markedly different from the city's midcentury boom.

Figure 10. Additions to Enron's headquarters in downtown Houston. Photo by Jeffrey Brandsted.

Figure 11. Opening day at Enron Field. Photo courtesy of Southwest Collection/ Special Collections Library, Texas Tech University, Lubbock, Texas.

Billions had been spent in construction, and in a sharp contrast to the days of vacant buildings during hard times in the 1980s, the vast majority of Houston's downtown office space had been leased. Not only were construction projects underway, but over 150 new restaurants and clubs had opened in the area. The number of residents had tripled in less than two years, and property values were rising. The message of downtown renewal was hard for Houstonians to ignore on opening day. A promotional book celebrating the Astros' new home invited fans to wander the neighborhood after the game and eat at new places serving Texas barbeque, Vietnamese cuisine, and Spanish tapas, or at a Mexican restaurant that had long been an area fixture. Besides dinner, there were now sake bars and jazz clubs. Some of Enron's workers could be counted among downtown's new residents. Younger employees were buying townhomes and apartments in Midtown, just on the east side of the Southwest Freeway, a road that earlier generations of energy

Figure 12. Downtown Houston in the late 1990s.

Key:
A: Enron Headquarters
B: Enron Field
C: Bayou Place
D: Spy Club
E: The Rice Luxury Apartments
F: Hogg Palace
G: Zydeco
H: The 43rd Restaurant
I: Solero

executives would have taken to quieter neighborhoods (Figure 12). Following the new bars, clubs, and restaurants opening in the city's center, young Enron workers were participants in the neighborhood's gentrification, and all the social problems that accompanied this process. In measurable ways, Houston's downtown was livelier. More than forty-eight hundred new residents had moved there over the course of the decade. For happy hours, Enron's traders favored the Front Porch, a bar on Gray Street in Houston's Fourth Ward.[76]

The opening game at Enron Field represented the culmination of a long process for Lay that had started with his work on the welcoming committee for the World Economic Forum a decade earlier. Fittingly, Lay's investment in the ballpark also reflected the ways in which business interests throughout U.S. cities were reimagining urban space as places that served their own needs. Older projects creating entertainment zones like Baltimore's Inner Harbor or Manhattan's South Street Seaport had fostered an entrepreneurial vision of urban renewal. Like these other cities, Enron could now offer potential employees life in "a city as vital and exciting as Enron is itself."[77] Lay reasoned that "the best talent and the brightest people may not be happy or be stimulated in a city without a center or a vibrant soul."[78] Even as all these spaces referenced the past, they were unmistakably remade spaces— Enron Field, the Inner Harbor, and South Street Seaport were bids to make their respective cities more competitive in luring capital and business investment.[79] A convention center attached to the ballpark was a clear signal of the commercial impulses behind Enron Field and downtown's transformation.[80] In addition to the ballpark, starting in 1997, the company had sponsored an annual Enron Earth Day music festival—an echo of the now-fading "green" image the firm's leadership had once embraced.

If these physical changes in Houston—from Enron Center to Enron Field—reflected the powerful influences of both Wall Street and Silicon Valley, they also paralleled linguistic and cultural shifts taking place inside the firm. Jeff Skilling had used investment banks as a model for his own organizational structure since the earliest days of the Gas Bank. By 2000, though, banking and finance had become a metaphor for the executive's approach to human resources. *Fortune* magazine, for instance, praised Skilling's ability to protect "knowledge assets" by creating a "flexible internal labor market" that rotated people throughout the company without changing titles or salaries. Descriptions of how Skilling had "securitized" the firm's "intellectual risks" by managing employees as if, like stocks or bonds, they were "part of a portfolio," revealed the extent to which financialization had taken root at Enron. The *Fortune* article's mixed metaphors, as well as on-the-nose discussions about risk taking in *Enron Business*, were emblematic of broader linguistic conflations beginning to take place at Enron.[81]

Alongside the language of investment banking, the jargon of Silicon Valley and management theory began to comingle, and their origins in different parts of the economy from different decades started to recede from view. As Skilling adopted terms like "optionality," "flexibility," and "networks," the distinctions among them—and among finance and computer programming—simply vanished. The flexibility that Skilling ultimately wanted was the product of obtaining as many options as possible. Indeed, this had been the firm's experience with options contracts that had been at the core of the Gas Bank's functioning. Metaphors from the world of finance slipped into the terminology Enron employees were using at the very moment the company's financing practices became even more complex. As they did, the logic of the firm's business changed.[82]

By the late 1990s, investment banks began including clauses in derivatives contracts that allowed one party to alter the terms of an agreement as interest rates changed, a practice that was termed "optionality."[83] Much as it had done in the past, Enron took its cues from Wall Street. In Houston, however, the word shed this specificity. The flexibility that the company's managers, such as Jeff Skilling, sought was directly linked to the idea of having options. In fact, the firm's strategy could now be summed up simply as acquiring "a portfolio of options."[84] The idea of options, of course, was more than just abstract. Including a number of different options in long-term contracts during negotiations had become central to the company's strategy.[85] For Skilling, the emphasis on optionality and flexibility meant business philosophies had to be completely reimagined. Now, Skilling declared, "the entire purpose of the business is to gain alternatives."[86] Such a focus on "options" deliberately deemphasized any sort of physical process or even providing a service—because that was the worst option. As Ken Rice told an interviewer for a case study, "physical assets are always the last resort" because building the physical asset (whatever that might be) was the most expensive action. The statement revealed how thorough the turn toward finance had been, as well as how Skilling and others were responding to the sense of speed and complexity the "new economy" fostered.

Material processes could fix the company in place for years, and "in a world that's moving real fast," Skilling had declared, "if you're stuck, you're

dead."[87] "You need flexibility in this world," he reasoned.[88] In describing the
strategies that Enron adopted during the 1990s for a University of Virginia
business school case study, Rice emphasized the need for "flexible contract
structures."[89] Likewise, Rice's 1998 presentation to the board of directors on
Enron Capital and Trade's electric utility strategy included building "peak-
ing" plants around the country to maintain "flexibility to decide the final
sites and equipment configurations."[90] "Flexibility" and "optionality" had become organizing concepts for developing strategies and allocating capital.

The new way of thinking and talking about business had also led to Enron's expansion beyond gas and electricity. Extending the "network" idea to
trading excess fiber optic, the company launched Enron Broadband Services
(EBS) in 2000. The plan, which would be called the "Enron Intelligent Network," entailed developing "flexible, market-based commercial solutions."[91]
In presentations to the board of directors, the familiar language of "flexibility" and "intermediation" surrounded descriptions of the unit. Enron Broadband Services also marked another shift in the firm's engagement with a
global economy. The broadband network that Skilling and others envisioned
linked cities in the United States with urban spaces in Japan and Europe.
Globalization was still a priority for Enron, but now that globalization was
not made up of environmentally conscious, sustainable development projects around the world, but rather high tech communications connecting
knowledge workers in Houston to other global cities abroad. Indeed, the
company's projections for the broadband business's growth rested on the expectation that the changes Ken Lay was pushing in Houston were also underway in cities around the world. The future success of Enron Broadband
Services, in other words, was dependent on a changing global economy. Even
though EBS lost $60 million in its first year, the optimistic rhetoric inside the
company continued to fuel an expansion into new businesses further and
further afield from pushing gas through pipelines.[92]

The influence of the new economy was clear. Enron had once been a "very
linear" business, Skilling noted, where a supply of natural gas was "hard-
wired" to a market. The preference for business over engineering that he had
first discovered as an undergraduate at Southern Methodist University was
still there. The "engineer's way" in creating an energy market was both expensive and inflexible. Instead of the hard-wired system that Skilling was
now turning away from, the company had, in effect, a portfolio system. "It's
a financial concept," he told his audience, almost as an aside. Taking a page
from the tumultuous lessons of the 1970s, Skilling compared the approach

Enron developed—pooling supplies—to airline restructuring. But in the description of the company's transformation, Skilling asserted that customers didn't care about the energy source, but rather some "function" like flipping a light switch. Much in the way Marx, in the nineteenth century, argued that the commodity form hid the labor and social relationships involved in production, by financializing energy and converting it into a tradable commodity, Enron had obscured the complex and potentially destructive relationship to the natural world that energy extraction and creation entailed. The source and production process, how things are made (even something as vaporous as energy from natural gas), disappeared—and with it, the company's older commitment to environmental responsibility.[93]

Triumphantly, the company had developed "flexibility from a portfolio of options," but the implications went beyond mere business strategy. Flexibility (or having options), one employee declared, meant the "ability to think freely" and "outside the box."[94] Such phrases revealed how the different strains of business thought were converging and collapsing on one another at Enron. However, much like the new marketing approach, the mantras "flexibility" and "optionality" were as ambiguous as they were ambitious.

Taken together, the loss of specificity presented a problem for the firm's next "vision." Skilling had come to see Enron as a company that applied a set of business principles to a "broader array of businesses." Drawing on a metaphor from the art world, Skilling told interviewers for the University of Virginia case study that while the "paint" and "brush stroke" remained the same, the "canvas" had gotten larger. Enron's corporate vision and approach now had "nothing to do with industry." Still, he and others were having trouble "articulating" the company's "core skill." Internally, he revealed, conversations about the vision statement tended to focus on "things about markets; things about new things; things about innovation; things about creativity." Though lacking clarity, Skilling's ruminations about the vision statement were near-perfect expressions of a business rhetoric centered around "creativity" that enjoyed a broad acceptance by the end of the decade.[95]

The new language permeated attempts to foster a new corporate culture at the company. At a time populated with genuine business celebrities, such as Apple's Steve Jobs, Enron's managers cultivated personas and images with a deliberately loud business aesthetic. For instance, at one meeting, Rebecca Mark (who had earned the moniker "Mark the Shark") made her entrance on a Harley-Davidson motorcycle.[96] Her closest rival at Enron, Jeff Skilling, had also fashioned a new style. In some ways, his transformation was even more dramatic. By the time Skilling compared Enron's business model to art, "creativity" had been a consistent and unifying theme in the corporate pageantry that characterized employee meetings. Once, a painter had taken to the stage and in a flurry of brushwork, started and completed a piece of art as music blasted out from speakers. As the color on the canvas dried, the company's management made its entrance with all the swagger of the Houston Rockets taking to the court.[97]

In 2001, *Enron Business* began running a series of features titled "Extreme Enron" about employees with unusual and dangerous pastimes. Employees could read about a coworker in customer service facing "alligators that jumped as high as their heads, black bears that weighed in at 500 pounds," as well as "countless water moccasins and panthers," while searching for wild orchids during his vacations.[98] According to the article, Enron employees spent their free time as hydroplane racers, mountain climbers, or, in the case of one notable example, an "all-around extremer."[99] Though they seemed like fluff pieces, these features were meant to show that "risk taking *is* an innate characteristic of Enron employees."[100] Risk, an organizing concept in the financial services sector, was now a deeply ingrained part of the firm's values, and the "Extreme Enron" features were attempts to fashion subjects that would prove economically productive.

The ethos of flexibility and optionality was proving to be infinitely expandable. To be sure, by 2000, the company had become the biggest participant in Europe in terms of buying and selling gas, though commodities themselves no longer mattered. The company's metals division, not gas or electricity, was its largest presence on Enron Online. Enron would now target "capital intensive industries" that needed "risk management products."[101] For instance, the firm launched Enron Credit to commoditize and trade unsecured credit. By the time that the expansion through Enron Online had come, the firm saw itself as a "market maker" that would make money through "high volatility" as well as "counterparties with shareholder pressure."[102] The connections among volatility, financialization, and Enron's business model were now explicit. However, if Enron Online was a success, it also compounded the firm's basic problems. Much in the same way Fastow was needed to securitize the volumetric production payments to ensure that money would flow back to Enron, Enron Online also created a problem because a vast amount of cash had to be on hand to settle up at the end of every trading day.[103]

These cash problems, however, were also dismissed using the same language. Andy Fastow, who was now the company's chief financial officer, began to concoct increasingly complex and elaborate financing schemes, referring to them as providing "financial flexibility" that helped connect them to the emerging Enron strategy. When, in 1999, Fastow began presenting these newer special purpose entities to the board of directors for approval, he explained that they would "possibly provide the Company with an alternative, optional source of private equity to manage its investment portfolio risk, funds flow, and financial flexibility."[104] Despite, or perhaps even because of, their inherent complexity, the board members considered the SPEs further evidence of the innovation that had become closely associated with the company. However, unlike the first Enron SPE, the Cactus Fund, which securitized the volumetric production payments, these newer funds were not connected to the company's original business.

LJM1, for instance, had been created to hedge a $10 million investment the company had made in an Internet company called RhythmsNetconnections in 1998. As with other technology companies in the late 1990s, RhythmsNetconnections' stock rose dramatically upon going public in 1999. However, Skilling was apparently concerned about the volatility of the stock. This was a problem, because Enron was contractually bound to hold its stake in the company for a specific amount of time. To minimize any potential loss, Andy Fastow created LJM1 in an attempt to hedge the initial holding. Though there were two genuinely outside investors, LJM1 was "capitalized" primarily with shares of Enron stock that it was obligated to hold for four years, but it could use the stock to secure a loan. Then, Enron created another SPE, LJM Swap Sub. LJM1 transferred cash and Enron stock to LJM Swap Sub (even though *this* SPE was supposed to be an "outside" participant in the hedge). Next, Enron and LJM Swap Sub entered into a "put option" agreement that gave Enron the power to require LJM Swap Sub to buy the shares of Rhythms NetConnections from Enron at an agreed-on price per share in June 2004. Much like JEDI II and Chewco, LJM1 failed to meet the 3 percent outside equity that was required by law.

Theoretically, Enron's initial investment was "hedged," meaning its risk was minimized by limiting the amount of money it stood to lose if Rhythms NetConnections' stock dropped. However, LJM Swap Sub's ability to buy the Rhythms NetConnections shares should Enron exercise its option was dependent on the value of Enron's stock remaining high (because this was LJM

Swap Sub's "capital"). Enron was hedging with itself. There was no true value grounding the deal.[105]

The precarious arrangement in the SPE did not go unnoticed. Almost immediately after hearing about the plan, Vince Kaminski, a PhD and managing director working in the RAC (risk assessment and control) group, raised concerns with Rick Buy, the division leader. In Buy's office, Kaminski used a "simple diagram" on a white board to explain what might go wrong, but such criticism was unwanted. Skilling himself told the concerned employee that because of complaints that Kaminski's group was acting "more like cops" than helping with deals, he was being transferred out of the risk control group. Even if he had stayed, though, Kaminski mostly likely wouldn't have been able to prevent what happened next.[106]

Even beyond what would later be called "noneconomic hedges," the SPEs had become critical to Enron's functioning in other ways. The pattern that Fastow had established with Chewco and LJM quickly spun out of control. What might have looked like brilliant intellectual achievements on paper or in diagrams were, at their root, convoluted and illegal schemes—but this did not stop their proliferation under Fastow. Ultimately, there were three thousand of them.[107]

In 2000, Fastow began creating SPEs called the Raptors (which included SPEs with names like "Harrier" and "Talon") and presented them to the board of directors as "risk management programs" that, through a new fund called LJM2, would help hedge against some of the company's volatile assets. LJM2, Fastow argued before the board, was an "alternative, *optional* source of private equity" that would give, again, more "financial flexibility." Indeed, in handwritten notes across the presentation, a board member had written that LJM2 would "Bring *quick* flexible equity." It was in that same script that the note taker wrote "LP will be traditional pension funds." So it was that the retirement payments of public teachers and other state employees throughout North America were brought into an unstable financial regime that was, to boot, being set up in such a way that built in specific conflicts of interest.[108]

As part of his plan, Fastow offered himself to serve as the general partner for these new special purpose entities. In essence, Enron's CFO would now also be negotiating deals with his employer. Later, many would regard the dual roles Fastow assumed as the most outrageous detail of Enron's history, and the contradiction of his two jobs was not lost on the board of directors. Though the arrangement's structure seemed to build in safeguards, that same handwriting noted that Norman Blake Jr., a board member, was "still concerned about" the "conflict of interest."[109] However, such reservations did not stop Fastow from assuming these newer responsibilities.

Though Fastow's dual role seemed to be a problem, the board of directors and the management team were willing to overlook it because the arrangement between Enron and LJM2 was that of an "internal marketplace"—an example of the same Wall Street wordplay that had become common at Enron. Such language normalized the ambiguity that came with Fastow's dual responsibilities. By 2000, board minutes had recorded discussions of "borrowing flexibility" when it came to the company's debt and credit.[110]

In establishing LJM2, a duo of executives working under Fastow, Michael Kopper and Ben Glisan, were made partners. Like the CFO, Kopper and Glisan would be working on both sides of the "internal marketplace." Fastow himself pledged to working for only three hours a week on behalf of the new corporation. Enron's chief accounting officer, Richard Causey, was tasked with approving any deals between Enron and LJM2, and controls, such as a document called a DASH (Deal Approval Sheet), were put in place. Still, these processes were not always followed. When Fastow's dual role finally became untenable, Michael Kopper resigned from Enron to take over LJM. But this did little to stop the overall unstable financing system.[111]

By the end of the twentieth century, the convoluted accounting techniques had become so widespread at Enron that Arthur Andersen hesitated to keep providing services for the company, though ultimately Enron remained a client. That other key members of Fastow's global finance group complicit in structuring the fraudulent SPEs, such as Glisan and Jeff McMahon, were former Arthur Andersen employees did not help matters. The Houston company had become Arthur Andersen's biggest client, and, frankly, the accounting firm needed Enron's business. Though the accounting techniques were unorthodox, when they were presented to the board's audit committee by Arthur Andersen in early 1999, the language about accounting techniques that "push[ed] limits" would not have been reason for alarm. The accounting language was similar to the rhetoric that was emerging in other quarters of the company (and in business discourse in general). Indeed, many board members regarded the accounting methods as further evidence of how Enron's leadership was charting fundamentally new territory. The term "integrated audit" (perhaps a reference to the "integrated circuit"), with its Silicon Valley overtones, covered over the inherent conflict of interest built into Arthur Andersen's work with Enron.[112]

This is not to say that everyone was comfortable with ideas like the "integrated audit." In fact, Arthur Levitt, the chairman of the SEC, was particularly concerned with an erosion of "auditor independence" and "the growth of nonaudit services and its potential effects on the audit function." It was crucial, he wrote to a member of Congress, "that auditors be independent not only in fact, but also in the minds of investors." But to some degree, Levitt's was a lonely voice.[113]

In a moment when the decade's innovations seemed to have permanently reshaped the rules of business, other policy makers were rethinking the rules of business reporting and accounting. In 2000, following a Senate hearing titled "Adapting a 30's Financial Model to the 21st Century," a number of senators wrote to the chairman out of concern that "current financial models only partially capture value in an economy where so much of corporate value is represented by patents, market access, human talent and intellectual property." In particular, the senators worried that older accounting techniques did not apply to newer companies. As the senators argued, "accounting standards will require significant modernization if they are to reflect value in today's economy." Much in the way the word "globalization" suggested the past was no longer an accurate guide, metaphor and language came to stand in as substitutes for looking to historical precedent and established practice.[114]

Fastow's increasingly creative and audacious financial schemes were also deeply connected to the new direction that Skilling was steering the company. Through these practices, Fastow was generating the flexibility that large, physical processes inherently lacked. As one slide from Fastow's October 1999 presentation to the board of directors noted, "Energy and communications investments typically do not generate significant cash flow and earnings for 1–3 years." Because of this, Fastow emphasized that "Enron must syndicate its capital investments in order to grow."[115] The connection between Fastow's presentation and Skilling's observations about how fast the world of business had become revealed why large-scale physical processes had become anathema to the company's upper management. The time pressures that production placed on the company would vanish into nothingness if the financing was right.

Increasingly, though, approval of such complex financing schemes became routine. By late 2000, the board consented to Fastow's plans for a third LJM partnership during an otherwise relaxed meeting in Palm Beach, Florida. It was an opulent affair. Members were ferried from airports to the

Breakers, a hotel modeled after Medici palaces, which stood at the edge of white Florida sands, not far from where the warm Atlantic waters ran up onto the shore. It was a fitting location. The Breakers was an artifact of the Gilded Age where Vanderbilts and Rockefellers had stayed. Now, Enron's meeting promised to rival nineteenth-century moneyed excess. Upon arriving, board members were advised to dress in "resort casual attire" for a cocktail reception followed by dinner on an open terrace. If that first night felt more like a vacation than a hard look at the company's finances and operations, that relaxed feel did not change. Save for one formal dinner, board members were encouraged to stay dressed in "resort casual attire." To be sure, while their spouses left the hotel for an "informal fashion show" and some "private shopping" at a boutique store the next morning, the directors did meet, though not for long. By one o'clock in the afternoon work was done. Directors spent the afternoon playing golf or taking a tour of the Everglades before concluding the first day with drinks and dinner. Guests awoke to a similar schedule the next day. Spouses and guests spent the morning on another private tour of a boutique followed by a tour of the hotel itself; board members sat through meetings that ended in the early afternoon. The rest of the day was spent instead on golf or a visit to the Flagler Museum. Dinner that night was taken aboard an evening cruise. As the moonlight danced across the waves gently lapping up against the hull of the ship, guests drank and dined. Directors on the Azurix board would meet the next morning, but the work was largely done. Tanned and relaxed, guests flew home on Enron planes the next day. There was little sense of the trouble ahead.[116]

Despite the tortured accounting logic and conflicts of interest, the SPEs enabled Enron to report enormous earnings. In 1997, JEDI II's investments accounted for 58 percent of Enron's net income, even though a court examiner later argued that the amount had been overstated. The pattern had been set. By 2000, there were hundreds of SPEs being used at the company with strange names like Hawaii, Aeneas, Bacchus, Heracles, Nahanni, and Marengo. By the end of the decade, these shell companies were set up to move assets around using a variety of derivatives transactions and to hedge against any drop in the value of assets sitting on the balance sheet. It was, in some ways, a fraud borne out of necessity. Because the firm had used mark-to-market accounting, the value for some of these assets—such as blocks of stock in a company or contracts for gas or broadband—meant that a degree of instability had migrated onto the company's balance sheet. Even a small depreciation of these assets would have been devastating for the

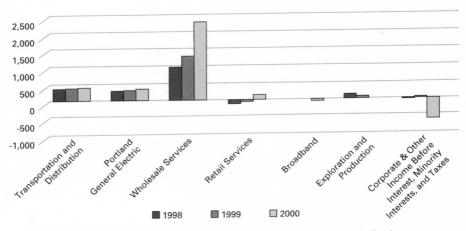

Figure 13. Enron's income before interest and taxes (in millions of dollars).
Source: Enron annual reports, 1998–2000.

company. By 2000, over a third of the assets the company held were marked to market.[117]

The motley collection of shell companies was crucial to the company in other ways as well. Much like the first Enron SPE, the Cactus Fund, kept cash coming to the Gas Bank, the schemes hatched in Enron Global Finance's offices papered over the basic cash problem that continued to vex Enron's operations. While the firm was using mark-to-market accounting to report deals as income at the start of a transaction, the actual cash came later in dribs and drabs. Indeed, through SPEs that entered into "prepaid forward contracts" with banks like Citibank and JP Morgan, and in deals with preposterous names, like Yosemite, Enron basically borrowed five billion dollars beginning in 1997. At the end of the decade, the practice had become unmanageable. Over half of the company's "funds flow" now came from these transactions. Such ways of raising capital without issuing stock (which might have hurt the share price), or debt (which would have hurt the company's credit rating), were crucial because Enron's various trading activities (which the company now listed as "wholesale" services in their literature) accounted for ever larger portions of the company's net income. Without this sleight of hand keeping the firm's credit rating aloft, the trading operation at the heart of the company's wholesale business could not have functioned (Figure 13).[118]

Likewise, the SPEs had become essential for propping up the very "brain-intensive" ventures that the business press had fawned over. Despite the great hopes Skilling had for them, both Enron Energy Services and Enron Broadband Services had been failures that had the potential to ruin Enron entirely. The degree to which Enron Broadband Services was threatening to hurt the corporation's overall earnings for the second quarter in 2000 pushed the unit into a deal with LJM2, which Fastow and Kopper controlled, to sell contracts to use some of the unused, or "dark," optic fiber EBS had but was unable to sell. LJM2 purchased the contracts through an SPE for $100 million, $30 million of which was cash. But Fastow's SPEs never offered permanent solutions. Though that deal may have temporarily saved EBS, by the end of that year, it was apparent that broadband was not going to be the roaring success that they had hoped for. The braided strands of transparent silica stayed unlit. Now, LJM2, after getting rid of one of the contracts, sought to exit the industry and transferred the languishing contracts to another SPE, Backbone Trust I. Much like many of the SPEs that were growing inside the firm, the details of these transactions involved a number of different steps and multiple SPEs. While Enron counted these transactions as sales, a derivative contract called a Total Return Swap, which, through a series of forward agreements, obligated Enron to pay Backbone Trust II, another Enron SPE. Often the final layer in the already convoluted arrangements, the swap meant that after the juggling routine involving assets, obligations, and cash, Enron was getting loans rather than seeing sales gains. Indeed, the Backbone deals, much like LJM1 and other SPEs, may have made the company look good, but they had managed to remove very little actual economic risk.[119]

Enron's "financial flexibility," "integrated audits," and "internal marketplace" had steadily pushed the company to the edge of ruin. Over the course of the late 1990s, Enron's managers increasingly relied on various SPEs to keep debt off the balance sheet, cash flowing through bank accounts, and earnings positive. By 2000, they formed the vast majority of the firm's income. Though Enron reported $979 million in net income for that year, $966 million of that total had come through SPEs with outlandish names like Whitewing and Marlin. Enron had, as the 2000 letter to shareholders proclaimed, "metamorphosed"—the company had become a gigantic fraud.[120]

Though most of the charade consisted of manipulating numbers in the company's records, at points the deception was more concrete. At the start of 1998, for example, Skilling, Lay, and Lou Pai escorted Wall Street analysts on a tour of the Enron Energy Services trading floor with secretaries and others pretending to work on unplugged computers to give the impression of a busy, vibrant workplace. Likewise, Fastow had found a path to personal wealth

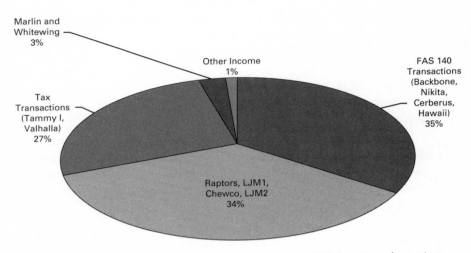

Figure 14. The effect of Fastow's special purpose entities (SPEs) on Enron's earnings in 2000.
Source: Enron Examiner Reports, University of Pennsylvania, Biddle Law Library, National Bankruptcy Archives.

through LJM by setting up a partnership with some coworkers called South-hampton to invest in the SPE. The name "Southhampton" (presumably a reference to the exclusive beach town on Long Island) reflected the scrambled geography at the heart of Enron. Because LJM was being run by Enron employees, they had a distinct advantage when dealing with the energy company, and LJM's profits reflected this. The Enron employees who formed the Southhampton partnership all made lots of money. Fastow himself had earned $45 million through his role at LJM.[121]

For the moment, though, the era's business ethos helped keep that fraud hidden. During the decade's last few years, when a stock price might have more to do with enthusiasm than economic performance, the Houston company's reputation among business journalists and analysts, as well as its marketing campaigns, produced tangible benefits. As if in unison, journalists, Wall Street analysts, and Silicon Valley boosters all proclaimed the end of the twentieth century to be a period of innovation, self-cannibalization, and transformation. And to these scribblers, prognosticators, and kingmakers, Enron appeared to have innovated, self-cannibalized, and transformed more than any other corporation. To be sure, the company's practices had changed, and the firm's marketing and corporate image reflected this.

However, these words and images had consequences inside 1400 Smith Street. The same sense of innovation and restlessness Peters and Waterman counseled in 1982 and that Kevin Kelly and other new economy writers described in apocalyptic grandeur was to be institutionalized at the company. Even beyond the success of Enron Online, and the enthusiasm with which the company had embraced new economy rhetoric, the company was adopting Silicon Valley ideals in other ways. Both Lou Pai and Louise Kitchen, for instance, were tapped to head up Enron Xcelerator. The unit, with its decidedly "new economy" name, was meant to develop new businesses. But there were other, more problematic elements of the "new economy" that had taken root at Enron.[122]

In northern California's start-up culture, the boundary between huckster and genius could be porous, and success in Silicon Valley could sometimes come down to little more than a game of confidence. Tales of heroic entrepreneurs abounded in the "new economy"—scrappy men and women who had to fly by the seat of their pants before making it big were a crucial part of the new economy mythology. At Enron, new economy vocabulary paved the way for supposedly sober-minded executives and corporate directors to authorize widespread fraud. Ultimately, though, failures like Enron Broadband Services had been transformed into sales. Yet Enron Global Finance could do only so much to hold off the impending disaster that the firm was hurtling toward. 2001 would be a very bad year for the company.[123]

CHAPTER 5

A Very Bad Year

For years, Kenneth Lay and Jeffrey Skilling had argued that regulations like the New Deal–era Public Utilities Holding Company Act were out of date in an economy defined by fast-moving global markets. By contrast, Enron had become celebrated for devising strategies that capitalized on the opportunities that this new global economy presented across the world. Still, if Enron symbolized the triumph of the late twentieth century's business developments, the company also inherited the era's instabilities and contradictions. As Enron expanded, risk, inconsistency, and instability proliferated inside the company. There might be enormous opportunity in managing (and confronting) risk, but by 2000 Enron had become an unstable organization facing intractable problems.

That year, as the public's giddiness over the "new economy" tipped into a nervous worry about overvalued stock prices, the firm became caught up in contentious battles with regulators and politicians over faltering energy deregulation in California. The state's deregulated electricity system may have started out as a great opportunity for Enron, but it ended up being a political nightmare. The company's former environmental image would come up against free market principles. By 2001 amid a full-blown crisis in the state, the company would be involved in a push to defend the idea of deregulation and market principles against an increasingly skeptical public in California.

Catastrophe on the West Coast marked the start of a multiplying sequence of troubles. Wall Street was placing new pressures on the company. Just as the focus on shareholder value drove the firm's dramatic transformation over the course of the 1990s, the pressure and demands that the investment community made on the firm as its share price languished accelerated Enron's demise. The calls to clarify the firm's accounting were consistent Wall Street demands. Enron under Skilling had thoroughly embraced financialization, and the financial community had been quick to valorize the firm's transformation. Now, that same world of investment banking hastened Enron's collapse. After the financial rot at the heart of the company was exposed, the ensuing negative media coverage culminated in Enron's bankruptcy at the end of 2001. While the California energy crisis would force Lay and Skilling to defend the idea of open markets, the quick-moving stock and bond markets would decide the firm's fate. The company would soon be undone by the very system it championed. But this process was far from view at the start of 2000.

After years of Lay, Skilling, and the firm's government affairs managers pushing for electricity deregulation, the campaign appeared to be working. After the state laid the legal groundwork for deregulation in 1996, Enron's government affairs unit considered electricity deregulation in California to be one of its greatest achievements. The idea of electricity deregulation was hardly controversial in Washington, and the government affairs unit seemed close to smoothing over the crazy-quilt patchwork of regulation that had long vexed Enron's managers. Outside of the United States, countries such as Japan and Brazil were considering similar restructuring, and Enron executives were already positioning the company to take advantage of such developments. In California, the company could point to the state as a model for the entire globe. However, the market in California presented distinct challenges.[1]

Though it was hardly identical to the deregulated natural gas market that gave rise to the Gas Bank, California's new system of buying and selling power centered on the spot market and its shifting prices. However, the California energy market was also different from the natural gas business. California Bill 1890 called for establishing the California Power Exchange (CalPX), which required investor-owned utilities (IOUs) "to buy all of their power in a newly created 'spot' market" as well as "forbidding IOUs from entering into long term, 'bi-lateral' contracts."[2] Because of this prohibition, Enron's traders could not offer the sort of long-term derivatives-based contracts that were at the heart of the Gas Bank's success at the beginning of the decade. What is more, while wholesale electricity had been deregulated, consumers remained protected by regulated prices for a set period of time. California, in other words, had an uneven and unpredictable market.

As the company began to operate in the state, Enron executives had to juggle two different ideals. Though California's market had implications beyond the state, the company's public relations strategy was built around local appeals, much as it had been in New Hampshire. Enron, the message went, would be a reliable corporate citizen and have a deep attachment to place. Californians needed to be happy with deregulation, and with the companies that would now do business in the state.[3]

Despite Enron's ties to Texas and Houston, in its official business with California, company officials downplayed these connections in order to not appear like an invading or hostile force. Rather than placing demands on California, Enron promised to adopt Californian values, emphasizing the firm's long-standing environmental image. Initially, many residents accepted the company's presence in their state.[4] However, any goodwill the company had managed to amass evaporated as electricity deregulation began to falter in California. Though at first the new electricity market seemed to run smoothly, problems in California began to appear on a local level as a hot summer loomed in 2000, and in May, "spot prices began to rise notably."[5] Such price movements in the wholesale market portended a looming disaster.

Problems first began in San Diego, where price protections for consumers were removed early. Almost immediately, the city's residents began to feel the pinch as the cost of power began to skyrocket. Before long, electricity prices in San Diego doubled.[6] The abstractions of "wheeling" electrons around the state turned out to pack a visceral punch. Suddenly unaffordable electricity fueled cries for an investigation just as problems spread beyond the city. While people in San Diego worried about prices rising for individual households, northern California's power supply became erratic.

On June 14, 2000, the first of several rolling blackouts hit the Bay Area. Throughout that summer, the state declared a "Stage 3" emergency. Beyond the rising energy prices, on August 1, the state experienced a record demand for power. As public discourse began to take shape, Californians began to feel themselves in a bind. Throughout the economic boom of the 1990s, not enough new power plants had been added to the state's electricity grid. By 2000, a quarter of California's electricity was coming from other states. Now, though, as technology development in the Bay Area became the most celebrated part of the U.S. economy, the need for more energy had only grown. Silicon Valley icons such as Intel were dimming their lights, and the situation in San Diego was only deepening.[7]

As the crisis unfolded, San Diego residents were quickly souring on both Enron and deregulation. By the middle of August, Catholic priests in the city were organizing candlelight vigils over electricity woes.[8] Letters to the editor in the *San Diego Union-Tribune* documented residents' anxiety and outrage. "Forget the new hotels, the booming tourism, the growth and prosperity San Diegans have come to view as theirs by right," one reader wrote to the paper; "it's over, folks."[9] The city, one irate citizen wrote the newspaper, was "being exploited by large out-of-state utilities, such as Enron."[10]

Being closely associated with the human suffering that deregulation brought to California was, of course, potentially disastrous for the company. Beyond any legal issues, deregulation on an international scale was at stake. Still, in the summer of 2000, the promise of national deregulation must have seemed within reach for Lay and Skilling. Even as federal relief was flowing into San Diego, President Clinton advocated for national energy deregulation. It was hardly a controversial point of view. In July, Senators Phil Gramm and Chuck Schumer introduced a bill that called for national electricity deregulation by 2002.[11] Even some skeptics of electricity restructuring conceded that it was too late for California to halt the process. As one pundit reasoned, the "toothpaste is out of the tube."[12] Californians' material experiences were turning out to be far from what Lay, Skilling, and others had predicted. Despite some national support for deregulation, state politicians in California were backing away from the marketplace. Loretta Lynch, president of the California Public Utilities Commission (CPUC), declared the experiment a failure. The sharpened rhetoric from state officials presented a new challenge for Enron's leadership. Though they were accustomed to extolling deregulation's virtues in the past, Lay, Skilling and other executives had to quickly mount a defense of free markets.

The message they ultimately settled on was that California had not really deregulated. "Despite a rocky start," one talking points memo read, "consumer choice and competition are working in California."[13] Other sections of the memo highlighted states (such as Texas) where deregulation was supposedly successful.[14] Enron's marketing and public relations team was working hard to shift the blame away from the company, and away from deregulation. "The complex structure that accompanied California deregulation was really re-regulation, not deregulation," they argued.[15] Perhaps even more so than in the past, the company's fortunes were bound up with the pace and progress of deregulation. In fact, advocating for national deregulation and achieving such restructuring in additional states were the government affairs unit's highest priorities.[16]

It was in this context of faltering support that threats began to mix with sunnier marketing messages. Though Enron's public relations efforts largely stressed the benefits of deregulation, the firm's spokespeople could also draw on the menace of interstate and international competition. As California lawmakers contemplated price caps, company executives warned that the steps would drive capital and potential power plants from the state, "taking jobs, [and] economic and reliability benefits." Instead, the company warned, "suppliers will sell outside California where markets are more predictable and prices are higher."[17] The state was on the wrong side of history, Enron's managers declared.

U.S. economic history was a long march of successfully deregulated industries including natural gas, trucking, airlines, and even railroads. Even though "de-regulation, free trade and markets" now occupied a "place in mainstream economic policy," California had been a "reluctant participant."[18] This was foolish and arrogant, Enron's managers and spokespeople cried. "Despite centuries of experience," one point from a memo read, "California believed it could create its own 'species' of market." The California experience was not, the document claimed, a failure of "markets" and "consumer choice." Rather, such a pure market that secured consumer choice had never really been introduced to the state.[19] Such company marketing memoranda claimed all the weight of logical reasoning and historical experience. The stakes were high.

Enron's goal of both domestic and international deregulation now hung in the balance.[20] California was supposed to be an example of how an open and unregulated power market could be an unambiguous good. Though writers for *Enron Business* hopefully noted that, "as more states and countries move toward complete deregulation, additional market opportunities will present themselves," California's well-publicized woes only made Enron's struggle more difficult.[21] In the wake of the California debacle, the company prepared to mount a "focused, strategic campaign" to "stabilize the fallout from California, promote competitive markets and improve public perceptions."[22] The company faced disaster if "government authorities" began "pulling away from their commitment to deregulation and open electric power markets."[23] Salvaging California wasn't simply a matter of recovering the company's prospects in the state, but also of maintaining the viability of its global strategy.

The company's public relations team, though, faced an uphill battle. Increasingly, journalists and politicians depicted the firm as a rapacious Texas company that had little regard for the state's citizens. In fact, Californians had good reason to be suspicious of Enron's operations in the state. Though the public would not learn about them until after the crisis ended, the company's West Coast traders had developed a number of trading strategies that exploited inconsistencies in the state's power market.

In the company's small office in Portland, Oregon, a group of traders led by Tim Belden was wringing money out of temporary glitches in the state's power system. Business units like the Gas Bank had developed ways to help customers mitigate price risk. By contrast, Belden's team depended on volatility as the means through which Enron could profit in the West Coast market. As he described it, Enron's West Coast energy trading profits were "completely dependent upon whether or not the prices went up or went down, depending on whether we bought or sold." In 2000, there was, as he put it, "chaos" in California's energy market (which Belden—along with other Enron executives—blamed on the way in which the state had organized it). However, because Enron had been systematically working toward a vast, unified space that money and megawatts could flow through, "chaos in California created chaos in the entire western market." At least in the short term, this was good for the company. As Belden put it: "The chaos drove high prices; and the high prices drove our profits." In a sense, these traders were simply finding the sorts of "arbitrage opportunities" that almost any finance student would read about in a derivatives textbook. Indeed, so-called arbitrageurs, traders who sought out such quick chances to profit, were crucial elements of the financial ecosystem that exposed anomalies and pushed prices toward their natural place. However, Enron traders had stepped beyond the muddy morality of exploiting loopholes.[24]

As they had operated in California, Tim Belden's team had developed numerous trading strategies that either artificially created congestion and then relived it through scheduling and ordering strategies that took advantage of problems in California's system. With titles such as "Fat Boy," "Death Star," and "Ricochet," the trades themselves were extraordinarily complicated, though many of them, on a basic level, revolved around creating congestion problems with the transmission lines, then scheduling flows of power that relieved the problem, and taking a payout from the state for the service. Belden was clearly aware that such strategies had a hazy legal status and discussed the potential risks with others at Enron.[25]

Long before such revelations, however, public antipathy toward the company played out in much more general terms as California journalists repeatedly pointed to Enron's out-of-state headquarters. One *San Francisco Chronicle* reporter depicted Ken Lay as a villainous figure gazing "out from his plush, 50th-floor office" with "Houston's downtown skyscrapers jut[ting] like sharp teeth against the overcast sky." Such rhetoric became increasingly common in the state's newspapers. Looking east from California across to Texas, Houston's role as a global center for energy services was hardly a welcome development. When the *San Francisco Chronicle* ran a story about the company with lines that read, "Enron's trading floors buzz all day long with frantic activity as . . . employees scan banks of flat-panel displays in search of the best deals," the threat of a "placeless" global capitalism hovered over the description. There was a menacing power in the sort of technological prowess the company seemed to project from Houston.[26]

Despite the bad press, a turn in political fortunes seemed to offer relief for the company. Though Enron's managers had quickly developed a good working relationship with the Clinton administration, it must have been a welcome change to have a Republican win the presidency in 2000. While both Carter and Clinton had overseen a significant rollback of business regulations during their tenures in the executive branch, the Republican Party had managed to appear like a much more natural home for businesses, and Lay had been actively involved in the party's politics since the early 1990s. Enron's chairman must have been particularly happy to have a Bush back in the White House. The political climate, it seemed, could not have been better for the company. Both Bush and his incoming vice president, Dick Cheney, were Texans with histories in the energy industry. Enron's jets (along with Halliburton's planes) served as transportation when Bush's supporters (including the Houstonian James Baker) arrived in Florida during the dispute after election night. The White House was again occupied by men with sensibilities close to Lay and Skilling's own approach to business—and Lay himself had a good rapport with the new president.[27]

To be sure, Lay and others at Enron did not shy away from pressing the administration, even when there were significant differences, such as concerning environmental policy. Throughout the first half of 2001, Enron officials discussed emissions and pollution policy with the White House and took part in meetings about renewable energy. Indeed, a good measure of contact between Enron and Washington early that year was through the company's involvement with the Clean Power Group, a trade organization that met with officials from the Environmental Protection Agency and the Council on Environmental Quality. Enron executives even discussed tax breaks for wind power with the White House. Aside from advocating for environmental policies that would benefit the firm, Lay and others at the company met with the vice president about his energy taskforce and the California energy crisis, where there was a great deal of consensus between the two.[28]

Much of what Enron advocated for during these months was well in line with the principles that had long formed the core of Lay and Skilling's economic philosophy. Throughout the second half of the 1990s, the company had approached electricity one state at a time, though they had always wanted a national system (not unlike what had happened to the gas industry in the 1980s). Skilling and Lay were—like some businessmen that came before them—system builders. What they wanted was for the Federal Energy Regulatory Commission (FERC) to exert more control over the country' energy grid. In short, what the company wanted was for the crazy-quilt energy system to be replaced by a central authority that could give firms greater access to energy, as well as override states' powers to inhibit power plant construction. In their recommendations to the energy taskforce, the firm's managers were seeking to further goals that they had long held that would have benefited the firm, but which would have also gone a long way toward rationalizing the country's energy system. Of course, Bush and Cheney also shared a market-based approach to energy, and Enron's executives were adamant (and Bush's team agreed) that price caps not be used to try to stop the crisis in California. It should have been of little surprise that the administration's energy plan, when it was finally released, reflected many of the policies that Enron's managers had advocated for. The image of the pair of Texans hashing out deals behind closed doors, though, was unseemly, and the crisis soon became a political issue.[29]

In an interview with the *San Francisco Chronicle*, one state senator declared that the state government "ought to be taking a hard look at how it is that California's pocket has been emptied into the pockets of Texas and Southern Corporations." The politician "nearly spit the word 'Texas'" the paper was careful to note. Similarly, reporters had little trouble describing Lay as a "Texas buddy of Bush." Though reductive, the conflation of Enron and Texas helped Californians to sort out the complex political-economic issues plaguing the state.[30]

In addition to supplying newspapers with stories, the company's close association with Texas (and Houston) was also turning out to be a useful piece of political rhetoric. As the relationship between Enron executives and California's state legislature continued to sour, Gray Davis, the state's governor, began to emphasize out-of-state companies that lacked any loyalty to Californians as a root cause of the problem. By the spring of 2001, the crisis showed no signs of abating. Significantly, Pacific Gas and Electric, the largest investor-owned utility in the state, filed for bankruptcy in early April.[31] Amid such acrimony (and with the prospect of another hot summer looming), Enron's managers tried to rally the state's business community to their defense. The firm's public relations team even circulated a form letter that California business people could send to Gray Davis and other state politicians. "As a prominent leader in the California business community, and a concerned California citizen," the letter began, "I am becoming increasingly impatient with the inability of our elected officials in Sacramento to mitigate our state's energy crisis."[32] Instead of bumbling regulators and elected representatives, the letter emphasized the need for a "competitive, efficient marketplace" where businesses could "retain the right to enter into competitive contracts for their energy purchases."[33] Lay and Enron were no longer offering themselves as trustworthy custodians of Californians' energy supply and environmental values. Instead, the company's leadership had fallen back on older rhetoric about a good business climate. "If California makes it attractive to do business in their state, they've got a chance of some of those turbines coming to California," Lay had told a newspaper in February.[34] On April 26, 2001, California declared a Stage 1 emergency, meaning "power reserves were at or below 7.5 percent of demand."[35] The situation remained tense.

Enron's public relations problems crested when the PBS news program *Frontline* ran an episode about the energy crisis in early June. Not unlike the local newspaper coverage, the broadcast pitted "electric cowboys" in Houston's "energy alley" against a suffering West Coast. Here, though, Enron's reputation as an industry leader meant bad publicity. The program repeatedly used an image of Enron Tower to stand in for the entire industry. California's woe, the report warned, was a harbinger of potential chaos across the country. Throughout the 1990s, the company's managers had advocated PUHCA reform and railed against the "monopolies" that electricity customers had lived under throughout the second half of the twentieth century. By contrast, the *Frontline* report noted that the country had not dealt with such an energy crisis since the New Deal. In light of California's problems and noting the business-friendly Texan in the White House, Lay and Skilling seemed more and more like the return of the Power Trust that led to PUHCA reform in the first place, rather than the modern-day trustbusters they claimed to be. California's energy crisis was threatening to become an argument about deregulation as a principle, and Enron was bungling the moment.[36]

Though the crisis eventually stabilized, the damage to Enron's reputation was significant. In fact, the CPUC had begun formally investigating power companies operating in the state. Any hope of reconciliation was quashed by a talk that Jeff Skilling delivered in late June to an audience at the Commonwealth Club in San Francisco, titled "The Arrogance of Regulation." Although Skilling criticized the Bush administration's policies and even (to an extent) offered kind words for Gray Davis, the overall mood was contentious.[37] Protesters were mixed in among the one hundred people in the audience, and before Skilling even began talking, an Oakland resident who had adopted the moniker "Agent Chocolate" planted a pie in his face.[38] Despite the rocky start, the executive remained defiant. Californians' anger was justified but misplaced, the man from Texas told them. Unscrupulous politicians, he claimed, were exhorting residents, "Blame the out-of-state power companies. They're from Texas. They're evil."[39] Skilling, though, had another culprit in mind. "The real cause of this crisis," he asserted, "was the regulatory structure put in place by the regulators—by the California Public Utilities Commission."[40] Mandates that the state's utilities purchase all the power that was available in the spot market were exacerbating price spikes. Regulators "arrogantly believed that they were smarter than the market," and Californians should be suspicious of attempts to reregulate the energy market, Skilling warned.[41] "The grand irony," he continued, "is that the regulators are now the people who California is turning to to solve this problem. They've screwed up the market, and now you're trusting them to fix it?"[42] Beyond seeking to discredit the state's lawmakers, Skilling's argument expanded to a general indictment of any attempt to regulate markets. "There is no reason to believe," his talking points went, "and every reason to doubt that government can do a better job than private industry in running an asset."[43] Invoking gas lines in the 1970s and even bread lines in the Soviet Union, Skilling warned that price controls "always have" and "always will" cause shortages.[44] Even worse, he cautioned, price controls might result in the flight of capital from the state.[45]

And indeed, though Skilling did not mention it at the Commonwealth Club, Enron's leadership was already looking for opportunities beyond California. In preparation for a meeting with New York's governor, George Pataki, the company's government affairs team prepared a set of talking points for Skilling emphasizing how the Empire State could benefit from California's problems by creating a better business environment while politicians and regulators on the West Coast were preoccupied with sorting out the electricity market mess. Even if other states were still exploring the idea of electricity restructuring, the crisis in California had "regional and global implications." Even abroad, California's experience was reopening questions about deregulation. In countries like Brazil, concerns about the California debacle were shaping the debate around whether or not to liberalize energy systems. Apart from a changing policy sensibility in regards to deregulation, Enron's connection to the state's energy crisis added to the challenges the company was already facing; the price of Enron shares was flagging.[46]

Though the price of the firm's common stock hit a high of over ninety dollars in August 2000, it had since declined. By June 2001, the price had dropped below fifty dollars.[47] The firm's managers were keen to disconnect the stock price from the bad press in California. "I'm trying hard (but failing) to shift the blame for our stock drop away from the bozos running California to the wacky broadband market," Jeff Dasovich in government affairs wrote to his colleagues in an e-mail.[48] Though a concern, the falling stock price was also a handy rhetorical device that could be used to defend the company in California. During his talk at the Commonwealth Club, Skilling had offered a chart that set the rising price of power in the state against Enron's languishing stock price to argue for the company's innocence, though the juxtaposition of how much West Coast electrons cost and the price of an Enron stock certificate failed to convince anyone that the company was running an honest business in California. Still, the presentation belied a persistent anxiety at the firm. Ever since the 1986 takeover bid, Enron's leadership had been haunted by the pressures that Wall Street placed on it. Since the 1980s, the power wielded by the financial services sector had only grown. Cable news channels now modeled the coverage of the stock market after the way ESPN covered football.[49] Enron's falling stock price could quickly become a news story that got out of control, and indeed, as bad as the company's problems were in California, they would soon be overshadowed by a larger crisis.

Though the 1980s and 1990s experienced one of the longest bull markets in U.S. history, by 2001, a nervous undercurrent had crept into discussions about the economy. As early as February 2000, financial magazines were beginning to write about the prospect of economic collapse.[50] Such jitters—particularly around Internet stocks—were reflected in the market. March 10, 2000, was a high-water mark for the NASDAQ stock index, which had been practically synonymous with the decade's technological innovations. During that day, the NASDAQ reached a record of 5132.52.[51] But this was not a plateau; it was a peak. By April 14, 2000, the NASDAQ had dropped to 3321.29.[52] The financial anxiety soon found its way onto the cover of *Newsweek* featuring two Alka-Seltzer tablets fizzing in a glass of water and the subtitle "Sobering Up about the New Economy." The NASDAQ's drop had been greater than the 1929 market crash. "If you could hurt yourself jumping out of one-story buildings," the article's author morbidly joked, "Silicon Valley parking lots would have been littered with the bodies of techies despairing over their vaporized stock options."[53] By the following year, confidence in the "new economy" was badly shaken.

As the NASDAQ dipped to 2781.30 toward the end of that January, fears of an impending recession surfaced in news stories.[54] The digital, knowledge-based economy appeared to be sputtering, and along with failing dotcom start-ups, Enron also came under scrutiny. Jim Chanos, an investor, had already shorted the company's stock, and publications that had once reliably championed the company's transformation now began printing critical pieces. An article in the September 20, 2000, Texas edition of the *Wall Street Journal*, titled "Energy Traders Cite Gains, but Some Math Is Missing," was especially prescient. The *Journal*'s reporter, Jonathan Weil, took issue with a number of energy trading companies' accounting practices, specifically mark-to-market accounting and the practice of claiming "unrealized gains." Significantly, Weil pointed out that even though Enron was reporting profits, without "unrealized gains the company would have reported a quarterly loss."[55]

However, the most prominent article was authored by a *Fortune* journalist, Bethany McLean, that appeared in March 2001, titled "Is Enron Overpriced?" Even though the company's stock was falling, the firm's P/E ratio still seemed inflated to the reporter. The full page photograph accompanying the article recalled many of the images that business publications (as well as the company itself) had used since 1997, depicting action on Enron's trading floor. The bodies of the traders moving about were slightly blurred, suggesting motion and high energy. In the foreground, one young trader sat in front of five large computer screens, each displaying Enron's businesses as charts, line graphs, and scrolling numbers. The accompanying caption also pointed to the company's ultimate transformation: "Some people liken Enron, with its massive trading operation, to a Wall Street securities firm." However, instead of signifying the triumph of "brain intensive businesses," the article's subtitle—"It's in a bunch of complex businesses. Its financial statements are nearly impenetrable. So why is Enron trading at such a huge multiple?"—framed the image in a negative light. Indeed, there was a direct connection between the overwhelming amount of abstract data in the photograph and the statement that Enron's businesses were "complex" and its statements "impenetrable." That the company's operations had become too complex was a criticism running throughout the piece. McLean pointed out Enron's arrogance early on in the article and quipped that even though the company's stock price was trading at a very high level, "Enron has an even higher opinion of itself." From this point, the journalist moved quickly to highlight the incomprehensibility of the company's practices.[56]

After noting that Enron "has been steadily selling off its old-economy iron and steel assets," she wrote that Enron's new business was usually described in "vague, grandiose terms like the 'financialization of energy.'" A little later, McLean argued that "describing what Enron does isn't easy, because what it does is mind-numbingly complex." These passages contained the first rumblings of the anxieties that Enron's collapse eventually unleashed. They registered the shift that Enron had taken, from an "old-economy" company with large, material assets (physical, tangible things) to the "financialization of energy"—a strange phrase that signaled the triumph of immaterial abstraction. By connecting strange phrases, complicated accounting, and a suspect business strategy, McLean offered a rebuke to Enron's celebrated lack of definition and anticipated the role that language would play in the public outrage that would soon engulf the company.[57]

While the 1999 letter to shareholders had boasted the failure of language, here the journalist was uneasy about it. For McLean, vague phrases rendered the business nearly impossible to describe. At the precise moment that information and symbols assumed dominion over the material world, as new economy boosters claimed, language failed. The description of the company's operations as "mind-numbingly complex" further connected the vagueness of language to the increasingly intricate manipulation of information. It was this very complexity that caused a loss of meaning. Inside the company, McLean's article was forwarded from e-mail to e-mail. "It is exactly what you have been worried about and now it is starting to catch Wall Street's attention," an employee wrote while sending it to Vince Kaminski, who had been quick to spot trouble when Fastow first proposed LJM a few years earlier. By the spring of 2001, it was clear that the firm was in trouble. Indeed, in April, the company's management informed the board of directors that more than half of the company's assets were not doing well, and that some of the international assets were worth less than reported. McLean's skepticism was justified.[58] As she would later reveal in her own coauthored account of Enron, after a brief, combative phone call with Jeff Skilling, Andy Fastow and two other executives made a quick trip to New York to meet with McLean. As she recounted, at the end of the meeting, Fastow had furtively asked her not to make him "look bad."[59] However, in the months that followed, the article was essentially ignored, and Enron, as a news story, more or less disappeared from *Fortune*'s pages beyond the typical coverage it had received up until that point.

On the contrary, Enron remained an object of praise in the business press. That August, *Business 2.0* ran a story titled "The Revolution Lives" in response to a critique of new economy rhetoric and philosophy that had recently appeared in the *Harvard Business Review*. Though *Business 2.0* had long indulged in techno-utopian flights of fancy, through its breezy, humorous tone and by conceding certain points made in the *Harvard Business Review*, "The Revolution Lives" revealed an anxiety that the new economic order had not actually come to pass. Yet amid the anxious undertone, the article's author offered Enron and Jeff Skilling as examples of a fundamental, revolutionary change. In Houston, the article suggested, "glimmers of a possible future are emerging."[60] Skilling himself even appeared on the magazine's cover, but the timing could not have been more ironic. That same month, the architect of Enron's transformation unexpectedly resigned. Perhaps he was exhausted. Earlier in the year, Skilling had publicly called a stock analyst an "asshole," raising questions about the CEO's mental state.[61] The outburst was a public display of one side to the man that some at the company had seen before. Kaminski, for instance, found that "it wasn't very useful trying to argue with" Skilling.[62] He was likely to stop the discussion. Those critical of their boss might find that interactions with him became brief and infrequent. Even if Skilling's short time as CEO had mercifully ended, the announcement did nothing to help the company's stock. At the end of July, shares of Enron had dropped over 45 percent since the beginning of the year. By the middle of August, the price was headed below forty dollars.[63] Though he initially cited personal reasons for leaving, the announcement caused a small flurry in the financial and energy trade press.[64] Journalists used words including "puzzling" to describe Skilling's exit, especially because, as many noted, Skilling's sudden departure meant that he would not receive a huge compensation package. Provocatively, within days of the announcement, John Emshwiller of the *Wall Street Journal* reported that one reason for Skilling's exit was the declining stock price.[65] In what would become a much-cited quote, Skilling called the stock price "kind of the ultimate score card."[66] Yet his departure was also intertwined with growing doubts about the "new economy." *InternetWeek*, for example, claimed that Enron's woes were caused by its close association with the web. The trouble in Texas was an indication that the digital world itself was under attack.[67] Such analysis, though, was largely a reflection of Silicon Valley myopia. The stock price was, in part, depressed because the cost of both electricity and natural gas was expected to drop.[68] For all of Skilling's efforts to disassociate the company's operations from a specific commodity, its fate remained tied to the physical world. To those watching the company closely, though, Enron's problems ran much deeper.

Wall Street analysts were not content to see Enron's problems as a temporary loss of investor confidence or drop in the price of a commodity. In the wake of Skilling's departure, investment banks issued calls for a fundamental change in direction. While a UBS PaineWebber equity analyst report characterized Skilling a "core force in the evolution of Enron (and open markets) over the past decade," the report also noted problems, including California and the broadband business, and that Enron had "lost substantial employee talent over the past 12-months."[69] Crucially, the report also called attention to a disconcerting and increasing "level of behind-the-scenes financial engineering."[70] Now, amid "increasing shareholder pressures" banking analysts hoped that there would be a "heightened sense of management urgency to hear and respond to overall Street desires" including "delivering a much cleaner and candidly-disclosed operating performance."[71] Though New York banks had been investors in Fastow's SPEs, Wall Street had grown uncomfortable with the derivatives deals between Enron and partnerships like LJM2. The convoluted financing was not the only problem. UBS PaineWebber had changed its eighteen-month target for the stock, expecting it to be lower than the price had been before the announcement. Other Wall Street firms were also reacting badly. Merrill Lynch had changed the firm's rating from a "buy" to a "neutral."[72] Even if the balance sheet was scrubbed clean, UBS had also noted that Enron faced a number of risks including "unfavorable changes in the regulatory environment."[73]

Within days of Skilling's departure, at least one industry journal hinted that Enron might once again be a vulnerable takeover target. As the trade journal *Energy Compass* ominously reported, "Sharks could now start circling the waters."[74] Rumors about an acquisition bid from Royal Dutch/Shell (which had previously tried to buy the firm) resurfaced.[75] Much in the way the hostile takeover attempts of the late 1980s had powerfully influenced Enron's development, now investment banks were demanding further changes at the firm. Just as it had done in other industries, Wall Street was attempting to shape the business to its own demands. Bankers were not alone in their discomfort with the company's finances. Skilling's resignation had also focused media attention on "heavy insider selling, indecipherable accounting practices, and a stream of executive departures."[76] The intricate financial and accounting structures that had been central to the company's transformation now appeared in news stories as untenable problems that had to be fixed. Publications such as the *New York Times* began echoing the criticisms that McLean had offered in March. In addition to the complexity that had now become a liability, "Enron," the *Times* reported, was in the "habit of selling assets and securities to closely related companies in 'related party' transactions."[77]

Discovering a Problem

These were precarious times for the Houston company. The "indecipherable accounting" that analysts were complaining about presented a big problem. Before Skilling's announcement, earlier that summer a company accountant named Sherron Watkins, who had transferred to Fastow's team from the faltering broadband unit, came across an item labeled "hedge-Raptor" while analyzing a spreadsheet of two hundred assets that the company was trying to sell. What she found as she looked at it further did not make sense. As she recalled during Lay and Skilling's trial, because the value of the Raptors had "tanked" and they "owed Enron a lot of money," it seemed as if "there were, apparently, some losses coming back to be borne by Enron." Confounded by the contradictory logic behind the Raptors, she set out to understand what she was looking at, meeting first with employees from Enron Energy Services who had "hedged the New Power Company with one of the Raptor structures." What she discovered horrified her. Realizing that Enron was "doing business with itself," Watkins came to the astonishing conclusion that she wasn't looking at "just aggressive accounting, but probably fraudulent accounting." Now, she remembered, she wanted to leave 1400 Smith Street.[78]

The next month, Watkins had lunch with a coworker who had gone to work for LJM, who revealed that the SPE was no longer invested in the Raptors, which shocked Watkins. The team at LJM "could care less what happened to the Raptors." The accountant felt even more urgently about the need to get a new job. Fittingly, Watkins made that decision the very day Enron announced Jeff Skilling's resignation.[79] Unnerved by all of it, Watkins e-mailed the firm's chief risk officer, Rick Buy, in the hopes of making "good use of the bad news about Skilling's resignation and do[ing] some house clean-ing" by "writ[ing] down some problem assets and unwind[ing] raptor."[80] Watkins confided that she was "horribly uncomfortable about some of our accounting in the past few years" and was "concerned some disgruntled employee will tattle."[81] She was not the only one troubled by the arrange-ment. Kaminski had refused to sign off on any valuation of the Raptors.[82] Ultimately, though, it would be Watkins, the worried accountant, who sounded the alarm bell.

Watkins also sent an anonymous letter to Ken Lay (who had temporarily resumed his role of CEO) warning him about the special purpose entities. In what would become an oft-quoted line, Watkins confessed that she was "in-credibly nervous" that the company would "implode in a wave of account-ing scandals." In particular, Watkins warned that the company would be in the spotlight because "the market just can't accept that Skilling is leaving his dream job." The false hedges Fastow had created in deal after deal had put the entire business in a dangerous position. The Raptors, which had been capitalized with Enron stock, were now faltering as the firm's share price dropped. "We are under too much scrutiny," she warned, "and there are probably one or two disgruntled 'redeployed' employees who know enough about the 'funny' accounting to get us in trouble." The memo apparently got Lay's attention. Before long, plans materialized to undo the knot of deriva-tives contracts tying the Raptors together. It would mean reporting losses in the firm's third quarter earnings, but Lay and others had to act. The com-pany Skilling had abandoned in August was in poor shape.[83]

The now-former executive's "loose-tight" culture had entirely unraveled. What remained was an ill-defined corporate structure. Lines of authority were unclear, and the signs of disarray were both big and small. After the company's brash moves into all sorts of markets, it was hard to find a person who understood all the products and services. An employee might be told to make up his or her own title for a business card. To a large degree, account-ability had collapsed. It had become a culture where one could hide without doing work. Likewise, the performance review committee process, which Skilling put into place early on, had devolved into an elaborate and cyni-cal exercise in office politics. Employees who were ranked in the bottom

10 percent of the company's workforce were dismissed, and the ranking determined the size of the bonus for those who remained. Scores between coworkers would sometimes be settled by giving workplace rivals bad reviews. The ability to lobby for good reviews was a necessary skill at Enron. Such dysfunction had taken its toll.[84]

By autumn a general gloomy rudderlessness among employees set in, according to internal documents. Some anxious workers had begun to look to the dismal stock price, which had bottomed out to under twenty-five dollars, as evidence of the company's troubles. As one employee put it while participating in a focus group the company commissioned, "People don't feel like they're getting the straight story right now, and the Street is sending back the same message." A sense of instability had begun to flow through Enron. "Sure, we live in unstable times," and "innovation and competition" was the pride of the company, but, a prepared report to the company's leadership argued, the falling stock price was feeding "insecurity and unease" among employees. Yet the sense of chaos and instability was not because of external pressure, but rather because these qualities had "become a part of Enron culture."[85]

To an extent, of course, creating a sense of instability had actually been a company goal. Skilling's management style had been deeply informed by the business literature of the 1980s and 1990s, which took aim at hierarchies and bureaucracies of any sort and replaced them with flat organizations and giddy cries of "creative destruction." As one employee noted during the study, "What people are defining as chaos now we would probably have defined as creativity and entrepreneurship a year ago. But the bloom is off the lily right now."[86] The marketplace in talent that Skilling sought to foster through various reorganizations and the PRC process in the 1990s had caused havoc and ruined morale. Indeed, even the terms that the company had pushed for years, such as "innovative," were now seen by employees as leading to chaos. In particular, employees sensed a lack of "corporate vision."[87] As it turned out, "The World's Leading Company" did not communicate much in terms of organizational direction. The malaise was also spilling out of the company's offices. The cynicism about the direction of the company that the focus group revealed was evident in other ways as well. When *Enron Business* published an employee-drawn cartoon car that let viewers know that when they "asked why," they would have to pay four times as much to get the correct answer, it was a clear indication of the ugly mood just under the surface at Enron.[88] Some Houstonians had also begun to sour a bit on Enron.

Even while celebrating the company's youthful image, it was difficult to keep criticism at bay. In an article for *Texas Monthly*, the journalist Mimi Swartz wrote, "The Enron skyscraper near the south end of Houston's downtown feels like the international headquarters of the best and the brightest." "Black, white, brown; Asian, Middle Eastern, European, African, as well as American-born," people buzzed around a lobby "throbbing with modernity." The other downtown oil offices seemed staid and "old-fashioned" by comparison. The globalization that Lay and Skilling had long pursued in Houston had arrived, and while the writer approved of the diversity the company represented, this passage also bristled slightly at the idea of importing workers from elite schools outside Texas, as opposed to hiring from venerable state institutions like Texas A&M. Beyond the lack of fealty to the Lone Star State, the globally mobile workers recruited to Enron had brought a crass materialism with them to Houston. With their outrageous paychecks and signing bonuses, Enron's new employees were filling up the lofts "being renovated close to downtown. (Enron people didn't live in far-flung suburbs. Suburbs were uncool and too far from the office.)" Swartz recast the downtown revitalization that had been praised in the pages of the *Houston Chronicle*, the *Houston Business Journal*, and *Enron Business* as morally suspect. Such moments were striking in an article that largely emphasized how Enron's business had been transformed from being, in Swartz's telling, populated by "cautious executives who dealt with tangible assets like pipelines" to an organization that now preferred "bold executives who dealt with intangible assets." What had become of downtown? Though she chose to close her piece with Skilling's grandiose prediction that Houston would soon be "the world's center of commodity trading," Swartz's article was shot through with ambivalence regarding the changes that Enron was ushering in. Giving Skilling the last word, though, made the article irrelevant. By the time *Texas Monthly* appeared on the newsstand, the firm's demise was well under way.[89]

As if to underscore the erosion of confidence in Enron during the early autumn weeks of fall in 2001, David Fleisher, an analyst for Goldman Sachs who had covered the firm for years at different banks, issued a report on the company that began by admitting that "investors have virtually given up" on the firm. Contrary to the pessimism that increasingly surrounded the Houston company, though, Fleisher argued that "perceptions toward Enron have tumbled far below reality." Problems including the California energy crisis and Skilling's resignation had hurt the share price, but the Goldman Sachs analysis maintained that the company was fundamentally a good business. Indeed, the document's persistent theme was that Enron's management team and accountants simply needed to clarify the firm's financial statements. From the outset, Fleisher insisted that "perceptions have hit bottom and are likely to turn with coming disclosures." Like other reports (and Watkins's recommendations), Fleischer emphasized the need for Enron to clarify and unwind some of the more complicated SPEs as a part of the upcoming third quarter earnings report. In fact, the Goldman Sachs document noted that "management has indicated to us that the company is working to restructure these transactions and that investors will see results on this score." The complexity that had been at the root of the firm's identity was now a decided liability. The stakes were high. Lay was expected to address the special purpose entities and, in general, clarify financial matters. However, the magnitude of the bad news Lay delivered was astonishing.[90]

On October 16, 2001, shortly after beginning a conference call about the earnings statement with financial analysts and reporters, Lay noted that the company would record "nonrecurring charges of slightly over a billion dollars." Some of the bad news had been expected. After all, Azurix had been such a failure that the once-celebrated Rebecca Mark had left the company under a cloud, and Enron Broadband Services had also been a disappointment. Still, shutting down the Raptors (which Lay coyly referred to as "certain structured finance arrangements with a previously-disclosed entity") accounted for $544 million of the loss. "In connection with the early termination," Enron's shareholder equity would "be reduced by approximately $1.2 billion." Though the number was high, Lay and others at Enron intended the announcement to be one of many steps the firm was now taking for the sake of transparency. Much in the way the 1986 takeover attempt forced a redirection to core competencies, Lay now explained that Enron's management was committing to "making the results of our core energy business more transparent to investors and not clouded by non-core activities." However, if clarity was the intended message, the call did not go well. Ironically, even the question and answer session was momentarily interrupted by crossed wires while Lay was in the middle talking, leading to a few moments of confusion. Though some analysts expressed concern over the losses Enron had just reported, the mood at the end of the call could hardly be described as one of panic or outrage. After all, the billion dollar loss had been swaddled in an overall sunny script. In retrospect, however, Lay's quick statement about "previously-disclosed entities," "shareholder reduction" and "nonrecurring charges" had set the course for Enron's demise.[91]

The next day, the *Wall Street Journal* printed an article written by John Emshwiller and Rebecca Smith, both of whom had regularly covered the company, calling attention to the losses in the announcement. Beyond the disappointing financial statement, the article called into question Enron's entire transformation under the now-departed Skilling's watch. "The loss," they noted in the opening paragraph, "highlights the risks the onetime highflier has taken in transforming itself from a pipeline company into a behemoth that trades everything from electricity to weather futures."[92] The line revealed the extent to which concern over Enron's entire style of business became intertwined with the more immediate occasion for Emshwiller and Smith's reporting on the bad earnings report and the confusing financial statements. The piece was the first of many the two wrote about the company's problems over the next two months.

Such coverage also gave voice to, stoked, and charted the growing loss of confidence in the company. Already impatient and uneasy stock analysts began demanding more answers, and a general theme of Enron's financial situation emerged. What management theorist David Boje calls a "dialogic dynamic" had emerged among financial reporters and analysts, amplifying the pressure on Enron's management. As analysts reacted to the journalists' coverage, Emshwiller and Smith would then report about the analysts' reactions. Such words directly affected the numbers crawling across trading desks.[93]

Because of the inherently symbolic nature not only of financial news reporting, but of Enron's transformed businesses, these news outlets, and the *Wall Street Journal* in particular, did not simply report on the company's collapse. Rather, Emshwiller and Smith were among the authors penning a story about Enron's fall in real time. The fragments that would make up the public and official narrative about Enron were now emerging from members of the financial community and gradually coalescing, primarily on the pages of the *Wall Street Journal*. Perhaps fittingly, a speculative impulse, rather than any individual "author," was forwarding the story. Narrative fragments, such as credit downgrades and analyst recommendations, were also bets on how the company's story would end. In the entirely "symbolic" world of finance, the story and the reporting of the story became indistinguishable. As credit or stock downgrades resulted from negative news coverage, these downgrades contributed to subsequent negative news stories. Within a week of the earnings report, shares of Enron dropped to under twenty dollars.[94]

The revelations and reports even turned recent advocates of the company into skeptics. Fleisher, the confident Goldman Sachs analyst, now worried about the sense that Enron was "hiding something" and publicly demanded that Lay "demonstrate to investors that your dealings are above board." In the *Wall Street Journal*, Emshwiller and Smith noted Lay's contrite response that Enron's management was "trying to be as transparent as we can."[95] The executive's statement, uncertain that the company itself could offer a clear assessment, was a stunning way to close the article. The past may have been obscured by baroque accounting logic, but the company's fate seemed increasingly clear. Even the announcement that Andy Fastow had been placed on a leave of absence (surely a formality ahead of the inevitable outright firing) did little to help matters.[96] Enron's fortunes had become an open question that was largely out of the control of its managers. Rather, investors were watching a public narrative about the firm develop and acting in anticipation of how events would unfold. Because financial measures, such as a P/E ratio, were in part indications of how optimistic stories about economies and companies were, losing authorship of these stories was dangerous for a firm like Enron.[97] In the days and weeks that followed, Lay insisted that he did not understand what had happened at his company.

At a meeting with the corporation's managing directors in the midst of the bad press coverage, Lay pledged his support for Fastow. The gesture, though, did not mean that the management was unified. After Lay, a nervous Kaminski walked to the podium and gave voice to all the problems he had with the Raptors. Fastow's schemes had been "improper" and "stupid." Good employees were resigning, he said. As he continued to insist that Enron's leadership had to "come clean," a hand rested on his shoulder. Greg Whalley, his boss, had come up to the podium and was now leading Kaminski away from the microphone. If the purpose of the gathering had been to rally the troops, it had not worked. As the stories from the *Wall Street Journal* continued, confidence inside the company evaporated. The situation outside of Enron's two towers was also deteriorating.[98]

On October 25, the *Wall Street Journal* reported an analyst recommending a "sell" on Enron's stock "because of uncertainties about the company's extremely complex financial structure."[99] By the end of the month, Moody's, the credit rating agency, had downgraded their assessment of the company. A few months after his departure, Skilling's worst fear had come true— Enron's managers were stuck. It was a grim time. Even inside the company, managers were scrambling to cash in on "deferred compensation benefits."[100]

As Emshwiller and Smith reported, if Enron's credit rating was to fall below investment grade, the company might default on billions of dollars worth of loans and "force it under the terms of various financial agreements to issue millions of shares of stock to holders of that debt, which would dilute the value of existing shares."[101] Now, as the reporters were diligently chronicling events, every news story threatened to further destabilize the company's position. The prospect of such a cause and effect was both ironic and unsettling. On Halloween, the reporters noted the carnivalesque nature of the company's fortunes, asking, "in the topsy-turvy world of Enron, what constitutes logic anymore?"[102] To be sure, this line was meant, at least to a degree, to be tongue in cheek, but it also pointed to a core anxiety about Enron's predicament.

This sense of unease was not limited to the financial press alone. The exasperation and uncertainty of the *Wall Street Journal* stories were echoed in Enron's November 8 earnings restatement. The special purpose entities that had been crucial to the company's success in building the Gas Bank were revealed to be more commonplace and more complex. Now, after unwinding the "Raptors" had inaugurated the company's woes, Lay and others tried to step back from the complicated and complex financial techniques that Skilling and Fastow had used. Amid cries of duplicity and demands for clarity, Enron's managers reexamined the many SPEs and discovered an accounting glitch. The governing accounting rules required that SPEs needed to have at least 3 percent of outside equity at risk. After a review of the extraordinarily complex SPEs Fastow and Enron had created, accountants at Arthur Andersen and Enron decided that they did not meet these requirements. The debt and losses sacked away in these SPEs would have to be reported. On November 8, Enron provided a financial restatement for the company from 1997 to 2001, plainly demonstrating that Enron had not been nearly as profitable as it had appeared to be over the past five years (Table 2).[103]

Not only did the document provide new numbers, but it also described the nature of the deals and how they were devised. However, the earnings restatement did not reestablish a sense of clarity and certainty as far as the firm was concerned. Sentences began with qualifiers such as "Enron now believes" and "to the extent information is available." Not long after the outrage around the earnings report erupted, Lay had been advised to put together an independent committee to examine the special purpose entities and release its findings. Indeed, such an action was probably the only hope the company had to reestablish its credibility. The committee, which was led by William

Table 2. Enron's reported net income, 1997–2000

	1997	1998	1999	2000
Originally Reported	$105,000,000	$703,000,000	$893,000,000	$979,000,000
Restated on November 8, 2001	$9,000,000	$590,000,000	$643,000,000	$847,000,000

Sources: Enron annual reports and Enron Form 8-K, November 8, 2001.

Powers, then dean of the law school at the University of Texas at Austin, and his team quickly began looking into matters. Ultimately, though, Lay and others at Enron had no way of knowing what the committee might find, compounding the sense of uncertainty in the November restatement. In one particularly telling passage, the statement read: "While the information provided herein reflects Enron's current understanding of the relevant facts, it is possible that the Special Committee's review will identify additional or different information concerning these matters." To be sure, the company's management did not know the extent of the problems they were facing. Fastow's partnerships had put the company in a very bad position. Because the hedges set up between Enron and LJM were faulty from the start, when deals were finally closed, Enron was forced to take a loss.[104]

However, Fastow's blatant obfuscation alone could not account for the uncertainty. Rather, the document's tone revealed the tenuous grasp the company itself had on its own activities. The unease about complexity and meaninglessness that had gripped journalists was also affecting Enron's managers. The revised earnings, though, did not put a stop to the company's troubles but accelerated the firm's decline. The company was in a fragile position, with the stock already trading under ten dollars since November 5. Though the story had largely been confined to the business press, by the end of the month, the accounting problems were being covered in newspapers beyond the *Wall Street Journal*.[105]

The *New York Times* and *Washington Post* were quick to emphasize the idea of complicated information but did not excuse the "many investors and analysts" who "were not curious about" the deals "when everything seemed to be going well." Enron's failure was damning evidence of a mode of production predicated on a willing suspension of truth and collective greed. Along with a creeping unease with the malleability of information that Enron had trumpeted in previous years, newspaper writers now added a sense of moral condemnation in their stories about the firm. Not only was Enron's "finan-cialization of energy" fraudulent, but it had been a fraud that many had gone along with. While newspapers saw Enron's stock collapse as justice, though, the decline compounded the misery for workers in Houston.[106]

In perhaps the cruelest twist, and through unfortunate timing, employ-ees had been locked out of their retirement accounts as the firm switched administrators. Now, an already disgruntled workforce could only watch helplessly as their savings—much of it in Enron stock—shrank. Lay tried in company-wide meetings to reassure employees, drawing a comparison to 9/11 that was widely derided, but to no avail. As Lay read aloud questions to a roomful of Enron employees, at least one worker wondered if the stately old PhD in economics and devout Christian had been smoking crack.[107]

Increasingly, the company's prospects looked grim. Though Lay reached out to members of the Bush administration about the company's growing problems, once officials in Washington decided Enron's failure would not have a broad effect on the nation's energy or financial system and would not hurt countries such as Japan and India, they simply let the Texas firm die. Even as the news coverage drove events, Lay and others at Enron attempted to stop a complete collapse through a merger with Dynegy, a smaller Houston energy company that many Enron employees regarded with disdain, but the deal quickly fell apart. Though some employees professed a perverse delight in the merger's collapse, that reaction was the last gasp of an otherwise vanishing loyalty to the company. Though Lay could expect periodic supportive e-mails from employees praying for him, his inbox was also filling with messages from other employees distraught and angry about their diminished retirement savings. By the end of November, the stock price fell below a dollar. Skilling had borrowed heavily from the investment banking community in remak-ing Enron, and throughout its history, Enron's managers had been keenly attentive to the firm's reputation on Wall Street. Now, however, the world of finance had issued its final judgment on the Houston company. It was worth-less. Enron filed for bankruptcy on December 2, making it the largest bank-ruptcy in U.S. history up to that point.[108]

By then, much of the work inside the two buildings on Smith Street had stopped anyway. As they waited for the inevitable axe, employees had spent their last days sending out résumés. When former trading partners lost con-fidence in Enron and refused to do business with the firm, the traders began to goof off. A football might sail across a room that had, just months earlier, buzzed with frenetic energy. People would take long lunches before leaving work early. It was not an orderly exit from the building when word officially came. There were lines of freshly unemployed workers waiting for the elevators with boxes piled up on top of rolling desk chairs, and as they left 1400 Smith Street, news vans and helicopters above the skyscrapers were waiting to convert their last day of work into background footage for the nightly news.[109]

However, media coverage did not end with the filing. The quick and dramatic bankruptcy signified something, but exactly *what* remained unsettled. Journalists, commentators, and letter writers all bemoaned the complexity of Enron's businesses, and what the firm's spectacular fall revealed about the country as a whole. News articles and letters to the editor were a tangle of moral judgments, a search for adequate reference points (such as the Watergate scandal and 1998's Long Term Capital Management financial meltdown), hostility toward intellectual sophistry, a distrust of politicians, disease metaphors, folksy aphorisms, and a panicked insistence on the power of objective truth. In all, journalists and others struggled to find modes of thought and representation in response to Enron's failure. These confused strands often appeared in the same articles as contradictory sentiments; at once blasting the company as sophisticated crooks who duped unsuspecting Americans, and condemning a morally lax culture all too willing to go along with such obvious hucksterism.

One example appeared in a letter to the *New York Times* worrying that "the loss of objectivity on Wall Street indicates an even wider problem: a culture that places very little value on truth." The entire country, the irate letter writer declared, had been "infected" with "the loss of objectivity." Only "measures of real value" could counter the phantasmagoric process of financialization that Enron seemed to embody. The letter's author was not alone in his prognosis.[110]

In an op-ed piece for the *New York Times*, columnist Richard Cohen laid the blame on U.S. society as a whole through an imagined conversation with his deceased, vaguely Capra-esque grandfather. The column pitted Cohen, here the defender of a sophisticated but fallen American culture, against the folksy wisdom of a less educated, plainspoken grandfather. In the column, when Cohen tried to explain Enron's business, the apparition retorted: "It sold smoke. . . . It sold the Brooklyn Bridge over and over again. It sold the uptown version of dream sheets and prayer handkerchiefs, only it used brokers and banks and not guys in fedoras and shiny suits. A bunch of con men." In this fictional exchange, Cohen began by adopting a tone of condescension,

insisting that Enron wasn't all bad, but the ghost had none of it: "Is that
how you college people talk? They lied." Cohen had found the roots of the
economy's corruption in language itself. The accounting statements that
had become a problem for so many were not merely confusing; they were
dishonest. The grandfather's apparition was more virtuous than Cohen
because his plainspokenness was unsophisticated. Despite (presumably)
lacking a formal education, he was able to get to an objective truth, the heart
of the matter, much faster. Awash in nostalgia, such condemnations of Enron and investing culture looked back to a simpler time, before the changes
that Enron (and its collapse) now seemed to embody.[111]

Even journalists who did not couch their take on Enron's demise in a
longing for the past reacted with a sense of alarm. The business and economics journalist Robert Samuelson focused on the manipulation of information as a systemic threat to capitalism as a whole. Though Enron seemed
destined to become a "metaphor for many of the sins of modern capitalism,"
that metaphor was simplistic and misleading. While capitalism was animated
by the "self-interest and the ingenuity of the human spirit," it was threatened
by humanity's darker impulses. Samuelson did not offer a critique of capitalism but rather condemned a degraded society that had threatened a system
that was, on some level, inherently moral. The journalist worried that Americans were now living in a time where "creative obscurity" had "become
commonplace" and was threatening capitalism.[112]

Samuelson's fears, however, were not shared by other writers, who remained confident that "Enron's demise" would "be little more than a blip."
Beneath what seemed like intimidatingly smart products like weather derivatives, "whatever that means," a columnist for the *Washington Post* added
sarcastically, Enron's rise and fall had the familiar and predictable feel of a
good, old-fashioned stock bubble that had popped. "If you live by the perception and the illusion of growth," the columnist concluded, "then you die
by it once reality sets in." Still, there had been a dramatic expansion of individuals and households investing in the stock market. The United States
could not "afford to preserve a system in which perception is more important than reality," though the writer gloomily assumed that his call was likely
to go unheeded.[113]

Many journalists called for a return to business activity that was rooted
in a simplicity that Enron's managers had lost sight of. The company's fall
was instructive because, as *Newsweek* explained to its readership, while it
"used complexity to its advantage on the way up," the firm "became a victim

of its own complex dealmaking on the way down."[114] Though the language and emphasis shifted from journalist to journalist, Enron had clearly exposed some fundamental anxieties about what had happened to the American economy.

In a sense, the troubles that Enron found itself in from 2000 through 2001 were not aberrant. The company's broadband business had failed, but technology companies in general struggled after the stock market bubble burst. Likewise, the Houston firm was hardly the only case of accounting fraud during these years. However, one would be hard pressed to find a better example of the new economy's internal combustibility. The company's missteps, first in California and then in the business media, revealed a number of key contradictions at the heart of the economic regime that Lay, Skilling, and others at Enron had championed for so long. Skilling in particular had enthusiastically embraced financialization and became famous for creatively applying a financial services model to other industries. However, as Enron became more embroiled in adopting financial strategies, their status as a credit-worthy trading partner, and their ability to raise money, was largely dependent on the view from Wall Street. Indeed, as a bankruptcy analysis of the firm later revealed, Enron was in a terrible bind—as they expanded their "financialization" into new areas, they could not afford to defy Wall Street demands. Because Enron had never really solved its cash problem, the company depended heavily on Wall Street's good graces. Now, however, as the company's reputation collapsed, so did its ability to operate. Wall Street, in a way, had both created and killed Enron. If, though, using Enron's collapse provided an opportunity to think systemically about what had become of the American business system, further revelations of criminal wrongdoing complicated matters.

CHAPTER 6

Making Enron Meaningful

Though the *Wall Street Journal*'s reporting played a decisive role in Enron's collapse, it was only toward the end of 2001 that the failure began to take on a significance beyond the business section of the morning papers. Ethereal problems like sour derivatives and earnings restatements did not focus public attention in the wake of the September 11 attacks. But by late November, some newspaper columnists worried that the corporation's implosion was indicative of a wider moral rot that had set in among Americans. Enron, as many of these writers had it, was the product of a country that was no longer concerned with "real value."[1] Investors hadn't been hoodwinked, such reasoning went. They had looked the other way. In such accounts, writers focused on issues of morality and fast-talking instead of the complexities of put options and special purpose entities. In December, other publications, such as *Time* and *Newsweek*, focused on the political implications of the firm's collapse.[2] But this was prologue. Enron's failure had been years in the making and involved so many different people that sorting it all out and explaining what had gone wrong would not involve just the press. Politicians would rush to respond to a business fraud that seemed to have sullied much of Washington as it fell. Reckoning with the firm's collapse was going to take a while. Surely, Enron was going to be one of 2002's biggest news stories.

By the end of January, the components of a compelling narrative were coming together. Not only did the Powers Report detail fraudulent activity inside the company, but Lay's long-standing connection to the Bush family allowed journalists to raise questions about political corruption. Likewise, if accounting irregularities were difficult to understand, fraud and document destruction were not. Sherron Watkins and her memo warning about a "wave of accounting scandals," as well as David Duncan, the Arthur Andersen accountant who had shredded Enron documents, were regularly featured in news reports. The company's collapse had all the familiar marks of a crime, a cover-up, and an abuse of power.[3]

The whole affair seemed destined to become a spectacle. Kenneth Lay's wife (and children) went on the *Today* program to claim her husband's innocence. The Lays, she insisted, were among the victims. Because they had invested so heavily in Enron, their family, too, was near bankruptcy. Through tears, she lamented that despite trying everything, her husband was unable to save the company. However, the chairman's battered reputation was beyond repair. Throughout the year Lay had sold Enron stock to pay down a line of credit Enron had extended to him. The timing of the stock sales, though, seemed like insider trading. By the end of month, Lay officially left the company. Enron's managers were on the defensive.[4]

When hearings in Washington, D.C., began the next month, most executives did little more than invoke their Fifth Amendment rights. Jeffrey Skilling, however, was unapologetic about his time at Enron, arguing that the company had been ruined by an emotional and unwarranted loss in investor confidence. If anything, it was the press that had visited calamity on the company, and he suggested that negative media attention had led one executive, Cliff Baxter, to commit suicide. However, much as he had done in California earlier in the year, Skilling had badly misread the public mood. Between the 9/11 attacks and an economy that was in recession, Enron had come undone at a time of high anxiety. Though most Americans had faith in their own employers, and many owned stock in the companies they worked for, the public was also convinced that Enron was not an isolated issue. At least one Gallup economist worried that renewed and tougher accounting standards after Enron might slow any economic recovery.[5]

Indeed, Enron's failure had created a wider suspicion about the stock market, and investors were concerned that Enron-like accounting across American business was a problem. The Gallup Organization had even begun referring to "Enronitis"—the idea that fears about more Enrons would further erode a waning faith in accounting practices, and hurt the stock prices of other companies—when tracking and analyzing investor confidence. Polling indicated that most Americans thought Enron's failure indicated a systemic problem. These fears were soon validated.[6]

Newspaper headlines in 2002 filled with stories of corrupt chief executives. In fact, there had been a marked increase in securities fraud among large, publicly traded corporations during the last few years of the twentieth century and the start of the new millennium. Tyco's chairman was exposed as a tax cheat. The head of the biotechnology company ImClone was facing insider trading charges. The CEO of Adelphia, a cable company, was probably headed for jail. Even Martha Stewart would find herself in trouble for insider trading. Such attention-grabbing scandals reflected a wider trend. When reporting these stories, journalists included polling suggesting that Americans no longer regarded CEOs as wise and trustworthy stewards of large corporations. By summer, at least one poll indicated that public attitudes toward business were far more negative than they had been in the past.[7]

Unbelievably, by the middle of 2002, Worldcom declared bankruptcy, displacing Enron as the biggest corporate failure in U.S. history.[8] Still, Enron retained a special symbolic power. In May, the unethical practices that traders had used in California (along with their colorful names like "Death Star") became public, deepening Americans' disgust with the company. For the Bush administration especially, the Houston company's collapse was a potential disaster. The president quickly learned to expect questions from reporters about his relationship with Ken Lay. Bush, for his part, would lean on his status as a Texan in trying to deflect questions. "I'm deeply concerned about the citizens of Houston who worked for Enron who lost life savings," he responded when pressed about the growing scandal in December.[9] Despite such protestations, the Texas connection was politically dangerous but unavoidable. Documenting all the administration's contacts with the company fell to another Texan who had followed Bush from the governor's mansion in Austin, White House Counsel Alberto Gonzales. Even after the scandal passed, one Democratic congressman wrote to the president that he worried the administration's ties to Enron, questionable stock sales while Bush was at Harken Energy, and Dick Cheney's time at Halliburton all suggested a "lax attitude toward corporate values."[10] A poll conducted by Bob Teeter, a longtime Republican pollster, clearly indicated that Americans thought the Bush administration had aligned itself with corporate interests at the expense of the public good.[11] Late-night comedians joked that the vice president was using the terror threat to avoid uncomfortable questions about any benefits Enron might have received from the energy taskforce.[12] The president's political opponents in D.C. also saw an opening. If the 9/11 attacks had temporarily quieted criticism of the Bush team, their connection to Enron was fair game. Henry Waxman, a Democratic congressman from California, demanded to know what sort of influence Enron's leadership had over the taskforce's recommendations.[13]

By the middle of January, "Enron" had become its own subheading in the "White House News Clips" that were sent to the president on a regular basis. Clearly aware of the potential fallout, the White House was closely monitoring public opinion. The potential political damage the firm's collapse could have done was enormous. Both parties were embarrassed to have received money from the company, but the Texas ties made it a particular problem for Bush's team. Newspapers were beginning to report that Karl Rove and the secretary of the army, Tom White, for example, had profited from stock sales before the company collapsed. Before joining the Bush administration, White had even worked at Enron as a vice president of Enron Energy Services. With Enron now a political liability, Lay would soon find that the company had no friends in D.C. Though Bush was the first American president with an MBA, the probusiness Republican was not about to defend a company that had led to such a public outcry.[14]

Administration officials were quick to point out that the company had not been granted any special favors, and, after determining that its collapse did not pose a systemic risk to the U.S. economy, the administration had let nature take its course. During his State of the Union Address at the end of January, Bush declared that "corporate America must be made more accountable to employees and shareholders and held to the highest standards of conduct."[15] Others in Washington were also scrambling toward a response to Enron's collapse.

Harvey Pitt, Bush's choice for chairman of the SEC, vowed to strengthen accounting oversight, though his ideological bias against more regulation was a persistent theme in press coverage.[16] In the Capitol building, Michael Oxley, a Republican congressman who chaired the House Financial Services Committee, remembered that other members of Congress were coming up to him with "horror stor[ies]" about investors who had lost everything."[17] The sense of urgency in the House of Representatives was fueled by a widespread anger. Even in his own conservative Ohio district, Oxley was hearing his constituents calling for a trial so Lay and the others could "hang."[18] Such anger was understandable.

When the special committee led by Bill Powers that Enron's leadership established at the end of 2001 released its findings in 2002, both lawmakers and the public learned the details of the SPEs that Enron had used throughout the late 1990s. The document, commonly called the "Powers Report," was devastating. Testifying before Congress, Powers himself described what the committee uncovered as "appalling." The report detailed Fastow's swindling (essentially a fraud inside the larger scandal) and faulted Enron for omitting important details in its initial disclosures of the SPEs (which appeared to violate SEC regulations).[19]

Beyond such damning revelations, the Texas lawyer offered detailed information on the SPEs and the multiple derivatives agreements inside each one. As Powers put it: "Enron purported to enter into certain hedging transactions in order to avoid recognizing losses from these investments. . . . These hedges were not real economic hedges. They just affected Enron's earnings statements by allowing Enron to avoid reporting losses on its investments."[20] Reporting such losses could be deferred with Fastow's SPEs, but the actual decrease in economic value remained. As the report noted: "The transactions may have looked superficially like economic hedges," but the reality was different.[21] Enron had become so intertwined with these companies that, "if the value of the investments fell at the same time as the value of Enron stock fell, the SPEs would be unable to meet their obligations and the 'hedges' would fail."[22] In effect, Enron had "hedged" with itself (prompting the financial restatements).[23] In their compiling of the report, the extreme complexity of these structures had left the committee unable to determine if the illegitimacy of SPEs (because they lacked genuine outside equity at risk) was intentional fraud or an honest mistake. The report also highlighted the complex and ultimately nonsensical logic that had come to define Enron.[24]

What bothered Powers even more was what his team saw as a "systematic" attempt to misrepresent the company's finances. Ultimately, his team had concluded that Enron's failure and the fraud that permeated the company was ultimately the result of a lack of oversight and direction from the company's leadership. Because the report was often quoted in congressional hearings that focused on other aspects of the corporate failure such as the board of directors' negligence and the too-cozy relationship between Enron and Arthur Andersen, the Powers Report definitively shaped public understanding about Enron.[25]

Despite the enormous complexity detailed in the document, the report's discovery of outright fraud offered a way to sidestep the quagmire of information confronting the news media tasked with explaining what happened. The details of the SPEs, with different corporations and partnerships linked together through loans, stock transfers, and derivatives contracts, were difficult to understand—but a confidence game was an easy concept to grasp.

The U.S. business scene appeared poised for a period of dramatic change. Arthur Andersen, whose fate was irrevocably tied with Enron's, was rapidly losing clients. In the spring, David Duncan, the Enron account's lead auditor who quickly became an object of scorn for spearheading a panicked burst of document shredding, pled guilty (making him an important witness against both companies). In August, Arthur Andersen was found guilty of obstruction of justice. By the end of the year, the accounting firm simply did not exist.[26] Gallup polls indicated a public appetite for new accounting regulation, and the president was pushing to sign *something* by the end of the summer.[27] In early July, Bush unveiled his "ten-point plan" to combat corporate fraud, a set of priorities for reform. With the president, and others, acknowledging the dramatic increase in the number of Americans invested in the stock market, most of his points were focused on providing accurate information through auditor independence, and providing individual investors with "prompt access to critical information."[28] Apart from the public declarations, privately, Democrats pressured the president for reform, writing that they were concerned about statements made by Karl Rove and SEC chairman Harvey Pitt "that legislation in this area is unnecessary."[29] Soon, Representative Oxley was leading the effort to write a new law, and politically ambitious legislators rushed to add amendments.[30]

The amendment process also presented an opportunity for grandstanding and populist outrage. "If Joe Sixpack is required to sign" a statement "verifying the information on his taxes," Zell Miller, the Georgia senator, thundered while proposing an amendment to the bill, "why shouldn't Josepheus Chardonay be required to sign that same oath for his big corporation?"[31] Though everyone on Capitol Hill was quick to condemn Enron, old political divisions died hard. Mitch McConnell, the Republican senator from Kentucky, for example, proposed an amendment "to provide for certification of financial reports by labor organizations and to improve quality and transparency in financial reporting and independent audits and accounting services for labor organizations."[32] Dick Armey, the Republican House majority leader, accused the Democrats' Senate majority leader Tom Daschle of hypocrisy for condemning Enron and calling for reform while holding up votes on legislation.[33] Some business interests were worried that Enron's collapse would lead to more regulation, warning Rove that "the Democrats are determined to paint these instances of corporate wrongdoing as a problem requiring more legislation as the solution; in fact, the problem is that too many laws have led corporate America to be more concerned with adhering to the laws of the land than in conducting their business according to a higher moral standard."[34] Another concerned writer wrote to Rove that while of course the administration should "prosecute the bad guys who hurt The Private Economy," the government must also take pains to "not strangle The Private Economy with over-regulation."[35] Enron's collapse had put the president in an awkward situation to say the least. Beyond the various and long-standing ties between Lay and the Bush family, to speak on matters of corporate responsibility meant a new round of questions from his own time in the private sector.

The president's signature on the final bill offered at least some sense of relief. At the end of July, the bill that would soon be known as Sarbanes-Oxley became law. By that point, reporters had largely stopped asking the president about Enron, but the process of legislating corporate reform had not been without tension.[36] One member of Congress who had been at the signing ceremony wrote to the president that she was "disturbed" that the president's interpretation of the law hinted at relatively weak protections for whistle-blowers.[37] Overall, though, Washington was ready to move on.

Many parts of the law were focused on shoring up a deteriorating faith in corporate accounting. Beyond establishing an accounting oversight board, Sarbanes-Oxley separated auditing from other accounting services, required the lead auditor on an account to rotate on a regular basis, addressed potential conflicts of interest with the audit committees of corporate boards, and compelled CEOs to personally certify their companies' financial statements. Other provisions in the law, such as new requirements for reporting off-balance sheet transactions, and criminal penalties for tampering with or destroying financial records, were clearly motivated by the particular causes of Enron's failure. However, the reform that quickly emerged from this moment of furious change revealed that an older logic in the government's approach to financial regulation was at work.[38]

Referring to both the insider trading scandals and savings and loans crisis of the 1980s, Oxley reasoned that Enron was the latest in a series of episodes revealing that "somehow the game is rigged against the average investor."[39] Enron, to be sure, was a bigger deal because the number of Americans participating in the stock market was much higher than it had been in the past. But it was not, for Oxley, a qualitatively different affair. Much like earlier bills such as 1988's Insider Trading and Sanctions Fraud Enforcement Act, the new law's emphasis was on policing bad actors like Enron. However, it did not challenge the broader systemic changes that had helped shape

Enron. From the perspective of most politicians, the task facing government in the wake of scandals like Enron was to "restore confidence in the markets."[40]

Alan Greenspan, who was chairman of the Federal Reserve, felt that such confidence was justified, though the implications of the Enron fiasco were clear and profound, because "an economy in which concepts form an important share of valuation has its own vulnerabilities." In a dramatic fashion, Enron revealed how "a firm is inherently fragile if its value added emanates more from conceptual than from physical assets." Events at the end of 2001 had demonstrated a fundamentally new problem that had accompanied the rise of the new economy. "The rapidity of Enron's decline is an effective illustration of the vulnerability of a firm whose market value rests largely on capitalized reputation," he told an audience at the Institute of International Finance in New York. Yet overall Greenspan was sanguine about the collapse. For the chairman, the absence of big shocks in the wake of Enron (as well as the mildness of the recession) demonstrated how expanded information technologies made the economic system safer. Before, the uneven spread of information led to "imbalances" that resulted in "pronounced economic stress" when those imbalances were finally fixed. "Today," Greenspan offered as a contrast, "businesses have large quantities of data available virtually in real time" and could "address and resolve economic imbalances far more rapidly." In a statement that echoed the language Jeff Skilling had used for years to describe Enron and that Fastow had used to justify more SPEs, Greenspan concluded that the "increased flexibility of the American economy" through "the combination of deregulation and innovation in the financial sector" was reason to rest easy. More specifically, it was the rise of ever more complex derivatives that blunted the potential wreckage from Enron's failure.[41]

Some investment bankers and regulators had taken a measure of comfort in the Wall Street firms that successfully hedged the risk associated with Enron's complicated financial fraud by employing complex new, unregulated derivative instruments called credit default swaps, which acted as insurance against bankruptcies. For Greenspan, Enron's collapse provided evidence of how effective this derivatives class was. In the immediate aftermath of the company's failure, the use of credit default swaps in Enron's case had worked to stop the financial fallout from the company's collapse. The Enron debacle, Greenspan's reasoning went, could have been far worse without them. In fact, for some at the Federal Reserve the use of these derivatives in the wake of Enron's collapse demonstrated that the growing and complicated derivatives market was "self-regulating." In other ways, Enron's failure had offered a reassuring glimpse of the complex inner workings of the modern financial system.[42]

In a December 2001 issue of *Fortune*, Bethany McLean noted that Enron's fall was hastened by credit rating downgrades from credit rating agencies that had "come to play a quasi-regulatory role in the market." As McLean noted as she closed her piece, "barring a few more Enron-caliber events, the credit-rating system" would probably not change. Indeed, McLean's sources for the article declared that the ratings agencies were becoming more responsive to the "forward-looking" equities market to balance out historical accounting data. The sense of sprinting into the future that had been celebrated inside Enron had survived the firm's bankruptcy. While politicians in Washington saw Enron's failure as having the potential to become a crisis of confidence in a functioning market, they were relatively untroubled by its expansion and shape, which now included both extremely complicated financial instruments and millions of Americans participating in the securities market through their retirement accounts. Instead, lawmakers emphasized the need to protect the market from episodes like the Enron scandal.[43]

Yet Greenspan, an influential voice, had gone one step further, using Enron to offer (an albeit qualified) affirmation of the "flexibility" and "creative destruction" that characterized political economy at the start of the twenty-first century. The chairman's statements offered a powerful reflection of how business and economic thinking had developed in the 1980s and 1990s. Like many others, he was content to let much of what facilitated Enron's transformation from a pipeline company into a fraudulent business remain in place.

For activists on the left, however, Enron's collapse represented a rare opportunity. Because of what they regarded as abusive and unethical practices in Dabhol, India, some liberal and progressive groups had been critical of Enron even before the bankruptcy. Now, the consumer activist Ralph Nader sought to use the firm's collapse and subsequent outrage to revive a twenty-year-old idea that had never gotten off the ground. It was an old fight for the aging progressive. In 1980, Public Citizen, Nader's public interest group, had tried (and failed) to mobilize Americans, calling for corporate reform with an event called "Big Business Day."[44] Ultimately, the day demonstrated how corporate interests had successfully organized and developed a winning response to activist criticism. In April 2002, though, Nader clearly thought the outrage over revelations at Enron (and the other corporate scandals) was an opportunity to reintroduce the event, which would now be called "Big Bad Business Day." The press release and mailing from Nader's group, Citizen Works, began: "The Enron/Anderson [*sic*] scandal has made it clear: we need a national campaign to stand up to corporate crime, fraud, and abuse."[45] Nader himself was unimpressed with the McCain-Feingold campaign finance reform bill that the president had reluctantly signed and wanted something more robust.[46] While there were events around the country (a group called the Houston Global Awareness Collective hosted one in Enron's hometown), Nader himself appeared at the Washington rally. Here, the rally included an oversized wood chipper with the Enron logo and the words "Democracy Shredder" on the side. The details of Enron's scandal were now providing anticorporate protesters with a new batch of iconography. However, much like the original "Big Business Day," the new event did not do much to galvanize the public. Still, it was clear that some sort of justice would have to be meted out. Even if Bush and Cheney seemed likely to avoid lasting political consequences, others in Washington were not so lucky. In early November, Harvey Pitt was forced to resign his chairmanship at the SEC.[47] Because Pitt was beset by the air of scandal, the Democratic senator Carl Levin wrote to the president that his "continued support of Mr. Pitt" was sending "the wrong message about the importance of corporate reform, investor protections, and strong government oversight."[48] Restoring confidence after Enron was proving to be a long process.

Outside of Washington, notes of protest were also coming from former Enron employees. A website, Laydoff.com, which had been founded by a former Enron worker, soon became a hub for frustrated ex-employees. The site would feature a number of different T-shirts and coffee mugs lampooning the company and giving voice to schadenfreude over the presumed fate of Ken Lay and Jeff Skilling. One design, for instance, called "Texas Justice" implied that the guilty parties should be executed. With its dark humor, the site reflected the same sense of discontent that Nader had tried to capture with "Big Bad Business Day." "Corporate America is very different today than it was during our parents' career building years," the home page read when the site launched in late 2001. The site's founders hoped that it would become the "working person's voice with regard to the ever-increasing corporate abuse of power at the hands of the hard working corporate masses. Laydoff .com would like to be the forum to expose financial and cultural abuses of corporate power by providing apparel to express our distaste for apparent unethical and unwanted behavior."[49]

While hawking T-shirts did not rise to the level of calling for political reform, Laydoff.com did become a venue for these former white-collar workers to make sense of what had been a jarring experience. In this way, Laydoff.com was an expression of anguish and distress. The site even featured a newsletter called the *Pink Slip* in April, as well as solicited contributions from Enron employees who hadn't been fired to donate some of their retention bonuses to the Ex-Enron Relief Fund Account.[50]

Laydoff.com was a harbinger of how the response to Enron would develop. Lay and Skilling were "villainous employers" who "ruined such a wonderful place to work."[51] By next May, Laydoff.com had posted survey results, presumably from former Enron employees. Many of them simply didn't trust Lay or Skilling, and many of them thought jail time was appropriate.[52] The company's leadership had clearly been cast as crooks and cheats.

A late summer Gallup poll revealed the fury of investors demanding jail time for corporate executives as the most important step in restoring confidence. If Martha Stewart couldn't escape the public's outrage, then clearly more than a few Enron executives might wind up in prison. Americans, it turned out, would not have to wait long. In early October, just a few months after Michael Kopper, who had helped run LJM, pleaded guilty to his involvement with the more outrageous accounting schemes, Fastow became one of the most significant players in the collapse to be charged.[53]

The next year, more criminal charges appeared for more Enron workers, including Fastow's wife, and his coworkers in Enron Global Finance, like Ben Glisan. Other former Enron executives, such as Ken Rice, who were associated with Enron Broadband Services, were also charged. Beyond individuals now in legal jeopardy, the corporation itself was meeting with a dismal fate as other companies began buying pieces of the former giant even as creditors rushed to collect their debt. The investment bank UBS Warburg, for instance, acquired Enron's trading operations. It was unclear whether or not what remained of the company—such as the pipeline network that ushered the company into existence—would operate or liquidate. Other, more symbolic sales also took place. Before the end of the year, the E sign at Smith Street was gone, and Enron Field had been renamed Minute Maid Park. The Houston company, for all intents and purposes, ceased to exist. Though the aftermath of Enron's collapse had been dramatic, the literal dismemberment of the company coincided with the diminishment of a reform impulse.[54]

By the summer of 2004 when Skilling, Lay, and others were criminally indicted, the word "Enron" lacked the same sense of political danger that it had possessed in 2002.[55] Even the president needn't have feared the topic. Though he did not name Lay, Skilling, or Fastow, the Enron executives were surely the "irresponsible citizens" he referenced while promoting his idea of the "ownership society" during his reelection campaign. Americans needed to own more—such as homes and stock portfolios—to weather the destabilizing episodes that had become routine in an era of globally interconnected markets and economies. In such speeches, Enron's collapse had become an argument in support of the political-economic sensibilities that had shaped (and warped) the company in the first place. When Bill Donaldson, who had replaced Harvey Pitt at the helm of the Securities and Exchange Commission, ended his tenure in 2005, the president sent him a handwritten note of thanks for "helping restore confidence in our markets."[56] This had been the goal from the start of the White House's response to Enron's failure, and as far as the president was concerned, the storm had long since passed.

Even the angry community of former employees at Laydoff.com retained a basic faith in the new economy. As the site grew, pages for networking and new business ideas appeared. By the middle of 2002, the site included a section called "New Business Ventures" that would provide "creative and entrepreneurial alternatives." Likewise, another section of the site was a forum dedicated to "entrepreneurial matters" such as "a startup looking for some venture capital or an established business looking for partners." What remained in the absence of sustained political upset was a good story.[57]

Substituting Mythology for Reform

As Representative Oxley put it, Enron's collapse had everything needed to grab public attention, and the revelations, from strippers to dangerous vacations and all manner of gross indulgence, made Enron—despite its abstractions—an irresistible topic. Over the summer, *Playboy* had even run an issue featuring ten women who used to work there, reinforcing the sense of sexual misconduct that would become associated with Enron.[58] Though the *Playboy* story was far more colorful, in Oxley's view Enron shared the theme of investor confidence that ran through earlier stock scandals.[59] In reflecting on why such a technical matter had become, after 9/11, the second biggest news story of 2002, *USA Today* commented that "the savings and loan scandal never delivered thrills like this."[60] The comment was telling in pointing out the human drama that made for great copy, but it also placed Enron as one of a longer line of financial scandals in the 1980s and 1990s. What set the company apart, the logic went, was the outrageous (and extraneous) detail.

In addition to villains such as Ken Lay and Jeff Skilling, the scandal had also produced a few heroes. Sherron Watkins had even been named, along with two other whistle-blowers, as one of *Time's* People of the Year at the end of 2002. Though the magazine reported that Watkins had been quick to sign a six-figure book deal, was lining up paid speaking engagements, and had arrived for the interview complaining about losing a designer scarf, the story depicted her as a plainspoken voice cutting through the convoluted business jargon and deceptive numbers swirling around Enron. It would not be long before morality tales or tragicomic farces would be fashioned out of such raw material.[61]

And sure enough, beginning in 2003, a spate of books about Enron began to appear. In a short space of time, there were so many books about the company that *Publishers Weekly* began evaluating each book's chances by the way its author was able to differentiate his or her tome from the others already on store shelves. These books were not intended to stand the test of time. Rather, the speed with which they were written and published suggested a rush to capitalize on the public's fascination with Enron. Likewise, more than one filmmaker would mine the company's history for material. If the Sarbanes-Oxley law made the company's collapse a matter of investor confidence, the books and movies about Enron made it a matter of humanism. Such narratives were cultural echoes of the political impulses behind Sarbanes-Oxley and the Powers Report.[62]

This was not the first time publishers had turned their attention to corporate scandal. Throughout the 1980s and 1990s, titles such as *The Predators' Ball*, *Barbarians at the Gate*, *Den of Thieves*, and *When Genius Failed* soon followed public revelations of corporate misconduct. The journalists and filmmakers who tackled Enron as a subject surely drew from this tradition but also looked back to older cultural narratives in an attempt to ask larger questions about political economy. However, these narratives ultimately fell short in this regard.[63]

Stories about business in the United States often reduced economic complexities to intimately human terms. Such stock narratives had the potential to shape Enron's significance in American cultural memory. For instance, in American literature the marketplace often appeared as a potentially immoral place that could corrupt individuals. Stories that turned on the corruption and redemption of a man on the make could be found in Gilded Age novels like *The Pit* and *The Rise of Silas Lapham* as well as Reagan-era movies such as Oliver Stone's *Wall Street*. Now, Enron was a useful vessel for retelling this much older story. For instance, the 2003 made-for-TV movie *The Crooked E* centered on the potential corruption of Brian, a young man working his way up Enron's corporate ladder even as it threatens his engagement to Courtney, a true and beautiful lass from rural Texas.[64]

Though early scenes in the movie depicted Brian as dealing with some sort of inner turmoil, he ultimately shed his sense of ethics, becoming "Enronized" and peddling a worthless derivatives contract to an unsuspecting executive at an old, industrial corporation who was practically the polar opposite of an Enron worker. While Brian was surrounded by the intoxicating chaos of Enron's trading floor (though the film's low budget only allowed for sparse set decorations), the rube on the other end of the telephone sat alone in a quiet office. Likewise, Brian's hair was rakishly tousled while the other man's hair was combed in a neat part. Sans tie, Brian's attire was also hip (in the preferred style of "Enronized" workers) while his opposite wore a traditional business suit. Even the technology surrounding the two was different. The Enron worker wore a (modern-ish) headset while the other executive held a cordless phone that was laughably out of date for 2003. True to many of the photographs and journalistic descriptions of Enron's offices and desks, the set of the Enron trading floor was filled with computer screens. By contrast, exterior shots of Enron's fictional client, Walderson Industries, included details such as smokestacks to imply that the company actually produced something. Despite the setup, however, what followed was not exactly a meditation on the perils of financialization.

The Crooked E ultimately rested on an older cultural trope that imagined women and the home as moral ballasts against the corrupting influence of the marketplace. Because of her moral grounding, Courtney reacted with alarm at the signs of her fiancé's "Enronization"—such as dining out on sushi with coworkers in lieu of returning to their apartment and her home-cooked pot of chili, or his purchase of a flashy new Lexus (and thus forsaking their battered, muddy Jeep). So rattled was Courtney by her future husband's transformation that she temporarily left him. Ultimately, though, Brian's redemption was secured when he rejected material abundance and returned to Courtney (once again driving the comfy old jalopy of a Jeep), who was shown working in a garden. Normalcy had been restored. Even more sophisticated takes on the company were powerfully influenced by this longer legacy of American fiction.

For instance, while the *New York Times* business reporter Kurt Eichenwald's book *Conspiracy of Fools* offered a condemnation of the corporation
and its executives, the book's form and stylistic conventions reaffirmed some
Enron executives as tragic heroes. In particular, older literary traditions informed the author's characterization of Skilling, who became "consumed by
depression" and alcoholism after being promoted to CEO. Later, Skilling's
melancholy deepened as he concluded that "the market did not 'like him.'"
Here, Skilling's behavior was beginning to affect his home life ("Carter [his
fiancée] felt terrible," the author confided to his readers). The man's physical
and mental health were also feeling the effects of the market—or at the very
least, the world of business. This connection to an unhappy personal life and
business success had some precedent. In Frank Norris's 1903 novel *The Pit*,
the protagonist, Curtis Jadwin, almost loses his wife—ignoring both her and
domestic life in general—as he becomes "addicted" to the market. Similarly,
in William Dean Howells's novel *The Rise of Silas Lapham*, the titular character becomes miserable even as his worldly fortune grows.[65]

As the new Enron stories indicated, the themes undergirding American
storytelling about business had remained remarkably stable even as American
business had become more complicated. To be sure, some Enron narratives
did take aim at the changes that Enron represented. In these moments, traces
of a much more powerful critique appeared as authors called attention to
the meaninglessness of the language and jargon that had drifted across the
pages of Enron documents.

In their book *24 Days*, Rebecca Smith and John Emshwiller, the two *Wall
Street Journal* reporters, focused on the financial complexity that could be
found in Enron's opaque and misleading financial statements. After the company's initial announcement of a billion-dollar loss, Smith read over ambiguous phrases like "structured finance arrangements with a previously
disclosed entity" and thought to herself: "What the heck was that?" Comb-
ing through documents, she found only "gibberish." Conflating the company's use of language and sketchy accounting, the book's central plot was
resolved as Ken Lay's "verbal calisthenics" lost their power to dazzle and ob-
fuscate. As the reporters wrote, many in the financial community "had been
ignorant to one degree or another about the inner workings of Enron. Company officials had used that lack of knowledge" and "played it like a musical
instrument." But this time, "bland reassurances and promises of great things
to come were no longer enough. Faith was being replaced by doubt. And
doubt could be deadly for a company that lived off credit." Such lines unmis-

takably inched toward condemning the very emphasis on image and imma-teriality that Skilling had championed during the company's heyday.[66]

The focus on language even popped up in the TV movie *The Crooked E.* In one scene, the hero, Brian, was unable to answer his future brother-in-law's question "What does that mean: virtual assets?" Brian's answer, "It's an asset that's not tied into any physical plant or product," did not satisfy. The brother-in-law's response—"Yeah, but what does it mean?"—offered a plain-spoken rejoinder to the business jargon that Enron employed throughout the 1990s. Amid the rural backdrop and among his future in-laws, Brian failed to communicate what it was he did, finally offering a flustered "it's really complicated to explain if you're not in business." The implication, of course, was that the phrase (and the thinking behind it) was nonsense. The assault on sophistry and pretension was even more direct when Texans took up pens.[67]

For example, *Texas Observer* reporter Robert Bryce tried to cast the failure as a tall tale from the Lone Star State in his book *Pipe Dreams.* Ultimately, though, the author suggested that the corrupting elements within the company were not native to Texas. In one passage, Bryce quoted a former employee as saying, "you had the old pipeliners and you had the New York–type financial traders." A little later, the writer again quoted the same executive as saying, "nothing mattered to the New York traders except the deal." In these mo-ments, the author betrayed a pride of place. The journalist could not help but admire Houston's swagger, calling it a "frontier" city with a "fearless 'can-do' spirit" that was missing in "Northern cities." Even if Lay was only the latest in a long line of Lone Star "energy baron[s] who willingly pulls his pants down," many of the company's bad practices were out-of-state imports. Perhaps coastal sophistication was to blame for the fall of the energy giant.[68]

Similarly, in her own account (coauthored with the Texas journalist Mimi Swartz), Sherron Watkins offered her direct and unadorned style of communication as an antidote to Lay's "unshakable faith in the power of appearances." The country needed more people like Watkins, the book im-plied, to halt the "whole sorry devolution of American capitalism at the end of the twentieth century" that had produced the "illusory tech bubble" and "the silly excesses." Ultimately, Swartz and Watkins used Enron to arrive at insights about U.S. culture as a whole, writing: "The mid to late 1990s prom-ised to be the era of the New Paradigm, when people were convinced that the rules of business, and even American life, were being rewritten." In roundabout ways, each of these texts took aim at some of the systemic changes that had enabled Enron's development. A character in a TV movie complaining about business jargon or frontier-town reckoning that a derivatives contract could be as much of a bluff as a bad hand in Texas Hold 'Em did not point just to fraud at Enron, but to business as a whole at the end of the twentieth century. However, such contemporary and potentially powerful critiques mixed uneasily with the human drama at the heart of these stories.[69]

These conflicted sympathies even appeared in what soon became the standard account of Enron's rise and fall, *The Smartest Guys in the Room*, coauthored by the *Fortune* journalists Bethany McLean and Peter Elkind. Perhaps more than any other book, *The Smartest Guys in the Room* offered a consistent rejoinder to the economy's financialization that helped shape Enron's development. Marking the passing of an earlier and more sensible way of doing business, the two authors lamented the demise of Arthur Andersen's old slogan, "Think straight, talk straight." The tragedy of Arthur Andersen and accounting was that, much like the natural gas business, the company was no longer "boring." In their account, the world of finance was always a disruptive presence. Indeed, the second chapter, entitled "Please Keep Making Us Millions," focused on the reckless and fraudulent trading run by two "rogue traders" (Louis Borget and Tom Mastroeni) in Valhalla, New York, in 1987 that nearly ruined the company. Though the episode was ultimately disconnected from Jeff Skilling's transformation of the company in the 1990s, McLean and Elkind used the event as an opportunity to foreshadow several themes. For example, the authors took Ken Lay's failure to fire the two even after they had been exposed as evidence of the CEO's own moral flexibility. McLean and Elkind also juxtaposed trading with the sort of large industrial processes that still typified Enron's business in 1987. As they wrote: "Enron Oil [the trading division that housed the two] as it was renamed, wasn't anything like the rest of the company's gritty industrial operations. It was the 'flashy' part of the business." They described Enron Oil's offices as "sleek and modern and sheathed in glass, a far cry from the more modest quarters favored by energy industry executives." This dichotomy, with "flashy" financial trading on one side and boring or even unappealing work on the other, was one of the book's constants. As McLean and Elkind wrote: "In more than location, the oil traders were closer to the freewheeling world of Wall Street than to the slow-moving, capital-intensive, risk-averse world of natural gas pipelines. Oil trading was about *trading*, not about oil." Of course, the trading schemes were soon revealed as criminal.[70]

This theme of financialization's destructive influence expanded in the book with Skilling's arrival. While McLean and Elkind conceded that his approach to the natural gas industry was visionary, they also faulted the executive for his dismissive attitude toward a practical approach to business. As they wrote: "What thrilled Skilling, always, was the intellectual purity of an idea, not the translation of that idea into reality." While that comment alone was not a negative, the authors immediately followed with the criticism: "he was often too slow—even unwilling—to recognize when the reality didn't match the theory." That Skilling was allowed to "create a place where raw brains and creativity mattered more than management skills and real world experience" was almost tragic. As if directly addressing Skilling himself, they wrote: "You can't build a company on brilliance alone. . . . You also need people who can implement those ideas." Indeed, McLean and Elkind seemed to pin Enron's eventual downfall on Skilling's almost blind commitment to knowledge work, noting that in the end his division would turn into a "chaotic destructive free-for-all."[71]

Though the authors clearly saw Skilling as the fountainhead of Enron's growing contempt for the older, less creative, and more concrete business operations, they also regarded others, particularly his protégés, as guilty of the same faults. McLean and Elkind presented Enron under Skilling's leadership as hopelessly chaotic and simultaneously contemptuous of "honest" work because it was not "intellectually pure." Through this focus on Skilling, *The Smartest Guys in the Room* inched toward a direct rebuke of the sort of business thought and strategy that Skilling had brought to Enron.[72]

As the reporters noted, the successes at Enron were encouraging an ultimately fatal hubris at the company. "Toward the end of the 1990s came unprecedented volatility," they wrote, "and for traders, volatility is one of the necessary ingredients for making outsize profits. And as trading profits soared, the traders became convinced of their own invincibility."[73] Elsewhere, the reporters offered other, similar details that depicted Enron's traders as boorish and arrogant and, in the end, lawless.

These themes of criminality and bluster also hung over the book's account of the California energy crisis. In describing the West Coast energy trader Tim Belden, they wrote: "He was, as they liked to say at Enron, intellectually pure—a trader who believed in the beauty of free markets and had no scruples when it came to exploiting inefficiencies to make money." Instead of laboring to create something of lasting and material value, he led "the effort to find exploitable loopholes" and worked "14-hour days learning the arcane rules of California deregulation." Ultimately, Belden found a "flaw" in the rules and conducted an "experiment" (setting up a particular power routing schedule across inadequate power lines) to see if his ideas were correct. Disaster followed. Once Belden proved that the state's energy rules could be exploited, he and the other traders rushed in, causing huge fluctuations in rates, rolling blackouts, and energy crises. Hubris and arrogance at the company had led directly to a public disaster.[74]

McLean and Elkind were perhaps even more critical and acidic when writing about Andy Fastow. With his "creative forms of financial chicanery," Fastow represented the most extreme example of the unstable approach to business that was becoming common at the company. Ultimately, Andy Fastow's case allowed the authors to frame structured finance as a con—nothing more. McLean and Elkind also called attention to Fastow's material excesses. They wrote that Fastow (full of "giddy, smug delight") and the entire staff of LJM had spent a "glorious time in the sun" vacationing in Los Cabos despite having defrauded the company. "And why not," the authors asked with indignation, "LJM picked up the $52,000 tab. And most of them had just made a fortune."[75]

Because McLean and Elkind largely blamed Enron's collapse on the culture of smartness that the firm shared with Wall Street, their book offered a direct rebuke to the image that Skilling cultivated over the preceding years. In a motif that ran throughout the book, the authors faulted him and others for dismissing traditional business structures in favor of a more chaotic and ultimately corrupt type of work and provided examples of older, more practically minded business people—ones without elite credentials and big ideas—who were pushed out of the company. In *The Smartest Guys in the Room*, such vestiges of the industrial economy were usually casualties of the new economy ethos of both newness in and of itself and, more to the point, the type of business practiced by the young, elite knowledge workers that Enron aggressively recruited throughout the 1990s.

McLean and Elkind's book was praised as a stellar example of business reporting. However, much like Sarbanes-Oxley, to a large degree *The Smartest Guys in the Room* was focused on individuals. The two *Fortune* reporters may have produced a sophisticated and detailed explanation of the company's development and failure, but they had also framed their story around flawed (and very specific) personalities like Jeff Skilling, Ken Lay, and Andy Fastow. In addition to the arrogance on display through the company's history, Skilling was a "gambler," Ken Lay disliked bad news and had a penchant for what might charitably be called situational ethics. Andy Fastow seemed not to have any moral compass to begin with. Much like other, less-developed Enron narratives, here interpersonal dynamics overshadowed systemic analysis. Political economy itself was not challenged. Because of this moderate political sensibility, the book would become awkward source material for the most widely seen narrative about the company, Alex Gibney's documentary film *Enron: The Smartest Guys in the Room*.[76]

Taking full advantage of the visual medium, Gibney juxtaposed images, commentary, and sound to achieve a decidedly visceral effect to represent California's energy crisis. Viewers were shown dice tumbling down a casino craps table, fading into an eagle's eye view of a spinning roulette wheel as a rock song blasted: "There's nothing wrong with the capitalism/ There's nothing wrong with the free enterprise." The camera moved over footage of Enron's energy trading floor, zooming in and out on rows and rows of people talking on telephones and headsets while their computer monitors displayed symbols and charts in an array of electric colors. These moments found Gibney reworking some of the basic iconography of financialization. Rather than the triumphant positioning of these images in Enron's marketing literature, Gibney invested these scenes with menacing undertones.[77]

Even apart from the California episode, deregulation was a prominent thread in the film, particularly the connection between Republican politicians and Enron executives such as Ken Lay. The first extended treatment of the executive noted (as many Enron narratives did) that Lay took his father's Baptist preaching and applied it to stumping for deregulation. In a section rich with symbolism, Gibney superimposed an old black-and-white photograph of Lay over various images of the Washington, D.C., landscape. Lay stood at what could be a lectern or pulpit, in the middle of speaking, one arm declaratively flung into the air. He might have been testifying, a suggestion aided by Peter Elkind calling him an "apostle for deregulation" and narrator Peter Coyote noting that Lay became "part of a new crusade to liberate businessmen from the rules and regulation of government." From there, the documentary moved to a clip of Reagan's famous line that "government is not the solution to our problem, government is the problem." In another clip, Reagan waxed rhapsodic about the "magic of the marketplace" as the film cut to an image of petroleum refineries before the jazz standard "That Old Black Magic" began to play. Coyote then elaborated on the point, explaining that "the magic power of deregulation pushed Ken Lay to found Enron in 1985." By linking figures such as Lay to a broader faith in deregulation, Gibney's film moved close to a systemic critique of political economy. Unlike its source material, the film was forthrightly political, and some conservative outlets such as the *National Review* blasted Gibney's film as liberal propaganda.[78]

Certainly, *Enron: The Smartest Guys in the Room* could provoke outrage among audience members. A film critic for the *Washington Post* reported that "just reviewing my notes . . . is making me physically ill."[79] Though it was hyperbolic, the reviewer suggested that *Enron: The Smartest Guys in the Room* was intended to be a visceral experience. Other, less evocative reviews noted the "dark humor" of Gibney's treatment and highlighted its righteous indignation. Several reviewers focused on what they deemed the "arrogance" and "greed" of the energy executives. One reviewer noted that a clip of Jeff Skilling getting hit in the face with a pie won cheers from a Houston audience filled with former Enron workers.[80] However, while other political documentaries displayed a coherent political worldview, Gibney's subject matter did not allow for a similar degree of clarity. McLean and Elkind were business journalists, not muckrakers, and their book reflected this distinction. To be sure, the filmmaker unequivocally condemned the sort of deregulation that Lay and Skilling had championed throughout their professional careers, but certain sections of the movie muddled this political sensibility.

In one section, comments from Peter Elkind that appeared just before the filmmaker launched into a critique of deregulation undercut Gibney's point. Not without some admiration, Elkind noted that Ken Lay was "way ahead of the curve" on deregulation, and that he "was thinking about energy markets that would be deregulated." Elkind even singled out the natural gas industry, which, he declared, was "shackled by regulation." To a large extent, the *Fortune* reporter was echoing what many have said about natural gas deregulation. Still, it is noteworthy that Elkind was not condemning deregulation as a principle, even though this was Gibney's intention.

Similarly clashing sensibilities emerged when Gibney took up McLean and Elkind's charge of corrosive intellectual arrogance at the company. This criticism of "smartness" as a business value pushed the film into an uncertain political and cultural terrain. Skilling-era Enron had been marked by advertising campaigns that boldly implored viewers to "Ask Why" and had been staffed with young MBAs from elite schools. The slogan in some ways did represent a turn in U.S. business rhetoric. One of the most powerful American traditions of criticizing new ideas came from business discourse. Writing in 1964, the historian Richard Hofstadter had argued that American businessmen harbored anti-intellectual values, regarding "success in some demanding line of practical work" as "much superior to, formal knowledge and expertise acquired in the schools."[81] This juxtaposition of business practicality and useless book smarts was never very far from the surface in *Enron: The Smartest Guys in the Room.*

For example, throughout the film Gibney featured interviews with Mike Muckleroy, a gruff, older executive who had been instrumental in saving the company from imploding during the 1987 Valhalla crisis. Muckleroy repeatedly appeared as a plainspoken, commonsense commentator on increasingly outlandish events with an unmistakable Texan drawl and a blunt, folksy manner. When the film turned to a consideration of the peer evaluation process that Skilling introduced, Gibney chose to show a close up on Muckleroy, who had gray hair and wore an open blue button-down shirt and no tie, as he scoffed, "I've never heard of any company yet that would be successful terminating 15 percent of their people every year, just to satisfy the fact that the other employees have to vote on 'em." Muckleroy operated as a marker for the sage, practical businessman pointing out the folly of big ideas. When compared to Skilling's decidedly modern appearance and "new economy" intellectual pretensions, Muckleroy came across as reassuringly old-fashioned. The air of nostalgia extended to other elements of the movie as well.[82]

For instance, just as Mike Muckleroy appeared as a commonsense rejoinder to financialization and increasingly outlandish business schemes, the director also highlighted the plight of an electricity lineman who suddenly became an Enron employee after the company acquired Portland General Electric in 1996. Gibney followed the lineman through his workday—driving a company van and wearing a hardhat. In these segments, the worker was often behind the wheel of his vehicle or just outside of it (an electricity pole usually in the background). All these details coded him as blue collar, providing a striking contrast to the younger, sharply dressed employees walking the halls of Enron's sleek, modern towers in Houston. Gibney tracked the hardworking lineman as he invested as much money in Enron as possible only to see his savings disappear when the stock collapsed. Moments such as these were packed with indignation and melancholy. Once again, the "everyman" had been duped by corporate greed.

Gibney's use of both the executive and the lineman as stand-ins for larger groups was striking in several respects. Both men, despite their differences, were casualities of Enron's "smart" and ultimately duplicitous way of doing business.[83] Though postwar industrial political economy was marked by business managers' pronounced animosity toward labor, such differences and distance between the two men shrank in the film.[84] There was no sense of irony in this conflation. Muckleroy might as well have been blue collar, while the lineman might have favored business-minded conservatism. In part because of his source material, Gibney's film presented a nostalgic, idealized portrait of an older, less complicated period in American business. The movie, like other Enron narratives, could only look backward. Such nostalgic notes confused and conflated a range of cultural stereotypes, including a progressive suspicion of large-scale business enterprise and the hard-nosed businessman's dim view of book learning.

Gibney's film ultimately earned over $4 million through its theatrical release and played in 146 theaters. For an unrated documentary about a business scandal perpetrated through arcane accounting practices, Gibney's film was a commercial success.[85] When the movie premiered at the Sundance Festival several months before the general release, at least one reporter described it as a "hot ticket."[86] But *Enron: The Smartest Guys in the Room* also marked a high-water point for narratives about Enron. That same year, when Kurt Eichenwald (who had covered Enron for the *New York Times*) published *A Conspiracy of Fools*, editors and others in the book industry began to worry about an oversaturated market for Enron stories.[87] New offerings more or less stopped coming, and Enron's place in popular memory began to harden.

To be sure, many Enron narratives were not overly simplistic or didactic. Details, such as Gibney's interview with a Houston pastor telling stories of unhappy Enron employees, hinted at complex inner worlds for almost everyone involved. Most retellings were shot through with a degree of ambivalence and even sympathy toward some of the personalities behind the collapse. McLean and Elkind, for example, treated Skilling as a tragic figure who alarmed his friends watching him come unglued as the company's fortunes declined. Even the last few pages of their book dwelled on an episode where Skilling was found drunk and confused in a New York City street after the company had come apart. Similarly, in his film, Gibney featured close-up images of Skilling looking haggard and worried, soft music murmuring in the background as interviewees used words such as "distraught" to describe Skilling's emotional state. In another sympathetic note in his film, the director lingered on an early black-and-white photo of a young boy (presumably Lay) atop a tractor as Peter Elkind explained how Lay liked to tell "a story later about sitting on a tractor dreaming about the world of business and how different it could be from the way things were for him and his family." After so much worldly success, it would be a sad decline for that poor boy imagining a better life beyond the horizon.[88]

In sum, these cultural documents contained the potential to offer a more thorough and systemic rebuke to the vagaries of financialization and the new economy than the narrowly focused reforms of Sarbanes-Oxley. However, older and more familiar cultural narratives about business overwhelmed these aspects and rendered Enron's collapse as a tale of individual corruption and redemption. They were, in other words, cultural reinforcements of the law Enron had inspired. Enron's memory, while an embarrassing episode in American capitalism, was not a moment for broader reflection. In fact, much in the way Alan Greenspan used Enron's failure to argue against further regulating the financial services sector, some of these books found comfort in the free market that Lay and Skilling had once championed.

At the end of *24 Days*, for instance, Smith and Emshwiller concluded that "Wall Street, that citadel of a freewheeling capitalism that was often perceived as amoral, had shown a surprising streak of Puritanical outrage about Enron's dishonesty."[89] The market itself had become an instrument of justice that punished Enron with each new revelation. In highlighting the market's intolerance for falsehood, *24 Days* ultimately affirmed the late twentieth century's political economy. That Wall Street culture may have exerted an enormous influence on Enron's transformation from a stable pipeline company to a fraudulent operation was lost in the book's conclusion. Enron, the reporters determined at the end of *24 Days*, was an aberration. That capitalism was left untroubled, though, was little comfort to former Enron executives who now spent their days meeting with lawyers in the hopes that they could stay out of jail.[90]

On December 13, 2005, Ken Lay stood in front of an audience at the Houston Forum, a local organization that hosted talks by prominent figures. The stakes of such a public appearance could not have been higher. Soon after the collapse, the Federal Bureau of Investigation assembled a taskforce to investigate what had happened at Enron.[91] As he noted in his address, Lay himself was potentially facing a prison sentence of 175 years. Lay was surely aware that stories about villainous business executives being written in books would play a powerful role in his own life, and during the talk, he offered up his own assessment of Enron narratives. "Most of what was and is still being said, heard or read," about Enron, Lay declared, "was and still is either grossly exaggerated, distorted, or just flat out false. But a time of political and public hysteria is not a ripe environment for truth." Much of the speech, which the embattled executive had originally entitled "Living in the Crosshairs of the U.S. Criminal Justice System" before settling on the slightly less hysterical "Guilty, Until Proven Innocent," was given over to a legal defense of his own involvement in the company, as well as dark warnings about "criminalizing" certain types of "business activities." This did not mean, though, that the executive thought all stories about the company were without merit. Lay even referred to Kurt Eichenwald twice, noting that as the "author of *Conspiracy of Fools*, shared with this same Houston Forum a few weeks ago, most of the seven charges against me could not even be brought in a civil case because they would be dismissed by the court before trial as being immaterial."[92]

Perhaps that author's conclusions offered the executive a measure of hope that passions would cool before the trial's start; but the "truth" about Enron had already been set in stone through the managing of a political crisis, in the Powers Report's description of fraud and abuse, and, finally, by the older and wider cultural practices of making sense of events through storytelling.[93] The content and shape of these Enron narratives meant that the company's collapse would be remembered as a case of corrupt, arrogant, and flawed individuals who fostered an ugly corporate culture while brazenly duping the public for years. To be sure, news of guilty verdicts and lengthy jail sentences reinforced this specific interpretation of Enron's history. As Jon Stewart, host of *The Daily Show*, a politically charged television comedy, remarked while interviewing Bethany McLean in 2009: "Enron, that's fraud."[94]

On the surface, that pithy explanation was accurate. Enron ended its life as a place that facilitated criminal activity at both the individual and institutional level. However, the comment (typical of how Enron was remembered) breezed past forces much bigger than the company itself, such as a new business language and sensibility that still enjoyed widespread acceptance. Enron had been a part of a process where business interests had solidified a neoliberal orthodoxy. Ironically, it was partly because Enron's collapse had been so singular and spectacular—because it was an undeniably good story— that the larger system of business thought and practice remained in place. Enron, the story went, was an exception, not the rule.

Conclusion

Learning from Enron

In 2006, while Kenneth Lay and Jeffrey Skilling stood trial, Houstonians could learn a lot about why the two men were fighting to stay out of jail. If one had five hours to spare, there was a bus and walking tour of places around the city connected to the defunct company. The tour departed at 10:30 in the morning from the Kirby Mansion, where fifteen years earlier Ken Lay had greeted foreign dignitaries during the World Economic Forum. From there, Sandra Lord, the tour's director, took visitors around the city, stopping at the Front Porch (once a popular hangout for employees), the courthouse where the two men were presently proclaiming their innocence, Enron's former headquarters at 1400 Smith Street (now occupied by Chevron), the Methodist church where Lay and his wife were members, and even some houses in upper-class Houston neighborhoods that had once been home to now-disgraced characters like Andy Fastow.

Throughout the tour, Lord added to the information she had taken from the Enron narratives and news coverage with her own observations. A shopper at Jus' Stuff (the thrift store Linda Lay opened after Enron's collapse), she noted, at one point would have been able to buy medals from Lay's time in the navy. The subject matter may have been dark, but the tour itself promised a jovial and light mood. Houston and Enron were bound to one another, though the tour director wanted her customers to end their day with a good impression of the city. Visitors could have their photograph taken with the Crooked E. Tour takers even left with promotional flyers for Gibney's movie that had been designed to look like stock certificates. Besides the tour, other Houstonians were trying to make light of the Enron scandal. Sometimes, though, the broader implications of Enron's life and death cut through the mirth making.[1]

That same year, *Enron—the Musical*, which was written and financed by Houston humorist Mark Fraser and performed by six community theater

actors, began playing in a church. Sharing the set with an old-fashioned
Christmas pageant, Fraser's production explicitly rejected the new Houston
and instead longed for the less complicated days of the Sunbelt city before
the bust and recovery in the 1980s. The musical's story line focused on a Houstonian everyman named "Ex-Enron" and his growing disillusionment with
the company. A telling line in the musical pointed to this sentiment when
Ex-Enron described Jeff Skilling as a "snake oil salesman" and the people he
hired as "a bunch of MBA snobs."[2] Not only did Fraser view Enron's collapse
as disastrous for Houston, but he blamed the late-century changes that Enron
exemplified and looked nostalgically back to the city's midcentury industrial economy and regional identity. By the time the musical opened, though,
Enron was no longer a hot topic in the city.

To be sure, the *Houston Chronicle* offered extensive coverage of Lay and
Skilling's criminal trial, but at the same time, even the creator of the Enron
tour sensed an "exhaustion" with Enron. With the country in the midst of
an unpopular war in Iraq that seemed to be dragging on, who wanted to take
a tour "about negative things?" Though it was marketed toward out-of-town
visitors, as of February, only locals had shelled out the thirty dollars to take
the tour. Besides, Enron's marks on the city's landscape were vanishing. Jus'
Stuff was now a business called the Import Warehouse. Enron Field was now
Minute Maid Park. Even the "E" outside of the company's old headquarters
was gone. As evidence of Enron's presence in the city continued to vanish,
the trial verdicts did offer a more definite conclusion. Skilling received a
harsh sentence, and Lay died of a heart attack in July, before beginning his
prison term. Still, the end of the trial did little to reignite interest in the company. It was not as if media outlets beyond Houston ignored the trial, but the
verdict was in some ways met with a shrug. The *New Yorker* writer Malcolm
Gladwell, for instance, published an article about it, but for Gladwell the trial
was little more than a foil to make a broader point about the information
age. The stakes simply did not seem as high as they had been when Enron first
collapsed.[3]

But even if most Americans forgot their outrage when it came to the
company, a shock to the global financial system would soon remind them of
the economic instability that they had first glimpsed with Enron. Two years
after Lay and Skilling's trial concluded, the next financial crisis arrived under
a deceptively familiar guise. Americans might have learned to be suspicious
of the wild promises of a Texas energy company upending an industry. Now,
though, money was pouring into good old-fashioned real estate. But this was

not a return to basics that so many thought was needed after Enron. Much in the way Jeff Skilling transformed the Houston energy firm by looking to Wall Street for organizational models, employees, and trading practices, a newfangled financial architecture stood behind that perennial American dream of home ownership.

Home loans were now connected to the global financial system through new products called mortgage-backed securities. The innovation pooled and chopped up mortgages that were then traded around the world. Through such an operation, the risk of providing a loan to an American of modest means was supposedly diluted. Just as Andy Fastow's special purpose entities ultimately magnified Enron's problems while promising to solve them, though, the sophisticated financing behind home loans was creating a precarious situation. Throughout the country unscrupulous mortgage lenders were giving loans to Americans who could not, in the end, afford them. This "subprime" market was meant to help families achieve financial stability by owning a home. Now, though, lenders were not even performing basic credit checks on borrowers. Adjustable-rate mortgages, loans that started off with easy-to-manage payments, would quickly overwhelm a poor family once the introductory interest rate expired. The problem, though, was much more pervasive. What would be a personal tragedy for a family with just such a mortgage also promised to be a global catastrophe as mortgage-backed securities built with such loans were being bought and sold by banks around the world. On top of that, credit default swaps, the derivatives that Alan Greenspan championed for containing the economic consequences of Enron's failure, proliferated alongside the shady, shaky home loans.

In some ways, it seemed as though things had only gotten worse since Enron. At least the credit rating agencies had declined to provide the energy company their best ratings. Now, though, all manner of convoluted financial derivatives received top scores. By 2007, the warning signs of impending crisis were growing. That summer, credit rating agencies were starting to downgrade risky mortgage-backed securities. The problems of offering adjustable-rate mortgages were becoming clear. The banks themselves were starting to shake. Most dramatically, when the bank Bear Stearns wobbled at the precipice of collapse, officials at the Treasury department and the Federal Reserve brokered a deal that allowed J. P. Morgan to take over the failing institution. This was just the start of a year when the entire global financial system came undone.[4] While the Enron scandal had ruined two companies, the subprime mortgage crisis threatened whole national economies. What became a global recession, unlike Enron's swift fall, slowly unfurled as a succession of increasingly ominous developments. Banks filing for chapter 11 bankruptcy threatened to become ordinary events.

Enron should have been a dress rehearsal for the bigger crisis, but the playbook the Bush administration used with Enron would not help in 2008. When the Houston company's troubles became apparent, the federal government had declined to step in. The personal political ties that Ken Lay had cultivated with the Bush family and other Texas politicians now in power were not enough to save the company. The Texas Republicans had stayed true to their laissez-faire economic philosophy and allowed the free market to exact its toll on the energy company. Enron died, and the absence of any wider financial fallout vindicated such a hands-off approach to matters of the market. When the crisis began to unfold, the Bush team would not be so steady. Already, the government had stepped in to help Bear Stearns and the government-sponsored entities Fannie Mae and Freddie Mac. However, in September, when it became clear that Lehman Brothers was on the verge of collapsing, the Bush administration returned to the tactics they had employed with Enron and simply stood back as the bank failed.

The result, though, could not have been more different from 2001. The stunning collapse of such an old bank set off a panic. Lehman Brothers became the largest bankruptcy in U.S. history, far surpassing Enron's. The effects of the investment bank's collapse were both immediate and severe. As the Federal Financial Crisis Inquiry Commission's report put it, "On the day that Lehman filed for bankruptcy, the Dow plummeted more than 500 points, $700 billion in value from retirement plans, government pension funds, and other investment portfolios disappeared." As the financial panic continued, it "plunged the nation into the longest and deepest recession in generations."[5] Banks and politicians were now scrambling to survive. Other banks disappeared or reorganized, and the government moved quickly to stabilize the insurance company AIG. After Lehman's failure, no one wanted to know what would happen if another giant company failed. What followed was high stakes political drama in Washington as the stock market continued to drop. Eventually, the legislature passed the Troubled Asset Relief Program, which the president signed into law.[6]

In a strange irony, George W. Bush, the first American president to hold an MBA, was forced to directly intervene in the market. He was, the president told one reporter, abandoning "free market principles to save the free market system."[7] It was an awkward and roundabout way of admitting that markets cannot be separated from the state. The economy, Bush's comments revealed, is always a political economy. The realization, though, had arrived too late. Right up until the collapse, both Republicans and Democrats regarded markets as near-perfect systems. It would be one of Enron's more tragic legacies that it did little to stop the development of an inherently risky and increasingly pervasive financial system. What should have been a warning bell in 2001 was instead, for some, a sign of the justice inherent to the market.

Much like Enron's collapse, the Great Recession was years in the making, with rampant risk taking, securitization, and, as the Federal Financial Crisis Inquiry Commission put it in their report, "exponential growth in financial firms' trading activities" and "unregulated derivatives."[8] However, there was one notable difference between Enron's demise and the subprime mortgage crisis. At least at first, the Great Recession did not produce the same explosion of narratives that Enron did.[9] "It's particularly tough to turn the most recent crisis into good entertainment," Daniel Gross wrote in the May 3, 2010, edition of *Newsweek*. The wounds were too recent, and besides, "the best and most enduring Wall Street entertainment hasn't been post-bull-market autopsies, but ripping bubble-era tales."[10] The lack of Great Recession narratives, though, did not mean that economic anxieties and a suspicion toward big business hadn't found their way into popular culture. There was even a new Broadway show that was opening that week: *Enron*.

Though new to U.S. audiences, British playwright Lucy Prebble's drama about the company had actually been playing in England for nearly a year. Prebble was drawn to the company because Enron ultimately became "that most theatrical of entities, just a game, an illusion, a system of belief."[11] For the play's director, Enron was a "peculiarly American" story with a "frontier kind of go-getting attitude" at its core.[12] With a good measure of artistic license, real life figures, such as Ken Lay, Andy Fastow, and Jeff Skilling, coexisted with fictitious characters, such as Claudia Roe, Skilling's nemesis and sometimes lover, who was based, in part, on Rebecca Mark. Likewise, the script blended well-known public statements with dramatic dialogue. However, the play's true thematic tension was between materiality and immateriality. As the stage directions instructed one of the Raptors—monstrous, corporeal manifestations of virtual corporations that ultimately ruined Enron—to menacingly toy with Skilling, Claudia Roe worried that "something is happening to business. At the beginning of this century. Things have started to get divorced from the underlying realities."[13]

Despite the theatrical blend of fact and fiction that mirrored the hazy line between illusion and reality at Enron, Broadway did not warm to the production. An early review for the *New York Times* savaged Prebble's creation. Perhaps, the reviewer conjectured, "British and American tastes don't always coincide," particularly "when the subject is American." Much like Enron itself, the review read, "the energy generated" by the play felt "factitious, all show (or show and tell) and little substance." The play closed in less than three weeks. In England, where the play had been a hit, critics were stunned. Its failure was a shame, one lamented. At a time when Americans were "gripped by the story of alleged misdeeds at Goldman Sachs," Prebble's play called attention to the public's "complicity in financial bubbles." The play's mixed success highlights Enron's strange afterlife in the wake of the Great Recession.[14]

For all the outrage the company once provoked, "Enron" is now a vague and uncertain referent. Politicians might still find the company's name invoked in attempts to conjure up the specter of political corruption. When the renewable energy company Solyndra failed, conservative writers tried (unsuccessfully) to characterize the firm as Obama's Enron. Likewise, references to the company's enthusiasm for the Kyoto Protocol can sometimes be found on right-wing websites as a way to discredit any attempt to mitigate the effects of climate change. In California, a connection to Enron can still cause headaches for local politicians.

For some former employees, the company represents a more complicated legacy. Rich Kinder, Enron's former president, is still a big presence in Houston. The company he left Enron to start, Kinder Morgan, is a successful firm. However, as of 2016, his corporate biography did not dare to mention a connection to his disgraced former employer. Other former Enron workers have not been so quiet.

Though Sherron Watkins, with both her book *Power Failure* and her subsequent career in public speaking about business ethics, is the most prominent example of an ex-Enroner to offer an interpretation of the company's history, more than a few self-published books about the episode offer evidence of how the company has been an avenue for a range of personal exploration. The author of *The Kingdom of Norne*, a satirical treatment of Enron that was framed as a children's book, was an electrical engineer whose wife had worked for Enron. Though an engineer by training, the author used the scandal to explore his "lifelong interest in doodling and sketching."[15] Writing with the nom de plume Busta Scam in 2006, the author dedicated his book to "all the hardworking Nornians."[16] That same year, David Tonsall, a former Enron employee, took the stage name N-Run and recorded a hardcore hip-hop album attacking "corporate America." Tonsall self-financed and released a CD, *Corporate America*, on the two-year anniversary of the company's bankruptcy. In his lyrics, Tonsall faulted Lay and Skilling for ruining the finances of honest employees, who he often referred to as the "pipeline boys." Beyond satirical children's books and a rap album, however, more ruminative explorations of Enron's legacy have also appeared from former employees.

Cindy Olson, for instance, published a book on her time with the company that takes the form of a religious awakening. "My career advancements and the challenges I encountered was part of God's plan," she wrote. Even Enron's collapse and the unpleasant experience of testifying before Congress had been "a blessing." Still, at the end of her book she confessed, "I believe that Enron was a great company."[17]

Robert Bradley, a former policy analyst for Enron, has written a trilogy of books about Enron through the lens of Ayn Rand's objectivist philosophy as well as his own libertarian worldview. Because of Enron, "interventionists and socialists alike," Bradley wrote, "now had a trump card to play against laissez-faire in theory and practice." But this conclusion made little sense, he argued. Enron's corruption and failure was not a product of capitalism, but another symptom of how far the nation had fallen from an ideal capitalism. Enron was a challenge to "get from what *was* to what *should have been*, and from what *is* to what *ought to be*." Enron, for Bradley, was a call for rededication to the works of Adam Smith and Ayn Rand.[18]

Mostly, though, Enron is remembered as a cautionary tale about fraud, arrogance, and ethics. Today, business undergraduates might watch *Enron: The Smartest Guys in the Room* for a required business ethics class, but they will graduate to work for companies that developed in the same atmosphere that produced Enron. There is a danger in cordoning off the Houston company's failure, chalking it up to a question of just ethics, or just oversight failure, or just accounting. The firm's collapse was born out of a specific historical moment when business managers were eager to push beyond the commonsense wisdom of the twentieth century and usher in a new age.

Starting in earnest in the early 1970s, the geography of industrial production began to shift away from the United States, and sectors that trafficked in information (such as financial services) assumed a more prominent role in economic life. Likewise, a renewed faith in free markets and deregulation began decades before Enron's collapse. Still, in an era when all these changes served to make capitalism more abstract and difficult to understand while simultaneously demanding an increased trust in its processes, Enron emerged as a rare concrete example of late capitalism's most troubling qualities. Because of its visibility in an otherwise abstract realm, the company became a vehicle for cultural expressions of outrage over undemocratic economic change and injustice. Yet the confused politics in the public outcry over the company and its failure to produce easy answers revealed the ways in which corporations have assumed a large and ambiguous role in public life. Older cultural ways of understanding proved inadequate when trying to navigate this peculiar historical moment.

Enron's collapse laid bare the inconsistencies and contradictions behind business thinking and action that developed at the end of the twentieth century, but it has proven to be little more than a brief pause in the entrenchment of a market-based view of the world. Demands to "ask why," which Enron's managers hoped would become a battle cry for businesses chafing against established practices, laws, and institutions, did not die with Enron. Rather, the neoliberal euphoria of the late 1990s is still very much with us. The "disruption" that Clay Christensen's 1997 book *The Innovator's Dilemma* describes has since become business orthodoxy in places like Silicon Valley.[19] On some level, this shouldn't be surprising. The rhetoric that Enron's managers adopted is powerful and seductive. But in its embrace of such language, Enron entered the cultural realm. Enron's cultural production was intended to help it establish and sustain a political-economic environment that would give the company every advantage it needed to amass a staggering amount of money. The message embedded in the company's cultural production was clear—that the market would be good for everyone as long as it was left to proceed without any oversight or constraints. In Enron's telling, even the turbulence that would accompany this market was a desirable effect. Yet such a cultural element challenges the orthodox view of a self-regulating economic system that is somehow separate from other facets of social and political life. Rather, political-economic systems cannot be established, and cannot function, without a great deal of cultural work. It is also through this cultural work that formerly abstract or invisible processes reveal themselves for challenge or protest.

If we are to prevent another corporate scandal—one that puts thousands out of work and leaves even more with uncertain retirements—we need to resist the urge to point the finger at a uniquely corrupt organization, and instead acknowledge the fact that companies like Enron are inextricably linked to larger cultural, political, and economic systems. Without critically examining how these corporations are enmeshed in such wider currents, we will find ourselves cheerfully "asking why" all the way to the next crisis.

NOTES

Introduction

1. Bruce W. Collins and C. Shawn Cleveland, "The Perils of Dismissing Enron as 'Different,'" ABA Section of Litigation Annual Conference, April 11–14, 2007, in Bruce W. Collins, *A Perspective on the Enron Trial* (Dallas: DeGoyler Library, Southern Methodist University, 2007), 11.

2. Collins and Cleveland, 10.

3. Transcript of Jury Trial Before the Honorable Sim Lake United States District Judge, vol. 2, February 1, 2006, 347.

4. "Federal Jury Convicts Former Enron Chief Executives Ken Lay, Jeff Skilling on Fraud, Conspiracy and Related Charges," U.S. Department of Justice press release (Washington, D.C., May 26, 2002), https://www.justice.gov/archive/opa/pr/2006/May/06_crm_328.html (accessed March 21, 2016).

5. Jim Yardley, "Influence Lost, Ex-Enron Chief Faces Congress," *New York Times*, February 3, 2002, http://www.nytimes.com/2002/02/03/business/03LAY.html (accessed March 21, 2016). Indeed, the temptation to dramatize Enron was noted by management theorist David Boje, along with Grace Ann Rosile, for instance, who note that after Enron's collapse, the company produced two different narrative modes, epic and tragic, to explain the failure, each with a very different political valence. See David M. Boje, Grace Ann Rosile, Rita A. Durant, and John T. Luhman, "Enron Spectacles: A Critical Dramaturgical Analysis," *Organization Studies* 25.5 (2004): 751–74.

6. Bethany McLean and Peter Elkind, *The Smartest Guys in the Room* (New York: Portfolio, 2003), 31.

7. Robert Bryce, *Pipe Dreams: Greed, Ego and the Death of Enron* (New York: Public Affairs, 2002), 94.

8. Kenneth L. Lay, *The Enron Story* (New York: Newcomen Society of the United States, 1991), 5; Bryce, 31.

9. Kurt Eichenwald, *Conspiracy of Fools* (New York: Broadway Books, 2005), 82. McLean and Elkind, 83.

10. Mimi Swartz and Sherron Watkins, *Power Failure: The Inside Story of the Collapse of Enron* (New York: Doubleday, 2003), 113.

11. Bryce, 87.

12. McLean and Elkind, 86.

13. Bryce, 30.

14. Kenneth Lay, "All Employee Meeting," October 23, 2001, SEC Historical Society, http://3197d6d14b5f19f2f440–5e13d29c4c016cf96cbbfd197c579b45.r81.cf1.rackcdn.com/collection/papers/2000/2001_1023_EnronAllEmployeeMeeting.pdf (accessed March 21, 2016).

15. See, for example, Malcolm Salter, *Innovation Corrupted: The Origins and Legacy of Enron's Collapse* (Cambridge, Mass.: Harvard University Press, 2008). *Enron: Corporate Fiascos and Their Implications*, ed. Nancy B. Rapoport and Bala G. Dharan (New York: Foundation Press, 2004), is another representative example of how legal and management scholars have addressed the company's collapse. Senate Committee on Governmental Affairs, Role of the Board of Directors in Enron's Collapse, 107th Cong., 2nd sess., 2002, S. Print 107–70, 8, 26.

16. For example, see Kim Phillips-Fein and Julian E. Zelizer, "Introduction: What's Good for Business," in *What's Good for Business: Business and American Politics Since World War II*, ed. Kim Phillips-Fein and Julian E. Zelizer (Oxford: Oxford University Press, 2012), 3–15, 7. As Christopher McKenna has pointed out, Enron's collapse does not fit well into Alfred Chandler's model of focusing on successful firms. Christopher D. McKenna, "In Memoriam: Alfred Chandler and the Soul of Business History," *Enterprise and Society* 9.3 (2008): 422–25. Likewise, Philip Scranton and Patrick Fridenson suggest that business historians have shied away from corporate fraud because of "the seeming uniqueness of each case and the apparent lack of theoretical resources to help frame broad questions." See Philip Scranton and Patrick Fridenson, *Reimagining Business History* (Baltimore: Johns Hopkins University Press, 2013), 127. However, some business historians, including Stephen Mihm and Matthew Hollow, have addressed issues of fraud and deceit. See Matthew Hollow, *Rogue Banking: A History of Financial Fraud in Interwar Britain* (New York: Palgrave MacMillan, 2015), and Stephen Mihm, *A Nation of Counterfeiters: Capitalists, Con Men, and the Making of the United States* (Cambridge, Mass.: Harvard University Press, 2009); Nelson D. Schwartz, "Enron Fallout: Wide, but Not Deep," *Fortune*, December 24, 2001, 72.

17. Richard White, *Railroaded: The Transcontinentals and the Making of Modern America* (New York: W. W. Norton, 2011), 375–78. Edward J. Balleisen, *Fraud: An American History from Barnum to Madoff,* (Princeton, N.J.: Princeton University Press, 2017), 5 .The connection between innovation and fraud was also a persistent theme at the German Historical Institute's 2014 conference on corporate crime, "Shady Business: White Collar Crime in History." See German Historical Institute, Conference Report, http://ghi-dc.org/index.php ?option=com_content&view=article&id=1420&Itemid=1230 (accessed March 21, 2016).

18. See Greta R. Krippner, *Capitalizing on Crisis: The Political Origins of the Rise of Finance* (Cambridge, Mass.: Harvard University Press, 2011), and Daniel T. Rodgers, *Age of Fracture* (Cambridge, Mass.: Belknap Press of Harvard University Press, 2011), 63.

19. David Harvey, *A Brief History of Neoliberalism* (New York: Oxford University Press, 2005).

20. For example, see Bethany Moreton, *To Serve God and Wal-Mart* (Cambridge, Mass.: Harvard University Press, 2009), and Benjamin C. Waterhouse, *Lobbying America: The Politics of Business from Nixon to NAFTA* (Princeton, N.J.: Princeton University Press, 2014). "Financialization" is a hazy term that can have multiple meanings and operate on different scales, from national policy changes to shifting strategies at individual firms. For an extended discussion of the concept, see Krippner, 27–57. Like that term, "globalization" has been the subject of much scholarly debate. Historians have challenged the idea that globalization is a fundamentally new phenomenon. It is not my intention here to engage this larger question about whether or not globalization is a new or a single process. Rather, I use it here as a historically situated idea that appeared new in the wake of the Cold War's end. Resituat-

ing Enron's history builds on many recent studies in the history of capitalism that have focused on the role of finance and financialization. Indeed, Louis Hyman has even argued that the history of capitalism must put capital itself "at the center of the story." See "Interchange: The History of Capitalism," *Journal of American History* 101. 2 (2014): 503–36, 517. See, for example, Jonathan Levy, *Freaks of Fortune* (Cambridge, Mass.: Harvard University Press, 2012), Louis Hyman, *Debtor Nation: The History of America in Red Ink* (Princeton, N.J.: Princeton University Press, 2011), and Julia Ott, *When Wall Street Met Main Street: The Quest for an Investors' Democracy* (Cambridge, Mass.: Harvard University Press, 2011).

21. Other scholars have also turned their attention to tracing the intellectual roots of neoliberalism and the "new economy." See Kim Phillips-Fein, *Invisible Hands: The Making of the Conservative Movement from the New Deal to Reagan* (New York: W. W. Norton, 2009), Daniel T. Rodgers, *Age of Fracture* (Cambridge, Mass.: Belknap Press of Harvard University Press, 2011), and Fred Turner, *From Counterculture to Cyberculture: Stewart Brand, the Whole Earth Network, and the Rise of Digital Utopianism* (Chicago: University of Chicago Press, 2006).

22. Though many history of capitalism monographs are broad in scope, there are some historians who have focused on single firms. See Bartow J. Elmore, *Citizen Coke: The Making of Coca-Cola Capitalism* (New York: W. W. Norton, 2014), and Moreton.

23. Recent studies in the history of capitalism have also focused on the politics of Sunbelt cities. See Elizabeth Tandy Shermer, *Sunbelt Capitalism: Phoenix and the Transformation of American Politics* (Philadelphia: University of Pennsylvania Press, 2013), and *Sunbelt Rising: The Politics of Space, Place, and Region*, ed. Michelle Nickerson and Darren Dochuk (Philadelphia: University of Pennsylvania Press, 2014).

24. Per Hansen is one business historian who has focused on the role of narratives and culture in shaping political economy and business organizations. As he and others have argued, the connection between narrative and finance is particularly strong. See Per H. Hansen, "From Finance Capitalism to Financialization: A Cultural and Narrative Perspective on 150 Years of Financial History," *Enterprise and Society* 15.4 (2014): 605–41. For an extended study from a literary critic, see Leigh Claire La Berge, *Scandals and Abstractions: Financial Fiction of the Long 1980s* (New York: Oxford University Press, 2015).

25. White, xxvii.

Chapter 1. Enron Emerges

1. Loren Fox, *Enron: The Rise and Fall* (Hoboken: John Wiley and Sons, 2003), 7.

2. Kurt Eichenwald, *Conspiracy of Fools* (New York: Broadway Books, 2005), 20.

3. Bethany McLean and Peter Elkind, *The Smartest Guys in the Room* (New York: Portfolio, 2003), 4.

4. Mimi Swartz and Sherron Watkins, *Power Failure: The Inside Story of the Collapse of Enron* (New York: Doubleday, 2003), 16–17.

5. Robert Bryce, *Pipe Dreams: Greed, Ego and the Death of Enron* (New York: Public Affairs, 2002), 16. Interestingly, in the book she coauthored with whistle-blower Sherron Watkins, Mimi Swartz echoed Bryce, writing, "Houston has never been conventionally pretty." Swartz and Watkins, 17.

6. Kenneth Lay to Pinkney Walker, September 29, 1967, University Archives, University of Missouri–Columbia.

7. Ibid.

8. Pinkney Walker to Kenneth Lay, March 28, 1967, University Archives, University of Missouri–Columbia.

9. Transcript of Jury Trial Before the Honorable Sim Lake United States District Judge, vol. 45, April 24, 2006, 14538.

10. *The Handbook of Texas*, s.v. "Allen, John Kirby" (by Amelia W. Williams), https://tshaonline.org/handbook/online/articles/fal21 (accessed March 21, 2016). *The Handbook of Texas*, s.v. "Houston Ship Channel" (by Marilyn M. Sibley), https://tshaonline.org/handbook/online/articles/rhh11 (accessed March 21, 2016).

11. Prior to the Civil War, Houston had a thriving slave market. Tyina L. Steptoe, *Houston Bound: Culture and Color in a Jim Crow City* (Oakland: University of California Press, 2015), 27–28, 60, 78–79.

12. Steptoe, 73; Tom Marsh, "Houston Union Station: The Great Hall Revealed," Astrosdaily.com, 1999, http://www.astrosdaily.com/history/houstonunionstation/ (accessed March 21, 2016); *Houston: Where Seventeen Railroads Meet the Sea* cover, Houston the Magnolia City, Special Collections, University of Houston Libraries, http://digital.lib.uh.edu/collection/p15195coll1/item/172/show/155 (accessed March 21, 2016).

13. Joe Feagin, *Free Enterprise City: Houston in Political-Economic Perspective* (New Brunswick, N.J.: Rutgers University Press, 1988), 60; Joseph A. Pratt and Christopher J. Castaneda, *Builders: Herman and George R. Brown* (College Station: Texas A&M University Press, 1999), 16; Feagin, 64.

14. Feagin, 66–69.

15. Christopher J. Castaneda, *Invisible Fuel: Manufactured and Natural Gas in America, 1800–2000* (New York: Twayne, 1999) 3, 84; Christopher J. Castaneda and Clarance M. Smith, *Gas Pipelines and the Emergence of America's Regulatory State: A History of the Panhandle Eastern Corporation, 1928–1993* (Cambridge: Cambridge University Press, 1996), 69–71; Louis Galambos and Joseph Pratt, *The Rise of the Corporate Commonwealth: United States Business and Public Policy in the 20th Century* (New York: Basic Books, 1988), 101.

16. Castaneda and Smith, 75.

17. Ibid., 75–79; U.S. Energy Information Administration, "Natural Gas Act of 1938," http://www.eia.gov/oil_gas/natural_gas/analysis_publications/ngmajorleg/ngact1938.html (accessed April 21, 2013); Galambos and Pratt, 100, 136; Richard H. K. Vietor, *Contrived Competition: Regulation and Deregulation in America* (Cambridge, Mass.: Belknap Press of Harvard University Press, 1994), 6–10, 101.

18. Joseph A. Pratt and Christopher J. Castaneda, *Builders: Herman and George R. Brown* (College Station: Texas A&M University Press, 1999), xii.

19. Harry Hurt III, "The Most Powerful Texans," *Texas Monthly*, April 1976, http://www.texasmonthly.com/politics/the-most-powerful-texans/ (accessed July 14, 2017).

20. Pratt and Castaneda, 162.

21. Ibid., 158–66. This is not to say that the Suite 8F Crowd's power in Houston was total. Other local businessmen, such as the head of Humble Oil and Refining, were influential but operated well clear of the Lamar Hotel, though the crowd never had a formal membership and other prominent Houstonians drifted in and out of the circle, including governors, mayors, and other businessmen. In this way, the 8F Crowd's approach to urban development reflected a much broader trend in the Sunbelt South. See, for example, Elizabeth Tandy Shermer, "Sunbelt Boosterism: Industrial Recruitment, Economic Development, and Growth

Politics in the Developing Sunbelt," in *Sunbelt Rising: The Politics of Place, Space, and Region*, ed. Michelle Nickerson and Darren Dochuk (Philadelphia: University of Pennsylvania Press, 2011), 31–57.

22. Kim Phillips-Fein, for instance, notes how conservative businessmen, particularly in the South and Southwest, worked to promote such ideals in the years following the New Deal. See Kim Phillips-Fein, *Invisible Hands: The Making of the Conservative Movement from the New Deal to Reagan* (New York: W. W. Norton, 2009), 68–71; Pratt and Castaneda, 167–70; Feagin, 246–47.

23. Shermer, 32; Robert S. Thompson, "The Air-Conditioning Capital of the World: Houston and Climate Control," in *Energy Metropolis: An Environmental History of Houston and the Gulf Coast*, ed. Martin V. Melosi and Joseph A. Pratt (Pittsburgh: University of Pittsburgh Press, 2007), 88–104, 95; Feagin, 156; Joel Garreau, *Edge City: Life on the New Frontier* (New York: Doubleday, 1988). Unlike, for instance, New York, with a city center that contains a vibrant cultural life and skyscrapers housing brainy pursuits such as finance, Houston's spatial layout from the midcentury on encouraged a suburban professional class that had largely abandoned the city. Many professional workers used the city's core primarily as a place of work. After World War II, oil fueled a working-class culture as refineries sprang up along the Buffalo Bayou. Historians Martin Melosi and Joseph Pratt write that Houston is an "archetypal twentieth-century city, which came into its own with the popularization of the automobile." Because of this the city's geography "is multinodal, decentralized, and expansive"—spatial qualities that contributed to some of the city's problems. See Martin V. Melosi and Joseph A. Pratt, eds., *Energy Metropolis: An Environmental History of Houston and the Gulf Coast* (Pittsburgh: University of Pittsburgh Press, 2007), 105.

24. As Kim Phillips-Fein notes, it was during this time that businessmen funded a number of new organizations devoted to such issues. Phillips-Fein, 58; Christopher D. McKenna, *The World's Newest Profession: Management Consulting in the Twentieth Century* (New York: Cambridge University Press, 2006), 72; Galambos and Pratt, 161–68.

25. Castaneda and Smith, 147.

26. Ibid., 184; Vietor, 120–21, 11.

27. Bret Benjamin, *Invested Interests: Capital, Culture, and the World Bank* (Minneapolis: University of Minnesota Press, 2007), 11–22; *Twentieth Century Petroleum Statistics* (Dallas: DeGoyler and MacNaughton, 1990), 136; Greta R. Krippner, *Capitalizing on Crisis: The Political Origins of the Rise of Finance* (Cambridge, Mass.: Harvard University Press, 2011), 89; Judith Stein, *Pivotal Decade* (New Haven, Conn.: Yale University Press, 2010), 251. See also Galambos and Pratt, 7.

28. Stein, 30; Krippner, 90; Edwin L. Dale Jr., "A World Effect," *New York Times*, August 16, 1971, http://search.proquest.com/docview/119210909?accountid=6667.

29. Daniel J. Sargent, "The United States and Globalization in the 1970s," in *The Shock of the Global: The 1970s in Perspective*, ed. Niall Ferguson et al. (Cambridge, Mass.: Belknap Press of Harvard University Press, 2010): 49–64, 49; Meg Jacobs, "The Conservative Struggle and the Energy Crisis," in *Rightward Bound: Making America Conservative in the 1970s*, ed. Bruce J. Schulman and Julian E. Zelizer (Cambridge, Mass.: Harvard University Press, 2008), 197–98; Bruce Schulman, *The Seventies* (Cambridge, Mass.: Da Capo, 2001), 7; Edward LiPuma and Benjamin Lee, *Financial Derivatives and the Globalization of Risk* (Durham, N.C.: Duke University Press, 2004), 67–68.

30. This abstraction of economic activity then allowed for the development of contracts like grain futures, a type of derivative. As William Cronon explains, futures contracts, an agreement to deliver grain on a future date, amounted to trading in a commodity that did not yet exist. Edward LiPuma and Benjamin Lee call these earlier forms of derivatives "production-based" because there was still a fairly direct relationship to the actual product. William Cronon, *Nature's Metropolis: Chicago and the Great West* (New York: Norton, 1991), 109–47. Edward LiPuma and Benjamin Lee, "Financial Derivatives and the Rise of Circulation," *Economy and Society* 34.3 (August 2005): 404–27, 411; LiPuma and Lee, *Financial Derivatives,* 77; Judith Stein notes that during the same time, industrial productivity was rising in both West Germany and Japan; Stein, 200.

31. Barry J. Kaplan, "Houston: The Golden Buckle of the Sunbelt," in *Sunbelt Cities: Politics and Growth Since WWII,* ed. Richard M. Bernard and Bradley R. Rice (Austin: University of Texas Press, 1983), 196–212, 198. As political scientists Robert Thomas and Richard Murray note, Houston's major industrial products "were several times more valuable than they had been a couple of years earlier." Robert D. Thomas and Richard W. Murray, *Progrowth Politics: Change and Governance in Houston* (Berkeley, Calif.: IGS, 1991), 49; Feagin, 81; Marsh; Roberto Marchesini and Joanne P. Austin, "Houston: Growth Center of the Southwest," in *Texas Metropolitan Area Profiles,* ed. Charles P. Zlatkovich (Austin: Bureau of Business Research, University of Texas at Austin, 1979), 73–78.

32. Hurt.

33. Ibid.

34. Charles P. Zlatkovich, Rita J. Wright, and Robert S. Moore, *Texas Fact Book 1978* (Austin: Bureau of Business Research, University of Texas at Austin, 1978), 41. U.S. Bureau of Labor Statistics, "Labor Force Statistics from the Current Population Survey: 1970–1982," http://data.bls.gov/pdq/SurveyOutputServlet (accessed February 2, 2015).

35. Transcript of Jury Trial Before the Honorable Sim Lake United States District Judge, vol. 37, April 10, 2006, 11863.

36. See Bethany Moreton, "Make Payroll, Not War: Business Culture as Youth Culture," in *Rightward Bound: Making America Conservative in the 1970s,* ed. Bruce J. Schulman and Julian E. Zelizer (Cambridge, Mass.: Harvard University Press, 2008), 52–70, 53–55; Bethany Moreton, *To Serve God and Wal-Mart* (Cambridge, Mass.: Harvard University Press, 2009), 148–60. Bethany Moreton has convincingly argued that during the 1970s, as the economic landscape was shifting and postwar prosperity began to wane, these business school programs, particularly those that were established in Sunbelt schools with working-class and first-generation college students, had the effect of realigning class interests with capital as opposed to labor, as well as providing students with the rationale for the increasingly unsteady economic landscape in the United States.

37. Transcript of Jury Trial Before the Honorable Sim Lake United States District Judge, vol. 37, April 10, 2006, 11865.

38. Milton Friedman, "A Friedman Doctrine—the Social Responsibility of Business Is to Increase Its Profits," *New York Times,* September 13, 1970, SM17. As Angus Burgin points out, Friedman's views on corporate social responsibility were wholly consistent with his general worldview. See Angus Burgin, *The Great Persuasion: Reinventing Free Markets Since the Great Depression* (Cambridge, Mass.: Harvard University Press, 2012), 190.

39. See Phillips-Fein; Schulman, 25; Daniel T. Rodgers, *Age of Fracture* (Cambridge, Mass.: Belknap Press of Harvard University Press, 2011), 49, 63; Neil Fligstein, *The Transformation of Corporate Control* (Cambridge, Mass.: Harvard University Press, 1990), 129, 155.

40. Though the Airline Deregulation Act became law in 1978, Kennedy's push for airline deregulation began a few years earlier in the 1970s. See Thomas McCraw, *Prophets of Regulation: Charles Francis Adams, Louis D. Brandeis, James M. Landis, Alfred E. Kahn* (Cambridge, Mass.: Belknap Press of Harvard University Press, 1984), 266; Krippner, 76; Stein, 251; Galambos and Pratt, 241–45; Vietor, 55; Angus Burgin and Kim Phillips-Fein are two scholars who regard this shift in attitudes as the triumphant culmination of a process that began in the wake of the New Deal.

41. Castaneda, 166; Stein, 208–9; National Energy Program Fact Sheet on the President's Program," April 20, 1977, American Presidency Project, University of California, Santa Barbara, http://www.presidency.ucsb.edu/ws/?pid=7373 (accessed February 1, 2015); Sanjay Bhatnagar and Peter Trufano, "Enron Gas Services" (Boston: Harvard Business School, 1994), 2; Vietor, 124.

42. Stein, 211.

43. Feagin, 51.

44. Marchesini and Austin, 78.

45. Transcript of Jury Trial Before the Honorable Sim Lake United States District Judge, vol. 45, April 24, 2006, 14542–43.

46. Jacobs RB, 197; see, for example, McLean and Elkind, 6, and Swartz and Watkins, 24; Transcript of Jury Trial Before the Honorable Sim Lake United States District Judge, vol. 45, April 24, 2006, 14543–45.

47. Laurel Brubaker, "Houston's Highest Paid Executives," *Houston Business Journal*, June 29, 1987, *Business Insights: Global*, http://bi.galegroup.com.proxy.libraries.smu.edu/global/article/GALE|A5165536/f078ff1754d6c54c6ab75b55cadf157b?u=txshracd2548 (accessed February 1, 2015). Wyatt was an aggressive force in the gas industry's merger movement, and Houston Natural Gas was not Wyatt's only takeover target in the 1980s. See also Castaneda and Smith, 251; Nelson Antosh, "Raiders Help Economy, Lay Says," *Houston Chronicle*, September 17, 1987.

48. Dean Starkman, *The Watchdog That Didn't Bark: The Financial Crisis and the Disappearance of Investigative Journalism* (New York: Columbia University Press, 2014), 87–92. For more on the takeover movement in the 1980s, see Karen Ho, *Liquidated: An Ethnography of Wall Street* (Durham, N.C.: Duke University Press, 2009): 129–56.

49. Federal Deposit Insurance Corporation, *History of the Eighties—Lessons for the Future*, https://www.fdic.gov/bank/historical/history/235_258.pdf (accessed February 2, 2015).

50. *Twentieth Century Petroleum Statistics*, 146–51.

51. Castaneda and Smith, 256–57.

52. Most natural gas pipelines in the United States are underground. Transcript of Jury Trial Before the Honorable Sim Lake United States District Judge, vol. 45, April 24, 2006, 14549.

53. Transcript of Jury Trial Before the Honorable Sim Lake United States District Judge, vol. 45, April 24, 2006, 14549.

54. Enron Corp., press release, April 10, 1986.

55. Tony Kennedy, "Irwin Jacobs Points to Minstar's Growth to Rebut Tag of Liquidator," *Associated Press*, March 13, 1987.

56. Judith Crown, "Enron Agrees to Buy Out Jacobs, Leucadia," *Houston Chronicle*, October 1, 1986.

57. United Shareholders Association, press release, "United Shareholders Association Chairman Comments on Enron Corp. Stock Buyback," October 20, 1986.

58. Indeed, Lay even relished the opportunity to call T. Boone Pickens a "corporate raider," saying "if it looks like a rose and smells like a rose." Both Pickens and Jacobs, along with others, disliked the term, seeing it as something of a pejorative. See Antosh, "Raiders Help Economy, Lay Says."

59. Bryce, 41–42.

60. Peter H. Frank, "Enron to Close Unit After Costly Trades," *New York Times*, October 23, 1987, D5.

61. Mark Carlson, "A Brief History of the 1987 Stock Market Crash with a Discussion of the Federal Reserve Response," http://www.federalreserve.gov/pubs/feds/2007/200713 /200713pap.pdf (accessed July 13, 2017); Barbara Shook, "Enron Moving Headquarters to Houston," *Houston Chronicle*, May 12, 1986.

62. Transcript of Jury Trial Before the Honorable Sim Lake United States District Judge, vol. 37, April 10, 2006, 11870.

63. Feagin, 97; Stephen L. Klineberg, "Houston's Economic and Demographic Transformations: Findings from the Expanded 2002 Survey of Houston's Ethnic Communities" (Houston: Rice University, 2002), 4.

64. George Getschow, "The Dispossessed," *Wall Street Journal*, November 12, 1982, 1. The problem of itinerant homeless encampments was not unique to Houston. Other Sunbelt cities were also experiencing these latter-day Hoovervilles, though it was particularly bad in Houston.

65. Tellingly, most of the foreclosed homes had been bought between 1979, when Houston's economy was still flying, and the downturn. James Drummond, "January Foreclosure Postings at Record," *Houston Chronicle*, January 17, 1986. Feagin, 98. For more on the recession in the early 1980s, see Stein, 265; Bonnie Britt, "Houston's Growing Number of Unemployed," *Houston Chronicle*, July 6, 1986; Steve Maynard, "Oil Prices Trim Income of Church," *Houston Chronicle*, February 7, 1986.

66. Britt.

67. Ibid.

68. M. Manfred Fabritius and William Borges, *Saving the Savings and Loan: The U.S. Thrift Industry and the Texas Experience, 1950–1988* (New York: Praeger, 1988), 97–100, 114; Bob Sablatura, "Tough Times Continue for Local S&Ls," *Houston Business Journal*, August 24, 1987, *Business Insights: Global*, http://bi.galegroup.com.proxy.libraries.smu.edu /global/article/GALE|A5274684/7bf3c7173e7a119d4cdf60a83dccdea1?u=txshracd2548 (accessed February 1, 2015).

69. Thomas and Murray, 56; James Drummond, "1986 Seen as Bleak Year for Real Estate," *Houston Chronicle*, January 16, 1986.

70. Transcript of Jury Trial Before the Honorable Sim Lake United States District Judge, vol. 37, April 10, 2006, 11875.

71. Thomas and Murray, 56.

72. Drummond. See also Bob Sablatura, "Where the $6 Million Went," *Houston Business Journal*, August 11, 1986, *Business Insights: Global*, http://bi.galegroup.com.proxy.libraries .smu.edu/global/article/GALE|A4406724/6a2cb5bb9cf7ddab1fe8caf1b72ecfd0?u=txshracd 2548 (accessed February 1, 2015).

73. Shook, "Enron Moving Headquarters to Houston."

74. Shook, "Enron's Move Here Will Add 720 Jobs," *Houston Chronicle*, May 13, 1986.

75. Ibid.

76. Ibid.

77. Judith Crown, "Consolidations Cushion Energy Industry Layoffs a Bit," *Houston Chronicle*, June 16, 1986.

78. Paul Burka, "Power," *Texas Monthly*, December, 1987, 216.

79. Ibid., 218.

80. Garreau, 3.

81. U.S. Census Bureau, "Geographic Mobility, Commuting, and Veteran Status," 1990 Census Population, Social and Economic Characteristics, Texas, table 143, p. 446.

82. Garreau, xiii.

83. Ibid., 245.

84. U.S. Census Bureau, "Nativity, Citizenship, Year of Entry, Area of Birth, and Language Spoken at Home," 1990 Census Population, Social and Economic Characteristics, Texas, table 138, p. 316.

85. As Thomas and Murray note, Houston's economic recovery was "rooted in a postindustrial economy with the impetus for growth coming primarily from an expanding corporate sector, technologically intensive industries, and a growing service economy." Thomas and Murray, 53.

86. Transcript of Jury Trial Before the Honorable Sim Lake United States District Judge, vol. 37, April 10, 2006, 11880.

87. Rusty Braziel, "Henry the Hub, I Am I Am—Understanding Henry Hub: How Changing Natural Gas Flows Will Impact the Benchmark," RBN Energy, https://rbnenergy.com/henry -the-hub-i-am-i-am-understanding-henry-hub (accessed February 2, 2015).

88. Transcript of Jury Trial Before the Honorable Sim Lake United States District Judge, vol. 37, April 10, 2006, 11880.

89. Ibid., 11884.

90. Transcript of Proceedings Before the Honorable Sim Lake and a Jury, vol. 37, April 24, 2006, 14557.

91. Swaps represent longer term relationships between two parties anchored by a series of forward contracts.

92. Transcript of Jury Trial Before the Honorable Sim Lake United States District Judge, vol. 37, April 10, 2006, 11884.

93. Lay had been thinking of Skilling for a while, later saying: "I started trying to recruit him into Enron as early as '88 or '89 for sure, but I never could quite put together the job that was exciting enough for him." Lay had long regarded recruiting top talent as crucial for business success, but in this case there was no guarantee that an offer would lure Skilling over to Enron. Transcript of Proceedings Before the Honorable Sim Lake and a Jury, vol. 37, April 24, 2006, 14558.

94. Transcript of Jury Trial Before the Honorable Sim Lake United States District Judge, vol. 37, April 10, 2006, 11886–87. Skilling's first hire was his former secretary at McKinsey.

95. McKenna, 192–215.

96. Thomas J. Peters and Robert H. Waterman Jr., *In Search of Excellence: Lessons from America's Best-Run Companies* (New York: Warner Books, 1982), 318.

97. Peters and Waterman, 318. Pai recalled that in the 1980s, "you did a deal and hoped for the best." What is more, some at the firm saw the rigid culture as stifling and, significantly, directly connected to industry regulation. Ken Rice, who would eventually run the company's broadband efforts toward the end of the 1990s, felt that early in its life Enron was little more than a "regulated utility," where employees ran "cost estimates" instead of "economic models." From there employees had to argue with regulators that the rate they came up with was "just and reasonable." "Culture 1," *Enron Case Study* (CD-ROM) (Hoboken, N.J.: John Wiley and Sons, 2002).

98. "Culture 1," *Enron Case Study* (CD-ROM) (Hoboken, N.J.: John Wiley and Sons, 2002).

99. At the start of the 1990s, the country was in the midst of a recession. However, that downtown was not nearly as severe as the economic collapse in the early 1980s. Thomas Peters, *Thriving on Chaos: Handbook for a Management Revolution* (New York: Harper and Row, 1987), xiii–xiv. Offering a path for customers to navigate "chaos and uncertainty" had been exactly what Skilling had done with the creation of the Gas Bank.

100. Thomas Peters, "Get the Structure Right First!" www.tompeters.com, October 19, 1990, http://www.tompeters.com/column/1990/005271.php (accessed September 4, 2013).

101. Ibid.

102. Michael Hammer, "Reengineering Work: Don't Automate, Obliterate," *Harvard Business Review*, July 1990, https://hbr.org/1990/07/reengineering-work-dont-automate-obliterate (accessed July 14, 2017). Peters had written approvingly of Hammer's article in his own column.

103. Ibid.

104. Antosh, "Raiders Help Economy, Lay Says."

105. Enron Corp., Form 10-K 1993, SEC EDGAR Database, http://www.sec.gov/edgar.shtml (accessed July 8, 2014).

106. Antosh, "Raiders Help Economy, Lay Says."

107. Nelson Antosh, "Rising Corporate Fortunes/Houston's List of Winners Grows," *Houston Chronicle*, October 8, 1990.

108. Ralph Bivins, "Enron May Build Downtown Tower," *Houston Chronicle*, October 9, 1991.

109. Enron Corp., advertisement, 1988, Houstonian Yearbook Collection, Digital Library, University of Houston, http://digital.lib.uh.edu/collection/yearb/item/19438/show/19411 (accessed February 1, 2015).

110. William H. Miller, "Vision Vanquisher," *Industry Week*, May 18, 1998, 37.

Chapter 2. Making Sense of the World After the Cold War

1. Daniel Rodgers notes that the rhetoric of the marketplace took on a sunny and optimistic hue over the course of the 1980s. Daniel T. Rodgers, *Age of Fracture* (Cambridge, Mass.: Belknap Press of Harvard University Press, 2011), 75.

2. Ibid., 245–48.

3. Quoted in R. W. Apple Jr., "The Houston Summit: A New Balance of Power," *New York Times*, July 11, 1990. http://www.lexisnexis.com, October 7, 2008, (accessed November 3, 2008).

4. Bob Tutt, "Summit Host Panel Sets Goal for City," *Houston Chronicle*, March 1, 1990, http://www.chron.com (accessed October 7, 2008).

5. Bob Tutt, "Summit Hosts Red Hot over Houston's Image," *Houston Chronicle*, June 8, 1990, http://www.chron.com (accessed October 7, 2008).

6. Betty Ewing, "Economic Summit Offices Open in Mansion," *Houston Chronicle*, April 6, 1990, http://www.chron.com (accessed October 7, 2008). This practice of juggling a sense of local place and global prominence is a typical neoliberal strategy for city booster-ism. On some level, hosting the World Economic Forum had the same effect as hosting the Olympics—a city's announcement that it was stepping onto the world stage. For more on the connection between the Olympic Games and neoliberalism, see Andrew Ross, *Nice Work If You Can Get It: Life and Labor in Precarious Times* (New York: New York University Press, 2009), 78.

7. Tutt, "Summit Hosts Red Hot over Houston's Image."

8. S. John Weimer, "Journalists Disdain Houston's Self-Promotions, Love Lavish Treat-ment," *Rice Thresher*, July 11, 1990, 6.

9. Robert Miller, "City Brings Out Best for Media Briefing," *Rice Thresher*, July 11, 1990, 5. "Summing Up the Summit," *Rice Thresher*, July 11, 1990, 8.

10. Noelle Vance and Shaila Dewan, "While Summit Jet-Set Lives It Up, Fourth Ward Knows None of It," *Rice Thresher*, July 11, 1990, 4.

11. Jay Yates, "Trickle-Down Explained," *Rice Thresher*, July 11, 1990, 3.

12. Elise Perachio and Shaila Dewan, "Summit Causes Merchants to Suffer, Despite Visi-tors," *Rice Thresher*, July 11, 1990, 6.

13. Lay, *The Enron Story*, (New York: The Newcomen Society of the United States, 1991), 7, 22–23.

14. Riley E. Dunlap and Rik Scarce, "Poll Trends: Environmental Problems and Protec-tion," *Public Opinion Quarterly* 55.4 (Winter 1991): 651–72, 652; Benjamin C. Waterhouse, *Lobbying America: The Politics of Business from Nixon to NAFTA* (Princeton, N.J.: Princeton University Press, 2014), 195–98; Meg Jacobs, "The Politics of Environmental Regulation: Business-Government Relations in the 1970s and Beyond," in *What's Good for Business: Busi-ness and American Politics Since World War II*, ed. Kim Phillips-Fein and Julian E. Zelizer (Oxford: Oxford University Press, 2012): 212–32, 226–27; Kevin C. Armitage, "State of De-nial: The United States and the Politics of Global Warming," *Globalizations* 2.4 (Decem-ber 2005): 417–27, 420.

15. Enron, "1988 Enron Annual Report to Shareholders and Customers" (1989), 5. With-out question, Enron's environmental commitments were largely self-serving. However, such self-interested motives do not necessarily negate the potential benefits of the resultant actions. As Bert Spector and others have noted, corporate social responsibility is frequently used as a way for a firm to gain some specific competitive advantage. See Bert Spector, " 'Business Re-sponsibilities in a Divided World': The Cold War Roots of the Corporate Social Responsibility Movement," *Enterprise and Society* 9.2 (June 2008): 314–36, 331.

16. Leo Marx, *The Machine in the Garden: Technology and the Pastoral Ideal in America* (Oxford: Oxford University Press, 1964), 23. The "pastoral ideal" is an early American studies

concept that was first articulated by Leo Marx in his 1964 classic, *The Machine in the Garden*. While subsequent scholarship has questioned the theoretical underpinnings of the "myth and symbol" school that Marx was operating under, the "pastoral ideal" as an ideological construct still has merit.

17. Enron, "1989 Enron Annual Report to Shareholders and Customers" (1990).

18. Indeed, *American Gas*, which was published by the American Gas Association, ran multiple articles about the environmental benefits of natural gas in the early 1990s. David Sicilia, for example, has demonstrated how U.S. chemical companies adopted a strategy of "accommodation" in response to public concerns over the environment in the 1970s and 1980s. See David B. Sicilia, "The Corporation Under Siege: Social Movements, Regulation, Public Relations, and Tort Law Since the Second World War," in *Constructing Corporate America: History, Politics, Culture*, ed. Kenneth Lipartito and David B. Sicilia (New York: Oxford University Press, 2004), 188–220, 206.

19. U.S. Environmental Protection Agency, *Overview—the Clean Air Act Amendments of 1990*, http://epa.gov/oar/caa/caaa_overview.html (accessed May 20, 2015).

20. *Time*, April 23, 1990, 2.

21. Dunlap and Scarce, 670. In the late 1980s and early 1990s, a variety of polls revealed that most Americans favored government action to protect the environment. Indeed, the greenhouse effect, holes in the ozone layer, acid rain, and a general concern over the state of the environment loomed large in U.S. culture in the late 1980s and early 1990s.

22. Barbara C. Farhar, "Trends: Public Opinion About Energy," *Public Opinion Quarterly* 58.4 (Winter 1994): 603–32, 611; Dunlap and Scarce, 664–67; Michael Boskin, interviewed by Russell Riley and Stephen Weatherford, George H. W. Bush Oral History Project, Miller Center, University of Virginia, July 30–31, 2009, https://millercenter.org/the-presidency /presidential-oral-histories/michael-boskin-oral-history-chair-council-economic (accessed July 14. 2017); Stephen J. Macekura, *Of Limits and Growth: The Rise of Global Sustainable Development in the Twentieth Century* (New York: Cambridge University Press, 2015), 272–73. However, Armitage argues that the Bush administration was adept at raising doubts about global warming. See Armitage, 422; Bobbie Greene Kilberg, interviewed by Russell Riley and Kathryn Dunn, George H. W. Bush Oral History Project, Miller Center, University of Virginia, November 20, 2009, https://millercenter.org/the-presidency/presidential-oral-histories /bobbie-greene-kilberg-oral-history-deputy-assistant (accessed July 14, 2017).

23. U.S. Environmental Protection Agency, "Cap and Trade: Acid Rain Program Results" (Washington, D.C., n.d.), https://grist.files.wordpress.com/2009/06/ctresults.pdf (accessed July 14, 2017).

24. Meg Jacobs, "The Conservative Struggle and the Energy Crisis," in *Rightward Bound: Making America Conservative in the 1970s*, ed. Bruce J. Schulman and Julian E. Zelizer (Cambridge, Mass.: Harvard University Press, 2008), 193–209, 228; U.S. Environmental Protection Agency. There were other reasons, of course, for a greater reliance on natural gas. Indeed, the recent Gulf War was a stark reminder that much of the nation's oil supply came from a politically unstable part of the world.

25. Enron Corp., "Enron Corp. Chairman Ken Lay Promotes Natural Gas in Testimony Before Republican Platform Committee," news release, April 13, 1992.

26. Ibid.

27. Even though the party (as well as the National Energy Strategy) called for ecologically dubious measures (such as drilling for oil in ANWR), party officials insisted that such actions could be undertaken in an environmentally sensitive way. "Energy, Agriculture and Environmental Issues," C-Span, April 13, 1992, https://www.c-span.org/video/?25564–1/energy -agriculture-environmental-issues (accessed December 15, 2016). Benjamin Waterhouse, for example, has argued that "the environmental movement had always been a global phenomenon." Waterhouse, 197.

28. Sicilia, 206.

29. The Competitive Enterprise Institute, for example, sent Bush a letter with numerous signatures urging him to stay away from the Rio conference. Letter, Fred L. Smith Jr. to George H. W. Bush, April 7, 1992, ID# 321395, FO006-16, WHORM: Bush Presidential Records, George Bush Presidential Library.

30. Armitage, 422.

31. Douglas H. Breese to George H. W. Bush, April 6, 1992, ID# S21394, FO006-16, WHORM: Bush Presidential Records, George Bush Presidential Library.

32. Draft speech, "Going to UNCED," 1992, ID# 323678, FO006-16, WHORM: Bush Presidential Records, George Bush Presidential Library.

33. Ibid.

34. Ibid.

35. Ibid.

36. Ibid.

37. Draft speech, "Going to UNCED," 1992, ID# 323678, FO006-16, WHORM: Bush Presidential Records, George Bush Presidential Library.

38. Kenneth Lay to George H. W. Bush, April 3, 1992, Department of Energy Records, http://energy.gov/sites/prod/files/maprod/documents/enron1992.pdf (accessed April 22, 2013).

39. Ibid.

40. In fact, many Americans wrote the president urging him to attend the Rio conference.

41. Willett Kempton, James S. Boster, and Jennifer A. Hartley, *Environmental Values in American Culture* (Cambridge, Mass.: MIT Press, 1996), 215. In the mid-1980s, the German sociologist Ulrich Beck had connected globalization and the environment by developing his theory of the "risk society." For Beck, industrial modernity was a world system that produced uncontainable risks. As he put it, "since the middle of the twentieth century the social institutions of industrial society have been confronted with the historically unprecedented possibility of the destruction through decision-making of all life on this planet." In fact, Beck went so far as to claim that this system—one that produced risks that increasingly did not respect national boundaries—could be characterized as "organized irresponsibility" as these risks are *enforced* "as a consequence of industrial action and production." See Ulrich Beck, *World Risk Society* (Cambridge, UK: Polity Press, 1999), 53–55.

42. Macekura, 9, 289–94; Yda Schreuder, *The Corporate Greenhouse: Climate Change Policy in a Globalizing World* (New York: Zed Books, 2009), 35.

43. United Nations, *United Nations Conference on Environment and Development, Rio de Janeiro, Brazil, 3 to 14 June 1992, Agenda 21*, http://sustainabledevelopment.un.org/content /documents/Agenda21.pdf (accessed April 22, 2013). See also Spencer R. Weart, *The Discovery of Global Warming* (Cambridge, Mass.: Harvard University Press, 2008), 161–62.

44. Early coverage of the Clinton administration's environmental efforts offered a contrast to the first Bush administration by referencing the "Bush Administration's obstructionist image" after the Earth Summit that made the United States look like a "global foot-dragger." See William K. Stevens, "Gore Promises U.S. Leadership on Sustainable Development Path," *New York Times*, June 15, 1993, C4, column 1.

45. Schreuder, 39–40.

46. Lay was hardly the only American businessman who saw opportunity in this green rhetoric. Indeed, as early as the mid-1980s, some businesspeople, such as the self-styled "new age entrepreneur" Paul Hawken, had been arguing that business and environmental goals did not have to be at odds with one another. In the early 1990s, with books including Hawken's *The Ecology of Commerce*, an ethic of sustainability further assumed an increasingly prominent place in business discourse. Paul Hawken, *The Ecology of Commerce: A Declaration of Sustainability* (New York: HarperBusiness, 1993); Donald R. Katz, "The Guru of the New Economy," *Management Review*, April 1985, 19; Martha Nichols, "Does New Age Business Have a Message for Managers?" *Harvard Business Review* 72.2 (March–April 1994): 52–54. Lay also connected gas to national security, stating that the Gulf War had revealed the country's vulnerability to "oil shocks" and "unstable energy supplies." Kenneth Lay, "Remarks by Dr. Kenneth L. Lay," Global Warming and the Earth Summit Alliance to Save Energy Conference, Washington, D.C., June 23, 1992, Department of Energy Records, http://energy.gov /sites/prod/files/maprod/documents/enron1992.pdf (accessed April 22, 2013).

47. Lay, "Remarks by Dr. Kenneth L. Lay."

48. "Republican National Convention AM Session," C-SPAN video, August 17, 1992, http://www.c-span.org/video/?31237–1/republican-national-convention-session (accessed July 16, 2017).

49. For instance, at the end of a reply to a letter Lay sent in the summer of 1992 to the deputy secretary of energy, Linda Stuntz, she wrote: "Ken, as always, it is good to hear from you. I trust that you will continue to provide your good counsel on matters of importance to the Department and the natural gas industry." Linda G. Stuntz to Ken Lay, August 4, 1992, Department of Energy Records, http://energy.gov/sites/prod/files/maprod/documents /enron1992.pdf (accessed April 22, 2013). "Energy, Agriculture and Environmental Issues," C-SPAN video, April 13, 1992, http://www.c-span.org/video/?25564–1/energy-agriculture -environmental-issues (accessed July 14, 2017).

50. Joel Makower, "Green from the Top Down," *New York Times*, January 30, 1993, 21, http://search.proquest.com.ezproxy.bu.edu/hnpnewyorktimes/docview/109227538 /7ACA00BA66454BCDPQ/3?accountid=9676; Holly Idelson, "Provisions: National Energy Strategy Provisions," *CQ Weekly*, November 28, 1992, http://library.cqpress.com.ezproxy.bu .edu/cqweekly/document.php?id=WR102409071 (accessed November 14, 2015).

51. Idelson; "1992 Democratic Party Platform," July 13, 1992, American Presidency Project, http://www.presidency.ucsb.edu/ws/index.php?pid=29610 (accessed July 16, 2017)

52. Terry Thorn to Hazel O'Leary, May 13, 1992, Department of Energy Records, http://energy.gov/sites/prod/files/maprod/documents/enron1992.pdf (accessed April 22, 2013).

53. Keith Schneider, "The 1992 Campaign: Issues—the Environment," *New York Times*, October 13, 1992, http://www.nytimes.com/1992/10/13/us/1992-campaign-issues-environment -clinton-bush-show-contradictions-balancing-jobs.html?pagewanted=all (accessed Novem-

ber 14, 2015). Bethany Moreton notes that a majority of the American public opposed NAFTA for much of 1993. See Bethany Moreton, *To Serve God and Wal-Mart* (Cambridge, Mass.: Harvard University Press, 2009), 255; David E. Rosenbaum, "Vice President Accuses Foe of Taking Stance for Personal Gain," *New York Times*, November 10, 1993, B15, http://search.proquest .com.ezproxy.bu.edu/hnpnewyorktimes/docview/109129242/41D04EC6BAF64EF7PQ/3 ?accountid=9676 (accessed November 14, 2015); see Waterhouse, 247, and Moreton, 255. As Sean Wilentz notes, a continental trade agreement that united these three countries had long been a presidential goal. Sean Wilentz, *The Age of Reagan: A History, 1974–2008* (New York: HarperCollins, 2008), 314.

54. Kristin Rankin, "Sustainable Development Assures Americans a Rosy Future," *Enron Business*, date missing, approximately 1993, Southwest Collection/Special Collections Library, Texas Tech University.

55. Rankin.

56. For more about efforts to shape attitudes toward global warming, see Armitage, 424–25.

57. Robert Shiller, *Irrational Exuberance*, 2nd ed. (Princeton, N.J.: Princeton University Press, 2005), 139.

58. Such images call to mind cultural studies scholar Frederick Buell's argument about the vast transformations in American environmentalism in the 1980s. To be sure, Buell has in mind an environmental backlash that was part of the Reagan Right. Still, it is worth noting that by 1992, an energy company headed by an avowed free marketer could present itself as an effective and dedicated environmental steward. See Frederick Buell, *From Apocalypse to Way of Life: Environmental Crisis in the American Century* (New York: Routledge, 2003), 5.

59. *Enron Business*, May 1994, Southwest Collection/Special Collections Library, Texas Tech University.

60. Mary Clark, "Promoting Natural Gas Underscores Enron's Environmental Activities on Capitol Hill," *Enron Business*, May 1994, 4, Southwest Collection/Special Collections Library, Texas Tech University.

61. Ibid., 5.

62. Hazel O'Leary to Terrence Thorn, August 2, 1994, Department of Energy Records, http://energy.gov/sites/prod/files/maprod/documents/enron1994.pdf (accessed April 22, 2013).

63. Ibid.

64. Louis Aboud, "Figuring Out the Climate for Change," *American Gas* 77.5 (June 1995): 38.

65. In general, corporate annual reports had, in recent years, undergone significant changes in form. Starting in the mid-1980s, annual reports had become flashier, with much more attention going into graphic design. In his business trend letter, John Naisbitt had noted the change in annual reports as a "small growth industry in itself." *John Naisbitt's Trend Letter*, August 7, 1986.

66. Enron, "1990 Enron Annual Report to Shareholders and Customers" (1991).

67. Thomas C. Hayes, "Bottom-Fishing in the Gas Patch," *New York Times*, May 19, 1991; Sanjay Bhatnagar and Peter Trufano, "Enron Gas Services" (Boston: Harvard Business School, 1994), 6.

68. "Enron Gas Services and Forest Oil Corporation Sign $44.8 Million Production Payment Agreement," PR Newswire, May 2, 1991; "Enron Gas Services and Zilkha Energy Sign $24 Million Production Payment Agreement," PR Newswire, May 22, 1991.

69. "Enron Gas to Supply Utility," *Houston Chronicle*, December 18, 1990, 5. Loren Fox argues that Enron had actually designed the first natural gas swap in a deal earlier in 1989. Loren Fox, *Enron: The Rise and Fall* (Hoboken, N.J.: John Wiley and Sons, 2003), 27. Enron Corp., print advertisement, n.d. Beyond prices that were hurting gas producers, FERC's lengthy process of deregulating the industry was causing problems for pipeline firms. Indeed, in 1992, Lay wrote to the White House about the problem. Letter, Kenneth Lay to Henson Moore, March 11, 1991, ID#315088, BE003-11, WHORM: Bush Presidential Records, George Bush Presidential Library.

70. Agreement between Enron Gas Marketing, Inc., and Northern Indiana Public Services Company, December 1, 1990, exhibit I-A in appendix to Jack I. Tompkins and George W. Posey to George H. Diacont and Robert A. Bayless, 11 June 1991, Securities and Exchange Commission, obtained through FOIA (Freedom of Information Act) request to the U.S. Securities and Exchange Commission.

71. Agreement between Enron Gas Marketing, Inc., and Banque Paribas, exhibit I-B in appendix to Jack I. Tompkins and George W. Posey to George H. Diacont and Robert A. Bayless, June 11, 1991, Securities and Exchange Commission, obtained through FOIA request to the U.S. Securities and Exchange Commission.

72. A derivatives swap is a series of forward agreements between two companies. Bhatnagar and Trufano; "Enron Gas Services' New Branded Products Provide Long-Term Natural Gas Supplies at Predictable Prices," Southwest Newswire, February 13, 1992.

73. As Louis Hyman notes, the roots of securitization were, like deregulation and financial derivatives, a product of the 1970s and an attempt to shore up a national economy that seemed to be stalling. See Louis Hyman, "American Debt, Global Capital," in *The Shock of the Global: The 1970s in Perspective*, ed. Niall Ferguson et al. (Cambridge, Mass.: Belknap Press of Harvard University Press, 2010), 128–42, 128. There was great irony in Fastow's background. Though Continental had become a leader in lending to energy companies in the 1970s, the bank collapsed in a spectacular fashion in 1984.

74. Though many of the special purpose entities that Fastow created were independent corporations, as a group, SPEs can have a number of different legal organizations. For example, they can also be set up as trusts. See Jalal Soroosh and Jack T. Ciesielski, "Accounting for Special Purpose Entities Revised: FASB Interpretation 476(R)," *CPA Journal*, July 2004, http://www.nysscpa.org/cpajournal/2004/704/essentials/p30.htm (accessed September 4, 2013); Gary Giroux, "What Went Wrong? Accounting Fraud and Lessons from Recent Scandals," *Social Research* 75.4 (Winter 2008): 1205–38, 1216.

75. The Star Wars reference was intentional. Fastow would often include such references in naming SPEs. "Enron and California Pension Fund in Energy Venture," *New York Times*, July 1, 1993.

76. Mary Clark "A Letter from the President and COO Rich Kinder," *Enron Business*, January 1994, 3; Kristin Rankin, "Enron and CalPERS Join Forces to Invest in Natural Gas," *Enron Business*, November 5, 1993, 7.

77. Even before setting this system up, the company had relied on a partnership with Bankers Trust to help Enron employees manage price risk. See Fox, 27–28. For a detailed explanation of

how ERMS managed such risk, see Bhatnagar and Trufano; "From a Fossil Fuel to a Commodity, Natural Gas Comes of Age with the Latest in Financial Marketing Tools," *Enron Business*, 1993, Southwest Collection/Special Collections Library, Texas Tech University, Lubbock, Texas.

78. Beverly Freeman, "Mark-to-Market Accounting: Endorsed for Risk Management Activities," *Enron Business*, May 1994, 8, Southwest Collection/Special Collections Library, Texas Tech University, Lubbock, Texas.

79. Jack I. Tompkins and George W. Posey to George H. Diacont and Robert A. Bayless, June 11, 1991, Securities and Exchange Commission, 1.

80. In later Enron narratives, the Securities and Exchange Commission's response was used to highlight systemic failure (in essence, that the agency never should have allowed Enron to use this kind of accounting).

81. Enron Corp., Form 10-K 1994, SEC EDGAR Database, http://www.sec.gov/edgar .shtml (accessed July 8, 2014).

82. Ibid.; Thane Peterson, "Natural Gas's Hottest Spot," *BusinessWeek*, March 8, 1993, 74–75; Bhatnagar and Trufano, 5–9; "Enron Unit Continues Sharp Growth in Use of Financial Tools for Gas," *Inside F.E.R.C.'s Gas Market Report*, October 8, 1993. For more about in complexity and business strategy, see Philip Scranton and Patrick Fridenson, *Reimagining Business History* (Baltimore: Johns Hopkins University Press, 2013), 67–72.

83. As some have pointed out, some projects, like the Cuiabá pipeline, were actually environmentally dubious propositions. See Derrick Hindery, *From Enron to Evo: Pipeline Politics, Global Environmentalism, and Indigenous Rights in Bolivia* (Tucson: University of Arizona Press, 2013).

84. The apparent incommunicability of the business unit's activities had also found its way into a 1993 Harvard Business School case study that cited a *Forbes* article critical of Enron Gas Services. Rather than agree with the *Forbes* article, though, the Harvard Business School case study's authors regarded the problem as evidence of an admirably sophisticated operation. See Bhatnagar and Trufano, 1.

85. Transcript of Jury Trial Before the Honorable Sim Lake United States District Judge, vol. 37, April 10, 2006, 11905.

86. Carol Hensley, "Enron Gas Services Savors the Success of Building on Opportunities in 1993," *Enron Business* January 1994, 4–5.

87. Ibid.

88. "What's in a Name?" *Enron Business*, October 1994, Southwest Collection/Special Collections Library, Texas Tech University, Lubbock, Texas. Roland Marchand has noted the significance internal corporate publications have for both internal and external corporate rhetoric, imagery, and identity. See Roland Marchand, *Creating the Corporate Soul: The Rise of Public Relations and Corporate Imagery in American Big Business* (Berkeley: University of California Press, 1998), 226–27.

89. "What's in a Name?"

90. Peter F. Drucker, "The New Society of Organizations," *Harvard Business Review* 70.5 (Septembe–rOctober 1992): 95–105, http://web.b.ebscohost.com.ezproxy.bu.edu/ehost/detail /detail?vid=5&sid=89db89d8-185c-4e1c-bc11-f22e5d09f488%40sessionmgr110&hid=124&bdata =JnNpdGU9ZWhvc3QtbGl2ZSZzY29wZT1zaXRl#AN=9301105369&db=bth (accessed November 14, 2015). For more on Drucker's early ideas about the role of the corporation in modern society, see Peter Drucker, *Concept of the Corporation* (1946; New Brunswick, N.J.: Transaction,

1993), 21; Michael Hammer, "Reengineering Work: Don't Automate, Obliterate," *Harvard Business Review*, July 1990.

91. Robert B. Reich, *The Work of Nations* (New York: Vintage Books, 1991), 174.

92. Gary Hamel and C. K. Prahalad, *Competing for the Future* (Boston: Harvard Business School Press, 1994), 28; Peters and Waterman.

93. Hamel and Prahalad, *Competing for the Future*, xii, 23, 25, emphasis in original.

94. Ibid., 33.

95. Kenneth Lay to George H. W. Bush, December 16, 1991, ID# 295446, FI010.02, WHORM: Bush Presidential Records, George Bush Presidential Library.

96. Benjamin Waterhouse has written that a similar tax plan proposed in the early 1980s revealed the ways in which executives at U.S. manufacturing firms failed to understand the drastic transformation the global economy had undergone. Indeed, the lobbyist championing the earlier tax plan, Charls Walker, was working closely with Lay on promoting the targeted ITC. Waterhouse, 229–32.

97. Kenneth Lay to Jeff Bingaman, September 26, 1994, Department of Energy Records, http://energy.gov/sites/prod/files/maprod/documents/enron1994.pdf (accessed April 22, 2013).

98. "Common sense" is a concept that Gramsci used throughout his work. See Antonio Gramsci, *Selections from the Prison Notebooks*, ed. and trans. Quintin Hoare and Geoffrey Nowell Smith (New York: International Publishers, 1971), 197, 323–25.

99. Mary Clark, "Enron Capital and Trade Resources Caps 1994 on Solid Ground," *Enron Business*, January 1995, 4–5; Mary Clark and Carol Hensley, "Enron Gas Services and Enron International—United in the Global Marketplace," *Enron Business*, September 1994, 2–3.

100. Enron, "1994 Enron Annual Report to Shareholders and Customers" (1995). To some degree, Enron would always retain a patina of environmentalism, and the company would never hesitate to strategically deploy "green" rhetoric when it proved useful. For example, in 1997, the company's annual report cover featured a close up of lush, vibrant green leaves.

Chapter 3. From Natural Gas to Knowledge

1. Department of Energy, "Audit Report: The U.S. Department of Energy's Solar Enterprise Zone," April 1998, 1, http://energy.gov/sites/prod/files/igprod/documents/CalendarYear1998/ig-0420.pdf (accessed April 22, 2013); Memorandum: Donald W. Pearlman Jr. to William H. White, August 11, 1994, Department of Energy Records, http://energy.gov/sites/prod/files/maprod/documents/enron1994.pdf (accessed April 22, 2013).

2. William H. White to Robert Kelly, January 24, 1995, Department of Energy Records, http://energy.gov/sites/prod/files/maprod/documents/enron1994.pdf (accessed April 22, 2013). This letter has apparently accidentally been filed with the Department of Energy's Enron records from 1994. It also revealed the extent to which Enron's nascent renewable units needed the government's partnership. Though Kelly and others were keen to develop a renewable energy practice, the economic viability of such ventures was possible only when the Department of Energy took steps like the ones in Nevada—offering itself as a customer for businesses that participated.

3. Timothy J. Mullaney, "Amoco's Solarex Venture to Merge with Enron Unit," *Baltimore Sun*, December 20, 1994, http://articles.baltimoresun.com/1994-12-20/business/1994354138_1_solarex-solar-cells-solar-power (accessed April 23, 2013). Some Enron narratives saw this as a cynical move to gain tax benefits. See Bethany McLean and Peter Elkind, *The Smartest Guys in the Room* (New York: Portfolio, 2003), 166–67.

4. Willett Kempton, James S. Boster, and Jennifer A. Hartley, *Environmental Values in American Culture* (Cambridge, Mass.: MIT Press, 1996), 114–15.

5. Mary Clark, "Change Is Imminent for the Nation's Electric Industry," *Enron Business*, July/August 1994, 4–5.

6. Mary Clark and Terrie James, "ECT's Powerful New Marketing Tool: Electricity Futures," *Enron Business*, April 1996, 3.

7. Mary Clark, "Open-Access Rule Puts U.S. Electric Utilities on Notice," *Enron Business*, May 1995, 2–3; U.S. Energy Information Administration, "Energy Policy Act of 1992," http://www .eia.gov/oil_gas/natural_gas/analysis_publications/ngmajorleg/enrgypolicy.html (accessed March 23, 2016); Paul Kemezis, "Setting the Rules for Electric Wheeling," *Chemical Week*, November 23, 1994, 24; Kenneth Lay to Roger B. Porter, January 15, 1991, WHORM: Bush Presidential Records, George Bush Presidential Library.

8. Barbara C. Farhar, "Trends: Public Opinion About Energy," *Public Opinion Quarterly* 58.4 (Winter 1994): 603–32, 609; Ann De Rouffignac, "Enron Ready to Retail Electric Power," *Houston Business Journal* 25.51 (May 10–16, 1996): n.p. Indeed, there is a longer history of older, regulated businesses fighting against deregulation in specific industries. See Mark H. Rose, Bruce E. Seely, and Paul F. Barrett, *The Best Transportation System in the World: Railroads, Trucks, Airlines, and American Public Policy in the Twentieth Century* (Philadelphia: University of Pennsylvania Press, 2010).

9. Clark, "Open-Access Rule Puts U.S. Electric Utilities on Notice."

10. Mary Clark, "Electricity Ruling Clears Path for Wholesale Wheeling," *Enron Business*, June 1996, 3.

11. Gaynell Dochne, "Enron Battles for Competition in Retail Electric Power Market," *Enron Business*, July/August 1996, 3, 8. Indeed, the specter of "monopolies" was one that Skilling even referred to during his trial. The way he saw it, the company's militaristic campaign was aimed at large utilities that were aligned against consumer interests. Significantly, the company had aligned with conservative lobbying organizations and think tanks such as the American Legislative Exchange Council (ALEC) and the Cato Institute.

12. Kenneth Lay to George W. Bush, February 15, 1995, George W. Bush Papers, Texas State Archives.

13. Kenneth Lay to George W. Bush, May 30, 1995, George W. Bush Papers, Texas State Archives.

14. Kenneth Lay to George W. Bush, July 11, 1996, George W. Bush Papers, Texas State Archives.

15. As David Harvey argues, a fluid sort of capitalism (the neoliberal ideal) results in "coercion" because of "inter-place competition for capital investment and employment (accede to the capitalist's demands or go out of business, create a 'good business climate' or lose jobs)." See David Harvey, "From Space to Place and Back Again," in *Justice, Nature and the Geography of Difference* (Oxford: Blackwell, 1996), 291–326, 299. For Harvey, this type of coercion is one step removed from outright violent oppression. However, the spatial implications are what I am interested in here. The demand is, much like the desires expressed in *Enron Business* articles, for a smooth, undifferentiated space (though Harvey will note that this then puts a secondary pressure on places to distinguish themselves in some manner from other places). It is this sense of coercion that lurks behind the neoliberal rhetoric of "freedom" and was, at times, more or less explicit in Enron's case. Significantly, the threat played out in geographic terms. These menacing comments can be read as Enron taking the frustrating patchwork of regulatory

regimes and leveraging them to its own advantage. Ironically, it was precisely the unfinished quality of neoliberalism that helped propel and accelerate its spread. The letters were examples of how neoliberalism is, as geographers Jamie Peck and Adam Tickell put it, a "strong discourse" that is "self-actualizing." See Jamie Peck and Adam Tickell, "Neoliberalizing Space," in *Spaces of Neoliberalism*, ed. Neil Brenner and Nik Theodore (Malden, Mass.: Blackwell, 2002), 33–57, 35.

16. Robert Barone et al., "Company Report: Enron Corp.," Kidder, Peabody and Company, July 7, 1994, p. 3, via Thomson Reuters/Investext, https://www.thomsonone.com (accessed January 16, 2016). Mary Quinn, "Enron Corp.," S. G. Warburg, April 27, 1995, p. 1, via Reuters/Investext, https://www.thomsonone.com (accessed January 16, 2016).

17. S. A. Parla et al., "Company Report: Enron Corp.," First Boston Corporation, February 8, 1994, 2–3, via Reuters/Investext, https://www.thomsonone.com (accessed January 16, 2016).

18. "The Western Energy Crisis, the Enron Bankruptcy, and FERC's Response," Federal Energy Regulatory Commission, n.d., http://www.ferc.gov/industries/electric/indus-act/wec /chron/chronology.pdf (accessed January 11, 2011); House Committee on Energy and Natural Resources, *Effects of Subtitle B of S. 1766 to the Public Utility Holding Company Act, on Energy Markets and Energy Consumers: Hearing Before the Committee on Energy and Natural Resources*, 107th Cong., 2nd sess., February 6, 2002, http://www.gpo.gov/fdsys/pkg/CHRG -107shrg80364/html/CHRG-107shrg80364.htm (accessed May 20, 2015).

19. Enron Corp., "Enron and Portland General Announce Pro-Competitive Merger," news release, July 22, 1996, 1.

20. Enron Corp., Form 10-K 1996, SEC EDGAR Database, http://www.sec.gov/edgar .shtml (accessed July 8, 2014).

21. Enron, "1995 Enron Annual Report to Shareholders and Customers" (1996), 6, 11.

22. Teresa Hurst, "Beyond Electric Restructuring," *Enron Business* 6 (1997): 2.

23. Ibid.

24. Ibid.

25. Kenneth Lay to George W. Bush, July 11, 1996, George W. Bush Papers, Texas State Archives.

26. Jeffrey Skilling to George W. Bush, February 9, 1996, George W. Bush Papers, Texas State Archives.

27. Letter, Kenneth Lay to George H. W. Bush, May 10, 1991, ID# 23823, WHORM: Bush Presidential Records, George Bush Presidential Library; Chetan Kapoor, "Powell to Participate in Baker Conference," *Rice Thresher* 83.6, ed. 1 (Friday, September 29, 1995), http://texashistory. unt.edu/ark:/67531/metapth246519/m1/1/zoom/?q=enron (accessed March 20, 2015); "Powell Receives Enron Prize," *Rice Thresher* 83.12, ed. 1 (Friday, November 17, 1995), http:// texashistory.unt.edu/ark:/67531/metapth246525/m1/11/zoom/?q=enron (accessed March 20, 2015). In future years, Lay handed out the award to such figures as Nelson Mandela. See Ben Weston, "Mandela to Visit Campus," *Rice Thresher* 87.7, ed. 1 (Friday, October 15, 1999), http://texashistory.unt.edu/ark:/67531/metapth246658/m1/1/zoom/?q=enron (accessed March 20, 2015).

28. Internal Revenue Service, Form 990: Return of Private Foundation: Enron Foundation, 1994. While the charitable arm of Enron also donated to environmental organizations, such as the World Wildlife Fund, the vast majority of the donations were in Houston. "Enron

Takes a Wider View on Diversity," *Enron Business* 2 (1999): 8. This program revealed the myriad ways in which the company, despite Republican ties, was adapting to the Clinton administration. Early on his presidency, Clinton's Energy Department, established the Entrepreneurs Networking to Realize Economic Power, or ENTREP, program to encourage partnerships between "energy-related major companies with minority business enterprises." Bill White to Duane Moody, October 22, 1993, Department of Energy Records, http://energy.gov/sites/prod/files/maprod/documents/enron1993.pdf (accessed March 25, 2016).

29. Transcript of Jury Trial Before the Honorable Sim Lake United States District Judge, vol. 45, April 24, 2006, 14502–3. Olson repeated many of these assertions in her own religiously inflected memoir. See Cindy Kay Olson, *The Whole Truth . . . So Help Me God: An Enlightened Testimony from Inside Enron's Executive's Offices* (Mustang, Okla.: Tate, 2008).

30. Enron Corp., print advertisement, 1994.

31. Stephanie Kolberg, "Cultivating Classiness: Trade Journal Instructions on Strip Club Upscaling," paper presented at the Business History Conference, Columbus, Ohio, March 2013; interview with former Enron employee, May 28, 2009. A word here about the use of oral histories is useful. Oral histories did not make up a substantial part of my research. When referring to oral history interviews with former Enron employees, I am referring to three separate interview subjects. Of course, such a small number does not come close to a statistically significant sample. There are many reasons for not pursuing oral history as a methodology. At the outset of my research, I intended to conduct more interviews but stopped after four. Oral histories are fraught sources to begin with, but Enron's notoriety and the existence of so many books (let alone the movie) meant that there would be an extra layer of mediation in these interviews. Indeed, as I quickly discovered, interviewees would sometimes misremember details, or, more often, frame some responses by referencing a book or the movie. Relying primarily on the archival record, I determined, would be far more preferable. However, these interviews did yield some personal memories and details about daily life at the company.

32. Harvey, "From Space to Place," 299.

33. Darrin Schlegel, "Albert Thomas Finally Arrives as Club Complex," *Houston Business Journal*, March 3, 1995, 1+. *General OneFile*, http://go.galegroup.com.ezproxy.bpl.org, (accessed November 25, 2015). See also Caleb Solomon, "A Night Life in Houston? It's About to Get a Boost," *Wall Street Journal*, March 8, 1995. Section *Texas Journal*; "What's New in Houston and the Gulf Coast Cities," *Successful Meetings*, 45.6 (May 1996): 131 (ProQuest Business Collection).

34. Darrell Preston, "Houston Oilers Sure County, City, Trying to Block Any Suit over Move," *Bond Buyer*, August 25, 1995, http://search.proquest.com.ezproxy.bu.edu/pubidlinkhandler/sng/pubtitle/Bond+Buyer/$N/45433/DocView/407403684/fulltext/4189F5C70B174BBEPQ/10?accountid=9676" (accessed March 25, 2016); Christopher McEntee, "Nashville Council Passes Measures to Aid Oilers' Move to City," *Bond Buyer*, October 12, 1995, http://search.proquest.com (accessed March 25, 2016); Darrell Preston, "Astros Confirm Talks About Possible Move," *Bond Buyer*, October 23, 1995, 3.

35. The company had, along with other businesses, donated money to Rice for new sports facilities.

36. John Williams, "11th Hour Pitch for Stadiums/ Business Leaders Tout Downtown Site," *Houston Chronicle*, October 28, 1996, http://www.chron.com (accessed February 25, 2010). By this point, Lay was no stranger to Houston's civic life. An article in the *Houston*

Chronicle mentioned Lay's success in bringing big events to the city, such as the 1990 Economic Summit and the 1992 Republican National Convention.

37. In fact, Lay was hardly the only voice advocating for a renewed downtown. For years, prominent Houstonians were working to rebuild the city's downtown. Bob Eury, interviewed by David Goldstein, Houston Oral History Project, Houston Area Digital Archives, Houston Public Library, October 23, 2008, http://digital.houstonlibrary.org/oral-history/bob-eury.php (accessed March 20, 2015).

38. Andrew Ross has even gone so far as describing the mid-1990s baseball stadium building as a "craze." See Andrew Ross, *Nice Work If You Can Get It: Life and Labor in Precarious Times* (New York: New York University Press, 2009), 88. The baseball stadiums had, since at least the 1960s, been seen as ways to sweep away urban blight and revitalize downtowns. Ben Lisle, " 'You've Got to Have Tangibles to Sell Intangibles': Ideologies of the Modern American Stadium, 1948–1982" (PhD diss., University of Texas at Austin, 2010), 322.

39. "Ballpark III—Fiscal Responsibility, Economic Opportunity Are There," *Houston Chronicle*, October 31, 1996, http://www.chron.com (accessed February 25, 2010).

40. John Williams, "11th Hour Pitch for Stadiums/Business Leaders Tout Downtown Site."

41. Ibid.

42. Ed Fowler, "Look No Farther Than Downtown," *Houston Chronicle*, October 30, 1996, http://www.chron.com (accessed February 25, 2010).

43. Howard Jefferson, interviewed by David Goldstein, Houston Oral History Project, Houston Area Digital Archives, Houston Public Library, May 15, 2008, http://digital.houstonlibrary.org/oral-history/howard-jefferson.php (accessed March 20, 2015).

44. Denise Culver, "New Construction, Higher Occupancy in Cards for '97," *Houston Business Journal*, December 27, 1996, 28+, *General OneFile*, http://go.galegroup.com.ezproxy.bpl.org, (accessed November 25, 2015). See also Bruce C. Webb, "Deconstructing the Rice," in *Ephemeral City: Cite Looks at Houston*, ed. Barrie Scardino, William F. Stern, and Bruce C. Webb (Austin: University of Texas Press, 2003): 292–304, 293–94.

45. John Williams, "Critics Balk at Ballpark Investment," *Houston Chronicle*, October 20, 1996, http://www.chron.com (accessed February 25, 2010).

46. John Williams, "Downtown: Betting on the Future," *Houston Chronicle*, October 12, 1997, http://www.chron.com (accessed February 25, 2010), 1.

47. Ibid.

48. Ibid.

49. Ibid.

50. *Houston: Where Seventeen Railroads Meet the Sea* Cover, Houston the Magnolia City, Special Collections, University of Houston Libraries, accessed March 21, 2016, http://digital.lib.uh.edu/collection/p15195coll1/item/172/show/155 (accessed March 21, 2016); Bob Eury, interviewed by David Goldstein, Houston Oral History Project, Houston Area Digital Archives, Houston Public Library, October 23, 2008, http://digital.houstonlibrary.org/oral-history/bob-eury.php (accessed March 20, 2015).

51. Enron, "1996 Enron Annual Report to Shareholders and Customers" (1996), 2–3, emphasis in original.

52. Robert J. Shiller, *Irrational Exuberance* (Princeton, N.J.: Princeton University Press, 2005), 2; Daniel T. Rodgers, *Age of Fracture* (Cambridge, Mass.: Belknap Press of Harvard University Press, 2011), 75.

53. As the geographers Neil Brenner and Nik Theodore point out, there is a split between the neoliberal ideal of a smooth space that capital can flow through, and what they term "actually existing neoliberalism." Brenner and Theodore argue that neoliberalized space resembles more of a patchwork of regulatory regimes than it does a space with a smooth, uniform character. Rather, they emphasize "the contextual *embeddedness* of neoliberal restructuring projects insofar as they have been produced within national, regional, and local contexts defined by the legacies of inherited institutional frameworks" and highlight the "contextually specific interactions between inherited regulatory landscapes and emergent neoliberal, market-oriented restructuring projects at a broad range of geographical scales." See Neil Brenner and Nik Theodore, "Cities and the Geographies of 'Actually Existing Neoliberalism,'" in *Spaces of Neoliberalism*, ed. Neil Brenner and Nik Theodore (Malden, Mass.: Blackwell, 2002), 2–32, 4, emphasis in original.

54. President's Council on Sustainable Development, "Sustainable America: A New Consensus for the Prosperity, Opportunity and a Healthy Environment for the Future," National Archives, 1996, http://clinton2.nara.gov/PCSD/Publications/TF_Reports/amer-chap7.html (accessed March 25, 2016).

55. Ibid.

56. Ibid.

57. President's Council on Sustainable Development, "Building on Consensus: A Progress Report on Sustainable America," National Archives, 1997, http://clinton2.nara.gov/PCSD/Publications/Progress_Report.html (accessed March 25, 2016); U.S. Environmental Protection Agency, "1997 SO$_2$ Allowance Auction," https://www.epa.gov/airmarkets/1997-so2-allowance-auction (accessed March 26, 2016); Stephen J. Macekura, *Of Limits and Growth: The Rise of Global Sustainable Development in the Twentieth Century* (New York: Cambridge University Press, 2015), 300.

58. Enron, "1997 Enron Annual Report to Shareholders and Customers" (1998).

59. Department of Energy, *International Energy Outlook 1998* (Washington, D.C.: USIA, 1998), 98; James Pierpoint, "Electric Deregulation Sparks 'Green' Power Demand," *Financial Post* (Toronto, Canada), August 13, 1997.

60. Board of directors meeting minutes and materials, February 11, 1997, box 1/folder 1, Enron Corp. board records (accession 2487), Hagley Museum and Library, Wilmington, Delaware.

61. The details of the Northern States Power Company's involvement in what would become the country's largest wind farm hardly followed from environmental concern. Dennis Lien, "NSP Wind Project Is Not Enough, Say Critics," *Saint Paul Pioneer Press*, September 26, 1998, Though most of the power for Northern States Power Company came from coal and nuclear plants, the large and diffuse wind farm on Buffalo Ridge in Minnesota was attracting both advocates and critics. Carol Ann Giovando, "Minnesota Wind Farm Steals California's Thunder," *Power* 142.5 (September/October 1998): 85; "Enron Wind Completes Largest Wind Power Complex," *Megawatt Daily* 3.180 (September 17, 1998).

62. Tom Meersman, "Tapping into Wind Power," *Star Tribune* (Minneapolis), September 24, 1998.

63. Department of Energy, "Wind Facility Provides Clean, Renewable Energy to Thousands in the Midwest," Department of Energy, September 24, 1998.

64. "Enron Tests Water with Azurix," *Financial Times*, September 26, 1998, http://www .lexisnexis.com.

65. Qtd. in Judy Corwin, "Global Perspectives from Enron's Rebecca Mark," *Baylor Business Review* 17.1 (Spring 1999): 2–5, 2–3.

66. The economist Robert Shiller has argued that this is the period of "new era" thinking. Shiller, 106. Likewise, the historian Daniel T. Rodgers has commented on the collapsible sense of time at the end of the twentieth century. See Rodgers, 230–31.

67. Board of directors meeting minutes and materials, February 11, 1997, box 1/folder 1, Enron Corp. board records (accession 2487), Hagley Museum and Library, Wilmington, Delaware. Board of directors minutes (partial), May 6, 1997, box 1/folder 4, Enron Corp. board records (accession 2487), Hagley Museum and Library, Wilmington, Delaware.

68. Much on the two slides was similar—suggesting that the May slide was simply a revision of the first.

69. Enron Corp., "NCPA and Enron Form Major Strategic Energy Alliance," January 15, 1997, http://www.lexisnexis.com (accessed November 18, 2006).

70. For more about consumer feedback loops, see Regina Lee Blaszczyk, *Imagining Consumers: Design and Innovation from Wedgwood to Corning* (Baltimore: Johns Hopkins University Press, 2000.). Board of directors minutes (partial), May 6, 1997, box 1/folder 4, Enron Corp. board records (accession 2487), Hagley Museum and Library, Wilmington, Delaware.

71. Board of directors minutes (partial), May 6, 1997.

72. Ibid. A megawatt is equivalent to one million watts.

73. Ibid. Interestingly, 1997 would turn out to be a terrible year for Enron's finances. In the wake of weak earnings, the stock had taken a bit of a tumble. Looking at coverage of the company following that year, many journalists referenced a post-1997 Enron. If, as Karen Ho suggests, the culture and power of Wall Street imposes a disciplinary regime on other corporations, in 1997, this seems to have happened to Enron. Until the company's spectacular fall at the end of 2001, the company would not disappoint Wall Street again. See Karen Ho, *Liquidated: An Ethnography of Wall Street* (Durham, N.C.: Duke University Press, 2009), 30.

74. Presumably, this designation meant that employees were being urged to read this article in particular. "Enron Playing a Key Role in Global Campaign to Reform Energy Services Trade Policies," *Enron Business* 1 (2000): 6, Southwest Collection/Special Collections Library, Texas Tech University, Lubbock, Texas.

75. Ibid.

76. Kenneth Lay to George W. Bush, October 6, 1997, George W. Bush Papers, Texas State Archives.

77. Kenneth Lay to George W. Bush, March 31, 1999, George W. Bush Papers, Texas State Archives.

78. Ibid.

79. "Enron in Global Marketplace," *Enron Business* 2 (1999): 5, Southwest Collection/Special Collections Library, Texas Tech University, Lubbock, Texas. Of course, much like other

free market advocates, Lay and Enron were often quick to link freedom and free markets in general.

80. Ibid.

81. "Enron's Government Affairs Group: A Two-Way Conduit to Regulators and Legislators," *Enron Business* 1 (1999): 8–9, Southwest Collection/Special Collections Library, Texas Tech University, Lubbock, Texas.

82. Lay's vision, though, was hardly unique. Rather, the executive's views were fairly standard for proponents of neoliberalism. As geographers Neil Brenner and Nik Theodore have noted, neoliberal advocates have always viewed "the world of market rules as a state of nature." The idea of the market as a natural state also works to deemphasize geographic variation, because advocates see the market as working "according to immutable laws no matter where they are 'unleashed.'" Given the ideology of a natural free market with universal laws, for a figure like Ken Lay it would make perfect sense that domestic deregulation should mirror international economic liberalization. For Brenner and Theodore, such a sensibility amounts to a vision of an unrealized utopia ("Cities and the Geographies of 'Actually Existing Neoliberalism,'" 35).

Chapter 4. Selling Instability

1. Malcolm Salter, *Innovation Corrupted: The Origins and Legacy of Enron's Collapse* (Cambridge, Mass.: Harvard University Press, 2008), 116–17.

2. Mimi Swartz and Sherron Watkins, *Power Failure: The Inside Story of the Collapse of Enron* (New York: Doubleday, 2003), 73, 151–52; Senate Committee on Governmental Affairs, Role of the Board of Directors in Enron's Collapse, 107th Cong., 2nd sess., 2002, S. Print 107–70, 40.

3. The economist Robert Shiller has noted that corporate earnings recovered from the 1991 recession around the same time that most Americans became aware of the Internet. Robert Shiller, *Irrational Exuberance*, 2nd ed. (Princeton, N.J.: Princeton University Press, 2005), 107.

4. Dean Starkman, *The Watchdog That Didn't Bark: The Financial Crisis and the Disappearance of Investigative Journalism* (New York: Columbia University Press, 2014), 145–46. Of course, there is historical precedent for such thinking. See Julia Ott, *When Wall Street Met Main Street: The Quest for an Investors' Democracy* (Cambridge, Mass.: Harvard University Press, 2011); Shiller 120. Economists George Akerlof and Robert Shiller note the importance of "confidence in a nation, a company, or an institution" and how that confidence rests on narrative. "Great leaders," they assert, "are first and foremost creators of stories." Indeed, Akerlof and Shiller go so far as to assert that on a macro level, stories "no longer merely *explain* the facts; they *are* the facts." The confidence in an economy, they argue, is directly related to stories. Directly referencing the Internet boom of the 1990s, the two write that confidence is a worldview and a "popular model of current events, a public understanding of the mechanism of economic change as informed by the news media and by popular discussions. High confidence tends to be associated with inspirational stories, stories about new business initiatives, tales of how others are getting rich. New era stories have tended to accompany the major booms in stock markets around the world. The economic confidence of times past cannot be understood without reference to the details of these stories." George Akerlof and Robert Shiller, *Animal Spirits: How Human Psychology Drives the Economy, and Why It Matters for Global Capitalism* (Princeton, N.J.: Princeton University Press, 2009), 51–54.

5. Thrift refers to these texts as the "cultural circuit" of capitalism. Thrift argues that business organizations became "cultural entities" that attempted to "generate new traditions, new representations" of themselves "and the world." Interestingly, Thrift also points to the role of rhetoric and visual style. It was also during this time that the company began aggressively advertising directly to consumers, as well as unveiling its now infamous "Big E" logo. See Nigel Thrift, *Knowing Capitalism* (London: Sage, 2005), 34. Indeed, rereading Lipartito's work in light of Thrift's observations suggests that culture was at the center of the "new economy." The figure of the entrepreneur was at the heart of new economy (and late-period Enron's) rhetoric. As Lipartito suggests, the goal of entrepreneurs (and entrepreneurial organizations) can be seen as getting the public and employees "to see reality in a new, unexpected way." See Kenneth Lipartito, "Culture and the Practice of Business History," *Business and Economic History* 24. 2 (Winter 1995): 35.

6. Skilling himself had no knowledge of this project. However, after the group successfully launched what became Enron Online, Skilling would use the episode as an example of the company's entrepreneurial culture.

7. Gilardi and Co., LLC, "Enron Corporation (ENRN Q) Common Stock Historical Price Table," n.d., http://www.gilardi.com/enron/securities/ (accessed July 9, 2014).

8. Kevin Kelly, *New Rules for the New Economy* (New York: Penguin, 1998), 2–3, 19. Though there is no direct evidence that Enron executives or employees were directly playing off of Kevin Kelly's style, Kelly still represents a good starting point here, because of his prominence within the new economy culture of the late 1990s. Not only was *New Rules for the New Economy* well received, but Kelly was also one of the founding editors of the magazine *Wired*, a major new economy outlet.

9. Ibid., 19.

10. Ibid., 113. Fred Turner argues that the pages of *Wired*, which Kelly edited, often made the connection between the new economy and the absence of regulation explicit. Fred Turner, *From Counterculture to Cyberculture: Stewart Brand, the Whole Earth Network, and the Rise of Digital Utopianism* (Chicago: University of Chicago Press, 2006), 208.

11. Thomas Frank, *One Market Under God: Extreme Capitalism, Market Populism, and the End of Economic Democracy* (New York: Anchor Books, 2000), 173–79.

12. Kenneth L. Lay, "Coming Soon to Your Home and Business: The New Energy Majors," in *Straight from the CEO: The World's Top Business Leaders Reveal Ideas That Every Manager Can Use*, ed. G. William Dauphinais and Colin Price (New York: Simon and Schuster, 1998), 255. Even if the gas itself was invisible, manipulating it necessitated large, industrial objects such as processing plants and lengthy pipelines.

13. Ibid., 254.

14. Tony Spaeth, "Fresh Faces for 1998," *Across the Board*, February 1998, http://www.identityworks.com/articles/Spaeth97.pdf (accessed December 8, 2013).

15. Rand himself died before Enron began using the new design. As it turns out, the logo needed to be modified after its introduction. The yellow that was originally used in the middle of the logo did not show up when letterhead with the logo was faxed or photocopied. The color was soon replaced by a shade of green See Michael Bierut, "The Smartest Logo in the Room," *Design Observer Group*, February 11, 2008, http://observatory.designobserver.com/entry.html ?entry=6237 (accessed December 8, 2013).

16. Paul Rand, maquette: "Presentation of a New ENRON Identity," August 1996, Paul Rand Papers, AOB 126, 2000-M-133 Acc, box 20, Robert B. Haas Family Arts Library, Yale University.

17. Rand maquette: "Presentation of a New ENRON Identity."

18. Elizabeth Arendall Tilney to Paul Rand, November 11, 1996, Paul Rand Papers, AOB 126, 2000-M-133 Acc, box 20, Robert B. Haas Family Arts Library, Yale University.

19. *Enron Case Study* (CD-ROM) (Hoboken, N.J.: John Wiley and Sons, 2002).

20. Thrift, 32.

21. Enron, "Enron Annual Report 1999" (1999), 2. Malcolm Salter has also cited this document as evidence of hubris and muddled thinking at the company. See Salter, 47–48. Indeed, the vague language would even prove to be a point of consternation for skeptical journalists. *Fortune* writer Bethany McLean would point to Enron's opaque language in a critical article on the company. See Bethany McLean, "Is Enron Overpriced?" *Fortune*, March 5, 2001, 122–26, 123. I want to stress here that the vagueness of language was not simply a matter of "rhetorical flourish." Years later, during his criminal trial, Jeff Skilling highlighted the problem of language and of describing what Enron actually did. Such dramatic pronouncements were accompanied by other, dramatic substantial shifts—such as internal reorganizations (there were so many of these that they became a joke among Enron employees) and renaming divisions.

22. Enron, "2000 Enron Annual Report to Shareholders and Customers" (2001).

23. Ibid.

24. Enron Corp., "Letter to Shareholders," 2000 Annual Report (2001), 4–5.

25. Kelly, 2.

26. "ETS Flying Under New Colors," *Enron Business* 6 (2000): 2, Southwest Collection/Special Collections Library, Texas Tech University, Lubbock, Texas. It is, of course, also significant that the letter described the change as a "cultural shift." While this phrase referred to the company's internal culture, it could easily have applied to the ways in which Enron was presenting itself to the outside world.

27. "Innovation 5," *Enron Case Study* (CD-ROM) (Hoboken, N.J.: John Wiley and Sons, 2002).

28. Ibid.

29. Rebecca Smith and Aaron Lucchetti, "Rebecca Mark's Exit Leaves Azurix Treading Deep Water," *Wall Street Journal*, August 28, 2000.

30. In her ethnographic study of investment banking practices, Karen Ho locates a distinct anxiousness around the term "globalization." As the word "global" began to appear at the beginning of corporate phrases and names, and as some investment banks opened more or less empty offices around the world to claim "global" status, Ho calls on scholars to "look critically at globalization as not simply a fact, but a hope, a strategy, and a triumphalist ideology." See Karen Ho, *Liquidated: An Ethnography of Wall Street* (Durham, N.C.: Duke University Press, 2009), 333–34.

31. In an October 2001 company-wide meeting, Lay and Greg Whalley, who replaced Skilling after his abrupt departure that summer, both noted that the company's international operations had shifted away from infrastructure projects in developing countries and toward trading markets in Europe. See Enron Corp., "All Employee Meeting," October 23, 2001, Securities and Exchange Commission Historical Society, http://www.sechistorical.org (accessed December 14, 2013), 8, 23.

32. Board of directors minutes, [October 7, 2000], box 2, Enron Corp. board records (accession 2487), Hagley Museum and Library, Wilmington, Delaware.

33. Ibid.

34. Thomas Friedman, *The Lexus and the Olive Tree* (New York: Random House, 2000), 288–89, 387.

35. Enron, "2000 Enron Annual Report to Shareholders and Customers" (2001), 12.

36. Ibid., 9.

37. Ibid., 13.

38. Board of directors minutes, [October 7, 2000], box 2, Enron Corp. board records (accession 2487), Hagley Museum and Library, Wilmington, Delaware.

39. Enron Corp., print advertisement, 1997. For the new marketing push, Enron used a different advertising company.

40. "Enron Asks Why?" *Enron Business* 2 (2000): 1, Southwest Collection/Special Collections Library, Texas Tech University, Lubbock, Texas.

41. Ibid.

42. Ibid.

43. Paul Rand maquette: "Presentation of a New ENRON Identity."

44. "Enron Asks Why?"

45. "Enron Commercial," http://www.youtube.com/watch?v=XZ8XM7JVpYw (accessed April 29, 2010).

46. Ibid.

47. "Enron Asks Why?"

48. "Enron "Why" Commercial," http://www.youtube.com/watch?v=pboh1SFk6TM&feature =related (accessed April 29, 2010). The building's image, like the entire ad, referenced "nonconformity" and was beautiful in the way it seemed to move (the structure was also known as "Ginger and Fred" because its form suggested that it was "dancing"). However, the image was also visual evidence of the global economic project of which Enron had become a part. A year later, Enron became a corporate sponsor for a Gehry retrospective at the Guggenheim Museum in New York. In a brief note in the exhibition book, Skilling wrote: "Enron shares Mr. Gehry's ongoing search for the 'moment of truth'—the moment when the functional approach to a problem becomes infused with the artistry that provides a truly innovative solution." Jeff Skilling, sponsorship statement, *Frank Gehry—Architect* (New York: Guggenheim, 2001).

49. "Enron Asks Why?"

50. Ibid.

51. Rosalee Fleming to Kelly Merritt, e-mail, December 11, 2000, Enron Email Dataset, Federal Energy Regulatory Commission. A word on sources is warranted here. Documentary evidence for this chapter and especially the next comes from the Enron Email Dataset that the Federal Energy Regulatory Commission made available during its investigation into the California energy crisis. Though the corpus, consisting of e-mails and attached documents from 1999 to 2000, represents a great resource, as an archive, it also presents an issue. Indeed, the e-mail dataset is fifty-five gigabytes of material—an enormous amount of information. Because of this size, even exhaustive qualitative research can only touch on a small portion of the overall dataset. Business historians Susanna Fellman and Andrew Popp have noted that because corporations generate numerous documents, there can be "an abundance of material" leaving

business historians "overwhelmed by sources" and "swamped with information." For Fellman and Popp, this poses a number of questions, including how to determine what is and is not relevant. In short, facing an "overflow" of material, in a corporate archive, the historian needs a sense of an archive's "geography" in striking a balance between "depth and efficiency." In order to make sense of the Enron Email Dataset, I adopted a strategy of first searching the inboxes of prominent figures, such as Kenneth Lay. As keyword searches through these inboxes yielded names that were clearly important, I searched these individuals' inboxes. Because the e-mail dataset is a network format, there is significant overlap in certain individuals' mailboxes, including entire conversation threads. In effect, certain e-mail inboxes served as hubs through which a good portion of relevant material passed. For clarity, I have opted to cite documents from the e-mail dataset as I would cite a document from a physical archive. If the authorship of a particular document is clear, I cite it as a memorandum. If the authorship is unclear, I cite the document attributing authorship to Enron Corp. See Susanna Fellman and Andrew Popp, "Lost in the Archive: The Business Historian in Distress," in *Coping with Excess: How Organizations, Communities and Individuals Manage Overflows*, ed. Barbara Czarniawska and Orvar Löfgren (Northampton, Mass.: Edward Elgar, 2013): 216–43, 217, 231. Much like the visual and rhetorical style found in the late 1990s annual reports, these commercials were a part of what historian Eric Guthey calls "New Economy Romanticism," which echoes "the very familiar narrative of American exceptionalism, which also celebrates the notion that radically atomistic individuals can achieve a clean break from the shackles of the past and from oppressive institutions in order to create a New World." Eric Guthey, "New Economy Romanticism, Narratives of Corporate Personhood, and the Antimanagerial Impulse," in *Constructing Corporate America: History, Politics, Culture*, ed. Kenneth Lipartito and David B. Sicilia (New York: Oxford University Press, 2004): 321–42, 324.

52. Qtd. in Brian O'Reilly, "The Secrets of America's Most Admired Corporations," *Fortune*, March 3, 1997, 62.

53. Guthey.

54. O'Reilly, "Secrets of America's Most Admired Corporations," 62.

55. Again, of course, this focus on the stock price is ironic because, as Malcolm Salter and others have pointed out, 1997 was the year that Enron had irrevocably slipped into fraud. One could argue that such media coverage only encouraged perpetuating fraudulent activity.

56. Erin Davies, "Enron: The Power's Back On," *Fortune*, April 13, 1998, 24.

57. "Just About Jeff," *Enron Business* 1 (2001): 7.

58. Interview with former Enron employee, May 28, 2009.

59. Wendy Zellner, "From Sleepy Utility to Online Turbotrader," *Business Week E.Biz*, September 18, 2000, 46.

60. Wendy Zellner, "Enron Electrified," *Business Week E.Biz*, July 24, 2000, 54.

61. Frank Gibney Jr., "Enron Plays the Pipes," *Time*, August 28, 2000, 38–39, 39.

62. Ibid., 38.

63. Board of directors minutes, [October 7, 2000], box 2, Enron Corp. board records (accession 2487), Hagley Museum and Library, Wilmington, Delaware; Brian O'Reilly, "The Power Merchant," *Fortune*, April 17, 2000, 148–60, 150; Gilardi and Co., LLC.

64. Gary Hamel, *Leading the Revolution*, 1st ed. (Cambridge, Mass.: Harvard Business School Press, 2000), xi, 213–14. Thomas Frank is one of those who has criticized such books for sacrificing intellectual rigor in favor of bombast.

65. Hamel, 214, 216.

66. Ibid., 217, 222 (emphasis in original).

67. Ann de Rouffignac and Laura A. Stromberg, "Energy Trading Giant Selects Downtown Headquarters Site," *Houston Business Journal*, July 18, 1997, *General OneFile*, http://go.gale group.com.ezproxy.bpl.org (accessed November 25, 2015); Ann de Rouffignac, "Power Market Surges in Houston," *Houston Business Journal*, February 28, 1997, *General OneFile*, http://go .galegroup.com.ezproxy.bpl.org (accessed November 28, 2015); Ann de Rouffignac, "Visions of Power: Jeff Skilling Is on an Innovative Mission to Make Enron Corp. the Top Trading Power-house in a Deregulated Electricity Industry," *Houston Business Journal*, March 7, 1997, 18A+, *General OneFile*, http://go.galegroup.com.ezproxy.bpl.org (accessed November 28, 2015).

68. "Abbreviations: Houston; New Building Ground Breaking Event," *Enron Business* 5 (1999): 3, Southwest Collection/Special Collections Library, Texas Tech University, Lubbock, Texas.

69. Stuart W. Leslie, "The Strategy of Structure: Architectural and Managerial Style at Alcoa and Owens-Corning," *Enterprise and Society* 12.4 (2011): 863–902, 864.

70. "Abbreviations."

71. While the term "campus" was a common way to refer to corporate offices in Silicon Valley, the term was also used in Houston's old Energy Corridor. Board of directors minutes, [February 13, 2001], part 1, box 2, Enron Corp. board records (accession 2487), Hagley Museum and Library, Wilmington, Delaware.

72. The facility was an EES customer, and the company had paid millions for the naming rights.

73. *The Making of Enron Field: 2000 Commemorative Program*, ed. Alyson Footer (Playa del Rey, Calif.: CWC Sports, 2000), 22, DeGoyler Library, Southern Methodist University.

74. "Just the Boost Downtown Houston Needed," *Enron Business* 2 (2000): 9.

75. Ibid.

76. *Making of Enron Field*, 42–43, 78–79; interview with former Enron employee, May 19, 2009; In truth, neither the company nor the team could claim full credit for the changes to downtown. Downtown growth was a national phenomenon. The racial makeup of downtown Houston was also changing, as more whites had moved into the area. Rebecca R. Sohmer and Robert E. Lang, "Downtown Rebound," Fannie Mae Foundation and Brookings Institution Center on Urban and Metropolitan Policy Census Note, May 2001, http://www.brookings.edu /es/urban/census/downtownrebound.pdf (accessed March 20, 2015).

77. "Just the Boost Downtown Houston Needed."

78. Ibid.

79. The political and economic implications behind these statements revealed a deep neo-liberal logic of interurban competition and rescaling. Referring to David Harvey's work, Jamie Peck and Adam Tickell write that "urban entrepreneurial" activities, such as the "reproduction of cultural spectacles, enterprise zones, [and] waterfront developments" reflect[s] "the powerful disciplinary effects of interurban competition." See Jamie Peck and Adam Tickell, "Neoliberalizing Space," in *Spaces of Neoliberalism*, ed. Neil Brenner and Nik Theodore (Malden, Mass.: Blackwell, 2002), 46; David Harvey, *The Condition of Postmodernity*, (Oxford: Basil Blackwell, 1989).

80. *Making of Enron Field*, 28–31.

81. Thomas A. Stewart, "Taking Risk to the Marketplace," *Fortune*, March 6, 2000, 424. As Louis Hyman has argued, in the early 1970s managers and consultants began to think about conglomerates as portfolios of assets, which significantly contributed to a financialized concept of a corporation. Louis Hyman, "Rethinking the Postwar Corporation: Management, Monopolies, and Markets," in *What's Good for Business: Business and American Politics Since World War II*, ed. Kim Phillips-Fein and Julian E. Zelizer (Oxford: Oxford University Press, 2012), 195–211, 204.

82. "Optionality in a Network," *Enron Case Study* (CD-ROM) (Hoboken, N.J.: John Wiley and Sons, 2002).

83. Robert Colvin, "New Rule Marks Major Shift in Investment Policy," *ABA Banking Journal*, July 1998, 48–50.

84. "Flexibility of Portfolio of Options," *Enron Case Study* (CD-ROM) (Hoboken, N.J.: John Wiley and Sons, 2002).

85. Ibid.

86. "Optionality in a Network."

87. "Flexibility of Portfolio of Options."

88. Ibid.

89. "Capabilities," *Enron Case Study* (CD-ROM) (Hoboken, N.J.: John Wiley and Sons, 2002).

90. Enron Corp., minutes of the board of directors, December 8, 1998, Herbert S. Winkour Jr., Enron Board Records Collection, Hagley Digital Archives, http://cdm16038.contentdm.oclc.org/cdm/compoundobject/collection/p15017coll21/id/3121/rec/15 (accessed December 14, 2013).

91. Board of directors minutes, [February 13, 2001], part 1, box 2, Enron Corp. board records (accession 2487), Hagley Museum and Library, Wilmington, Delaware.

92. Of course, it is not unusual for a new line of business to operate at a loss after launching. However, the losses at EBS fit a broader pattern of failure—and hiding that failure—at Enron. Board of directors minutes, [February 13, 2001], part 1, box 2, Enron Corp. board records (accession 2487), Hagley Museum and Library, Wilmington, Delaware.

93. "Innovation 2," *Enron Case Study* (CD-ROM) (Hoboken, N.J.: John Wiley and Sons, 2002).

94. "Flexibility of Portfolio of Options."

95. For an extended analysis of new economy rhetoric, see Frank, 170–251.

96. Sandra Lord, "Information About Rebecca Mark Jusbasche," 2006, box 2, folder, 76, Discover Houston Tours Records, Woodson Research Center, Rice University, Houston, Texas.

97. Interview with former Enron employee, May 28, 2009.

98. Sarah Palmer, "Extreme Enron," *Enron Business* 4 (2001): 12, Southwest Collection/Special Collections Library, Texas Tech University, Lubbock, Texas.

99. Ibid., 13.

100. "Extreme Enron," *Enron Business* 2 (2001): 4, Southwest Collection/Special Collections Library, Texas Tech University, Lubbock, Texas.

101. Board of directors minutes, [October 7, 2000], box 2, Enron Corp. board records (accession 2487), Hagley Museum and Library, Wilmington, Delaware.

102. Board of directors minutes, [February 13, 2001], part 1, box 2, Enron Corp. board records (accession 2487), Hagley Museum and Library, Wilmington, Delaware.

103. Senate Committee on Governmental Affairs, Role of the Board of Directors in Enron's Collapse, 7.

104. Finance committee minutes, August 9, 1999, box 1/folder 15, Enron Corp. board records (accession 2487), Hagley Museum and Library, Wilmington, Delaware.

105. For a detailed description of the LJM1 deal, as well as Enron's other SPEs, see William Powers et al., "Report of Investigation by the Special Investigative Committee of the Board of Directors of Enron Corp."

106. Transcript of Jury Trial Before the Honorable Sim Lake United States District Judge, March 14, 2006, 7951–59.

107. Senate Committee on Governmental Affairs, Role of the Board of Directors in Enron's Collapse, 23.

108. Executive committee minutes (partial), June 22, 2000, box 1/folder 21, Enron Corp. board records (accession 2487), Hagley Museum and Library, Wilmington, Delaware.

109. Ibid.

110. Finance committee minutes, May 1, 2000, box 1/folder 20, Enron Corp. board records (accession 2487), Hagley Museum and Library, Wilmington, Delaware.

111. Senate Committee on Governmental Affairs, Role of the Board of Directors in Enron's Collapse, 29–34.

112. Ibid., 18–19; U.S. Bankruptcy Court, Southern District of New York, *In re Enron Corp.*, chapter 11, case no. 01-16034 (AJG), "Third Interim Report of Neal Batson, Court Appointed Examiner," Enron Examiner Reports, University of Pennsylvania, Biddle Law Library, National Bankruptcy Archives, 20; Senate Committee on Governmental Affairs, Role of the Board of Directors in Enron's Collapse, 57.

113. Arthur Levitt to Billy Tauzin, May 24, 2000, SEC Historical Society, http://3197d6d14b5f19f2f440-5e13d29c4c016cf96cbbfd197c579b45.r81.cf1.rackcdn.com/collection/papers/2000/2000_0524_TauzinLevitt.pdf (accessed July 15, 2017).

114. Rod Grams et al. to Arthur Levitt, July 28, 2000, ID#16245, folder: Bill Donaldson [folder 1], FOIA 2014-0357-F: Records created by or sent to William Donaldson, SEC chairman, courtesy George W. Bush Presidential Library, National Archives and Records Administration.

115. Enron Corp., minutes of the board of directors, August 9, 1999, Herbert S. Winkour Jr., Enron Board Records Collection, Hagley Digital Archives, p. 23, http://cdm16038.contentdm.oclc.org/cdm/compoundobject/collection/p15017coll21/id/3680/rec/2 (accessed December 16, 2013).

116. Board of directors minutes, [October 7, 2000], continuation, part 1, box 2, Enron Corp. board records (accession 2487), Hagley Museum and Library, Wilmington, Delaware; Breakers Hotel, https://www.thebreakers.com (accessed December 15, 2016). The hotel had been rebuilt after a fire in 1925.

117. Salter, 136–37; U.S. Bankruptcy Court, Southern District of New York, *In re Enron Corp.*, chapter 11, case no. 01-16034 (AJG), "Second Interim Report of Neal Batson, Court Appointed Examiner," Enron Examiner Reports, University of Pennsylvania, Biddle Law Library, National Bankruptcy Archives, 120–21, 23–24a.

118. U.S. Bankruptcy Court, Southern District of New York, *In re Enron Corp.*, chapter 11, case no. 01-16034 (AJG), "Second Interim Report of Neal Batson, Court Appointed Examiner."

119. U.S. Bankruptcy Court, Southern District of New York, *In re Enron Corp.*, chapter 11, case no. 01-16034 (AJG), "First Interim Report of Neal Batson, Court Appointed Examiner," Enron Examiner Reports, University of Pennsylvania, Biddle Law Library, National Bankruptcy Archives, 118–22.

120. Sifting through Enron's finances, of course, can yield different interpretations. For instance, the court appointed examiner in Enron's bankruptcy case judges that SPEs account for 96 percent of Enron's reported net income for 2000. This figure is calculated by deducting $936.7 million, not $966 million, from Enron's total reported number of $979 million. In its evaluation, the examiner credited Enron $29.7 million from a group of SPE transactions collectively labeled "Share Trusts." According to this estimation, Enron could legitimately claim $42.3 million in net income for 2000. Regardless of the status of the "Share Trusts," only $12.6 million, or 1 percent, of Enron's net income for 2000 was realized without the use of an SPE.

121. John Conyers Jr. to George W. Bush, August 13, 2002, folder 535045, FOIA 2014-0221-F: Records sent to, sent by, or received by President George W. Bush between January 2001 and December 2002 regarding Enron, Jeff Skilling, Kenneth Lay, and Andrew Fastow, courtesy George W. Bush Presidential Library, National Archives and Records Administration; Senate Committee on Governmental Affairs, Role of the Board of Directors in Enron's Collapse, 36–37.

122. Board of directors minutes, [February 13, 2001], part 1, box 2, Enron Corp. board records (accession 2487), Hagley Museum and Library, Wilmington, Delaware.

123. Jonathan Coopersmith has observed that the line between fraud and legitimacy is often hazy for technology startup companies. See German Historical Institute, Conference Report, http://ghi-dc.org/index.php?option=com_content&view=article&id=1420&Itemid=1230 (accessed March 21, 2016).

Chapter 5. A Very Bad Year

1. Of course, the 1990s had brought smaller successes, such as the program in New Hampshire. Much like Enron's actions in New Hampshire and Texas, the drama that unfolded between Enron and California as the company bought and sold energy in the state's newly deregulated energy market in the late 1990s and the opening years of the twenty-first century reveals the instability of space and place as categories under neoliberalism. From 1996 to early 2001 (before the company's complete collapse), the traces of dynamic, relational, and multiple understandings of space and place were revealed in the relationship between the company and the state.

2. "The Western Energy Crisis, the Enron Bankruptcy, and FERC's Response," Federal Energy Regulatory Commission, http://www.ferc.gov/industries/electric/indus-act/wec/chron/chronology.pdf, n.d. (accessed January 11, 2011).

3. This public relations strategy recalled a longer tradition in corporate-public communications. Roland Marchand argues that during the twentieth century, large and increasingly decentralized businesses attempted to ingratiate themselves to communities as "good neighbors" in order to "cast an aura of familiarity over ever-more-complex economic and spatial relationships." This same attempt to produce a sense of closeness could be found throughout

Enron's public relations efforts in California. Roland Marchand, *Creating the Corporate Soul: The Rise of Public Relations and Corporate Imagery in American Big Business* (Berkeley: University of California Press, 1998), 349.

4. Though many news stories referred to Houston as the company's headquarters, others seemed to suggest that locating Enron was a more difficult task. For example, the company was one of three in an October 2000 story in Escondido, California's *North County Times*, titled "California Power Companies Report Sizzling Third Quarter." One line in the article's opening paragraph was telling: "Three of the companies that generate and sell electricity in California." Dan McSwain, "California Power Companies Report Sizzling Third Quarter," *North County Times*, October 19, 2000, http://www.ebscohost.com (accessed November 28, 2006).

5. "The Western Energy Crisis, the Enron Bankruptcy, and FERC's Response." As this FERC report ultimately concluded, there were multiple causes for the dramatic increases in energy prices, including "a low rate of generation having been built in California in the preceding years making California dependent on imports of electricity; northwestern drought conditions resulting in lower than expected water runoff for hydropower generation; a rupture and subsequent capacity constraints on a major pipeline supplier of natural gas to California markets (California was heavily dependent on gas-fired generation due to state air standards); strong economic growth and thus increased electricity demand throughout the west; and unusually high temperatures coupled with an increase in unplanned plant outages of older plants that were being run to meet increased demand in California." However, the report also found that "some energy companies attempted to manipulate wholesale electric and gas markets."

6. In other parts of the state, there were also problems, though consumers were protected from the rising prices.

7. "The Western Energy Crisis, the Enron Bankruptcy, and FERC's Response"; John Woolfork, "Power Demand Nears Record; Blackouts Averted," *San Jose Mercury News*, August 20, 2000, http://www.lexisnexis.com (accessed July 10, 2014).

8. John Woolfork, "Residents Cutting Corners Since Power Deregulation; Electric Prices Jolt San Diego," *San Jose Mercury News*, August 14, 2000, http://www.lexisnexis.com (accessed July 10, 2014).

9. Carolyn Wheat, letter to the editor, *San Diego Union-Tribune*, August 19, 2000, http://www.lexis-nexis.com/ (accessed November 18, 2006).

10. William Brotherton, letter to the editor, *San Diego Union-Tribune*, August 19, 2000, http://www.lexis-nexis.com/ (accessed November 18, 2006).

11. Lawrence L. Knuston, "Clinton Pushes for Energy Relief," *West County Times* (California), August 24, 2000, http://lexisnexis.com (accessed July 10, 2014). The bill did not pass. *Consumer Empowerment and Electricity Deregulation Act of 2000*, HR 2886, 106th Cong.

12. "Kilowhat?!$ Plug in Other Options," *San Jose Mercury News*, August 8, 2000, http://lexisnexis.com (accessed July 10, 2014).

13. Enron Corp., "Talking Points Draft 3," n.d., Enron Email Dataset, Federal Energy Regulatory Commission.

14. Ibid.

15. Ibid. Of course, when dealing with the state and regulators, the company made a more sophisticated argument. For example, under Robert Bradley's direction, Enron's people would

attempt to counter academic voices arguing that electricity deregulation was a bad idea. Robert Bradley to Richard Shapiro and James D. Steffes, "Joskow Critique," April 24, 2000, Enron Email Dataset.

16. Enron Corp., "Government Affairs—the Americas: Top 'Ten' Objectives for the Year 2000; North America," May 4, 2000, Enron Email Dataset.

17. David Parquet, "Consideration of Price Caps Reduction—Meeting of the Board of Governors of the California ISO," June 28, 2000, Enron Email Dataset.

18. Steve Kean to Kenneth Lay, "Cal Talking Points—Presentation.doc," December 4, 2000, Enron Email Dataset.

19. Ibid.

20. "EES Muscles in Big," *Enron Business* 6 (2000): 5, Southwest Collection/Special Collections Library, Texas Tech University, Lubbock, Texas.

21. Ibid.

22. "Advancing Electric Competition . . . Enron Is Hot on the Campaign Trail to Affect Policy and Public Opinion," *Enron Business* 2 (2001): 12, Southwest Collection/Special Collections Library, Texas Tech University, Lubbock, Texas.

23. Ibid.

24. Transcript of Jury Trial Before the Honorable Sim Lake United States District Judge, March 1, 2006, 5059–64.

25. Though the Federal Energy Regulatory Commission would eventually issue a report determining that California's power market had been manipulated, at first the firm's lawyers had a difficult time determining the legality or impact of many of the strategies. Still, there could be little doubt that the trading strategies were not helping the state's energy woes. For instance, some trading moves, such as buying power in California and then selling it outside of the state for a higher price, had potentially "contributed to California's declaration of a "Stage 2 emergency" in early December. Memo—December 8, p. 3; Rick Shapiro and Tim Belden, recorded phone conversation, Threads Enron Database, https://enron.threads.uk.com/detail/edit/by/email/id/454701 (accessed March 26, 2016).

26. David Lazarus, "Enron's Chief Denies Role as Villain," *San Francisco Chronicle*, March 4, 2001, http://www.lexis-nexis.com/ (accessed November 18, 2006).

27. Sean Wilentz, *The Age of Reagan: A History, 1974–2008* (New York: HarperCollins, 2008), 421. Some authors would point out that Lay even offered the Bush campaign use of Enron's jets. Robert Bryce, *Pipe Dreams: Greed, Ego and the Death of Enron* (New York: Public Affairs, 2002), 272.

28. Alberto Gonzales to Joseph Lieberman, May 22, 2002, https://www.gpo.gov/fdsys/pkg/CHRG-107shrg86405/pdf/CHRG-107shrg86405.pdf (accessed June 23, 2016).

29. Minority Staff, House Committee on Government Reform, *How the White House Energy Plan Benefitted Enron*, 107th Cong., 2nd sess., 2002, 2, 6; Minority Staff, House Committee on Government Reform, "Fact Sheet: The White House Energy Plan Reflects Seven of Eight Recommendations in Enron Memo," 107th Cong., 2nd sess., 2002, 5.

30. Robert Salladay, "California Shivers—Texas Smirks," *San Francisco Chronicle*, February 20, 2001, http://www.lexis-nexis.com/ (accessed November 18, 2006). Of course, this is not to deny the somewhat tongue-in-cheek tone to the article. For example, after quoting tensions between the two states, Salladay, in faux-California lingo, wrote: "Harsh, Texas dudes. Is California experiencing some sort of karmic retribution?" In effect, this news coverage

amounted to a vernacular articulation of Doreen Massey's critique of cyberspace. As Massey notes, "the world of physical space and the world of electronically mediated connection do not exist as somehow two separate layers, one (in what is I suspect a common mind's eye imagination) floating ethereally somewhere above the materiality of the other." Indeed, Massey goes on to argue that points of access to cyberspace are always rooted in a physical location. It was this connection that Californian journalists highlighted in references to the Houston skyline, Enron Tower, and even the corporation's trading floor, the very moment when Enron traders *in Houston* were, through this ostensibly "ethereal" world of cyberspace, having a direct, material impact on California. Doreen Massey, *For Space* (London: Sage, 2005), 96.

31. Laura M. Holson, "California's Largest Utility Files for Bankruptcy," *New York Times*, April 7, 2001, New York Times (1923–Current File), http://search.proquest.com/docview/91958200?accountid=9676 (accessed March 26, 2016).

32. Enron Corp., "CA Constituent Letter to Gov. Davis.doc," April 3, 2001, Enron Email Dataset.

33. Ibid.

34. Just as Lay had written to Bush in the mid-1990s about the perils of regulation, in California Lay began publicly voicing neoliberalism's threats, rather than promises. No longer the "good neighbor," Lay began to reflect Harvey's observations about the pressures mobile investment capital could put on a place. Salladay; David Harvey, "From Space to Place and Back Again," in *Justice, Nature and the Geography of Difference*, ed. David Harvey (Cambridge, Mass.: Wiley-Blackwell, 1996), 291–326.

35. "The Western Energy Crisis, the Enron Bankruptcy, and FERC's Response.".

36. "The California Crisis," *Frontline*, PBS, 2001.

37. Chris O'Brien, "Energy Executive Says Davis Isn't to Blame in Crisis Enron CEO; Also Is Critical of Bush Policies," *San Jose Mercury News*, June 22, 2001, http://lexisnexis.com (accessed July 10, 2014).

38. Rick Jurgens, "Enron Exec Get Chance to Say 'I Told You So,'" *Contra Costa Times*, June 22, 2001, http://lexisnexis.com (accessed July 10, 2014); O'Brien.

39. Enron Corp., "The California Story.doc," June 25, 2001, Enron Email Dataset.

40. Ibid.

41. Ibid.

42. Ibid.

43. Ibid.

44. Ibid.

45. Ibid.

46. Howard A. Fromer to Rick Shapiro, "Memo and Talking Points for Pataki Fundraiser," June 1, 2000, Enron Email Dataset; Luiz Maurer, e-mail to Jennifer Brockwell, September 27, 2001, Enron Email Dataset.

47. Gilardi and Co., LLC, "Enron Corporation (ENRN Q) Common Stock Historical Price Table," n.d., http://www.gilardi.com/enron/securities/ (accessed July 9, 2014).

48. Jeff Dasovich, e-mail to Sur Nord and Lara Leibman, July 31, 2001, Enron Email Dataset.

49. Starkman, *The Watchdog That Didn't Bark: The Financial Crisis and the Disappearance of Investigative Journalism* (New York: Columbia University Press, 2014), 151.

50. Bill Steigerwald, "Money, ASAP Warn of Crash Ahead," *Pittsburgh Post-Gazette*, February 24, 2000, http://lexisnexis.com (accessed March 12, 2009).

51. Bill Mann, "Where Were You When the Bubble Popped?" *Motley Fool*, March 10, 2005, http://www.fool.com/investing/value/2005/03/10/where-were-you-when-the-bubble-popped.aspx (accessed February 24, 2011). While March 10, 2000, was the NASDAQ's high point, the stock index began to drop immediately afterward.

52. Google Finance, "NASDAQ Composite Historical Prices," http://www.google.com/finance/historical?cid=13756934&startdate=March+1%2C+2000&enddate=May+1%2C+2000 (accessed May 7, 2009).

53. Allan Sloan, "The $2.1 Trillion Market Tumble," *Newsweek*, April 24, 2000, 22–26.

54. Wayne Rash, "Enjoy the Recession of '01 and You'll Feel Better—Really," *InternetWeek*, January 8, 2001, http://lexisnexis.com (accessed March 12, 2009). Google Finance; David R. Francis, "How the Bottom Fell Out of the U.S. Economy So Quickly," *Christian Science Monitor*, January 25, 2001, http://lexisnexis.com (accessed March 12, 2009). Interestingly, the article points to the media and communications as contributing to the bad environment, arguing that the speedy travel of bad news complicated matters.

55. This article is sometimes cited as the one that "broke" the Enron story. However, its focus is much narrower than that of other early critiques of the company. What is more, as some have pointed out, the article ran in the *Wall Street Journal*'s regional edition, lacking widespread circulation. Likewise, Peter Eavis, a writer for the financial website TheStreet.com, had been a consistent critic for some time. Jonathan Weil, "Energy Traders Cite Gains, but Some Math Is Missing," *Wall Street Journal*, September, 20, 2000, http://factiva.com (accessed March 23, 2009).

56. Bethany McLean, "Is Enron Overpriced?" *Fortune*, March 5, 2001, 123. Some writers point out that Chanos approached McLean about the story. See Kurt Eichenwald, *Conspiracy of Fools* (New York: Broadway Books, 2005).

57. McLean.

58. At the same time, McLean also rejected Skilling's emphasis on "brain intensive businesses." She paraphrased Fastow as saying that the company still, at the end of the day, delivered natural gas, a physical commodity, and mentioned that "in order to facilitate its plan to trade excess bandwidth capacity, Enron is constructing its own network." Indeed, these details underscored the central contradiction of the informational economy—such traffic in information could be facilitated only by large material objects and spaces. Though it was muted, McLean's article hinted at tensions that would later rise to the surface, in effect making Enron a convenient site for some to voice anxiety about the post-1973 informational economy just below the technological euphoria of the previous decade. I am not arguing that McLean intends some Derridian meditation on the nature of language here. However, it is striking how the traces of Derrida's insights about the indeterminacy of meaning in a signifying system, such as language, dovetails nicely with McLean's turns of phrase. McLean, 126; Li Sun, e-mail to Vince Kaminski, February 23, 2001, Enron Email Dataset. Another e-mail referred to the article as "garbage." Cindy Derecskey, e-mail to Jeff Dasovich, February 3, 2001, Enron Email Dataset; Senate Committee on Governmental Affairs, Role of the Board of Directors in Enron's Collapse, 107th Cong., 2nd sess., 2002, S. Print 107–70, 12.

59. Bethany McLean and Peter Elkind, *The Smartest Guys in the Room* (New York: Portfolio, 2003), 325, 321–23.

60. Jerry Useem, "The Revolution Lives," *Business 2.0*, August/September 2001, 74; Michael Porter, "Strategy and the Internet," *Harvard Business Review*, March 2001, 62–78.

61. McLean and Elkind, 325.

62. Transcript of Jury Trial Before the Honorable Sim Lake United States District Judge, March 14, 2006, 8118.

63. Gilardi and Co., LLC. In what was, by many accounts, a rough patch for Enron (including an industrial accident that killed three employees in England), bad press even beyond California began.

64. In later accounts, authors would give much weight to Skilling's announcement, though a review of newspaper coverage from around this time suggests that the reaction was fairly mild.

65. John Emshwiller, "Enron's Skilling Cites Stock-Price Plunge as Main Reason for Leaving CEO Post," *Wall Street Journal*, August 16, 2001, http://factiva.com (accessed April 27, 2009).

66. Ibid.

67. Robert Preston, "Enron a Victim of Irrational Pessimism," *InternetWeek*, August 27, 2001, http://factiva.com (accessed April 27, 2009).

68. Alex Berenson, "A Self-Inflicted Wound Aggravates Angst over Enron," *New York Times*, September 9, 2001, http://lexisnexis.com (accessed July 10, 2014).

69. Ronald Barone, "UBS PaineWebber Research Note," UBS PaineWebber, August 15, 2001, Enron Email Dataset.

70. Ibid.

71. Ibid.

72. Emshwiller.

73. Barone.

74. "Enron Offline," *Energy Compass*, August 17, 2001, http://lexisnexis.com (accessed July 10, 2014).

75. Ibid.

76. Berenson.

77. Ibid.

78. Transcript of Jury Trial Before the Honorable Sim Lake United States District Judge, March 15, 2006, 8139.

79. Ibid., 8141–44.

80. Sherron Watkins, e-mail to Rick Buy, August 14, 2001, Enron Email Dataset.

81. Ibid.

82. Transcript of Jury Trial Before the Honorable Sim Lake United States District Judge, March 14, 2006, 7967.

83. Sherron Watkins, Memorandum to Ken Lay, August 2001, SEC Historical Society, http://www.sechistorical.org/museum/papers/2000/ (accessed July 10, 2014). Watkins was not the only employee who was getting nervous about Enron. As at least one employee e-mailed Lay, "as an employee and a stock holder of Enron, I'm very concerned with what's going on

within our company." Sammy Williams, e-mail to Kenneth Lay, September 25, 2001, Enron Email Dataset.

84. Interview with former Enron employee, April, 30, 2009.

85. Frank Luntz, memorandum to Ken Lay, October 19, 2001, 9, Enron Email Dataset.

86. Ibid.

87. Though the memorandum was delivered to Ken Lay after the firm's Q3 earnings statement, undoubtedly, the actual focus group was conducted before October 16, 2001. Other more specific problems some felt at the company was that deal makers often got promoted, which was not always a good thing. As Luntz put it, employees were frustrated by seeing deal makers with no managerial experience gain power within the firm. The peer-review process, or PRC, system that Skilling had introduced had also become a problem for the firm. Indeed, as the focus group had found, "Employees associate the PRC with Jeff Skilling and the last thing you want is for that negative association to shift to Ken." Ibid., 5.

88. "Cartoon Craziness Contest," *Enron Business* 3 (2001): 23.

89. Mimi Swartz, "How Enron Blew It," *Texas Monthly*, November 2001, 136–39, 171–78, 138.

90. Fleisher later assumed an infamous role in Enron narratives for his defense of the firm. David Fleisher, "Neg. Perceptions Hit Bottom and Catalysts Appear at Head," Goldman Sachs, October 3, 2001, 1, SEC Historical Society, http://www.sechistorical.org/museum/papers/2000/ (accessed July 10, 2014).

91. Transcript, Enron 3rd Quarter 2001 Earnings Statement Conference Call, October 16, 2001, http://www.usdoj.gov/enron/ (accessed on May 7, 2009).

92. John R. Emshwiller and Rebecca Smith, "Enron Jolt: Investments, Assets Generate Big Loss," *Wall Street Journal*, October 17, 2001, http://factiva.com (accessed January 22, 2009).

93. David Boje's concept of "antenarrative" proves instructive. Boje intends the term to indicate two different concepts. First, "antenarrative" is an early stage of narrative development when "people are still chasing stories, and many different logics for plotting an ongoing event are still being investigated." Rather than a structurally coherent story, antenarrative implies a "fragmentary" state. As Boje puts it, "a wandering audience chases storylines in multiple and simultaneous stages." David M. Boje, *Narrative Methods for Organizational and Communication Research* (London: Sage, 2001), 4–5. However, Boje also intends "ante" as a "'bet' on the future, a prediction of an end-state." Indeed, in both senses of the term, "antenarrative" was removing agency from the company itself. David M. Boje, "Reflections: What Does Quantum Physics of Storytelling Mean for Change Management?" *Journal of Change Management* 12.3 (September 2012): 253–71, 257.

94. As journalism professor Dean Starkman notes, "the symbolic nature of finance makes for a kind of relativism" because "much of business journalism boils down to an argument about value: How much is something worth, in dollar terms, now and in the future." As Starkman puts it, "the key 'facts' of financial news—value, money, securities—are human constructs." Starkman, 42–43; Gilardi and Co., LLC.

95. John R. Emshwiller and Rebecca Smith, "Enron May Issue More Stock to Cover Obligations," *Wall Street Journal*, October 24, 2001, http://factiva.com (accessed January 22, 2009).

96. U.S. Bankruptcy Court, Southern District of New York, *In re Enron Corp.*, chapter 11, case no. 01-16034 (AJG), "First Interim Report of Neal Batson, Court Appointed

Examiner," Enron Examiner Reports, University of Pennsylvania, Biddle Law Library, National Bankruptcy Archives, 120–21, 4.

97. Robert Shiller, *Irrational Exuberance*, 2nd ed. (Princeton, N.J.: Princeton University Press, 2005), 85–143.

98. Transcript of Jury Trial Before the Honorable Sim Lake United States District Judge, March 14, 2006, 7971–76.

99. John R. Emshwiller and Rebecca Smith, "Enron Replaces Fastow as Finance Chief," *Wall Street Journal*, October 25, 2001, http://factiva.com (accessed January 22, 2009).

100. U.S. Bankruptcy Court, Southern District of New York, *In re Enron Corp.*, chapter 11, case no. 01-16034 (AJG), 120–21, 4.

101. John R. Emshwiller and Rebecca Smith, "Enron Debt Is Downgraded by Moody's," *Wall Street Journal*, October 30, 2001, http://factiva.com (accessed January 22, 2009).

102. John R. Emshwiller and Rebecca Smith, "With Enron Stock Trading at Book Value, Some See Company as a Takeover Target," *Wall Street Journal*, October 31, 2001, http://factiva.com (accessed January 22, 2009).

103. The "Special Committee" here refers to an investigative team led by William Powers. William Powers et al., "Report of Investigation by the Special Investigative Committee of the Board of Directors of Enron Corp.," February 1, 2002, 2.

104. Ibid.

105. Gilardi and Co., LLC.

106. Floyd Norris, "Plumbing Mystery of Deals by Enron," *New York Times*, October 28, 2001, http://lexisnexis.com (accessed February 22, 2009).

107. Kenneth Lay, "All Employee Meeting," October 23, 2001, SEC Historical Society, http://3197d6d14b5f19f2f440-5e13d29c4c016cf96cbbfd197c579b45.r81.cf1.rackcdn.com/collection/papers/2000/2001_1023_EnronAllEmployeeMeeting.pdf (accessed March 21, 2016).

108. Alberto Gonzales to Joseph Lieberman, May 22, 2002, https://www.gpo.gov/fdsys/pkg/CHRG-107shrg86405/pdf/CHRG-107shrg86405.pdf (accessed June 23, 2016); Gilardi and Co., LLC.

109. Interview with former Enron employee, May 18, 2009; interview with former Enron employee, April 30, 2009.

110. Interestingly, on a formal level, this letter vaguely resembles a jeremiad. Daniel Freedenberg, letter to the editor, *New York Times*, December 2, 2001, http://lexisnexis.com (accessed February 22, 2009).

111. This train of thought would emerge later as an ugly by-product of attempts to come to terms with Enron and the informational economy—a creeping hostility toward intellectualism in general. Richard Cohen, "Enron's 'Con,'" *Washington Post*, December 4, 2001, http://lexisnexis.com (accessed February 22, 2009).

112. Robert Samuelson, "Enron's Creative Obscurity," *Washington Post*, December 19, 2001, http://lexisnexis.com (accessed February 22, 2009).

113. Lanny J. Davis, "Enron? We're Missing the Point," *Washington Post*, January 6, 2002, http://lexisnexis.com (accessed February 22, 2009).

114. Allen Sloan, "Digging into the Deal That Broke Enron," *Newsweek*, December 17, 2001, 48–49, 48. Sloan, again writing for *Newsweek*, was surely trafficking in some degree of schadenfreude in reporting how Enron had stumbled (a sentiment that was shared by others, owing largely to the company's arrogant posturing throughout its heyday). Nonetheless, the

statement also reflected an uneasiness toward complicated symbolic manipulation (one that would become increasingly pronounced as time moved on).

Chapter 6. Making Enron Meaningful

1. Such assessments were also shared by readers who sent in letters to the editor. See, for example, Daniel Freedenberg, letter to the editor, *New York Times*, December 2, 2001, http://www.lexisnexis.com.

2. Because of this, the language of and rhetorical references to Watergate began to appear.

3. For example, see David S. Hilzenrath and Peter Behr, "Enron Chief Got Early Warning," *Washington Post*, January 15, 2002, http://www.lexisnexis.com.

4. "The Enron Scandal," *USA Today*, January 22, 2002, LexisNexis Academic; Dan Morgan and Peter Behr, "Enron Chief Quits as Hearings Open," *Washington Post*, January 24, 2002, http://www.lexisnexis.com.

5. Baxter, who had retired from the company, had suddenly found himself the center of media attention because Watkins mentioned him in her anonymous letter to Ken Lay as another insider who was uncomfortable with some of the company's practices. Dennis Jacobe, "Enronitis: Are Workers Immune?" *Gallup Tuesday Briefing*, February 12, 2002. One Gallup study even suggested that Enron's collapse might give a boost to union membership. Ben Klima and Chris McComb, "Unions in the Age of Enron," *Gallup Tuesday Briefing*, February 19, 2002.

6. Polling indicated that many investors were less interested in stock investments and more interested in other investment vehicles like real estate, bonds, and CODs. In March, though, optimism about the stock market rebounded from February. Dennis Jacobe, "Investors Have Been 'Enroned,'" *Gallup Tuesday Briefing*, February 26, 2002, http://www.gallup.com/poll/tb/finanComme/20020226b.asp; Jacobe, "Enronitis."

7. Andrew W. Lo, "The Gordon Gekko Effect: The Role of Culture in the Financial Industry," Working Paper 212267, National Bureau of Economic Research, June 2015, 15–16, http:www.nber.org/papers/w21267 (accessed July 15, 2017). Thank you to Eric Hilt for pointing out this research. Allan Sloan, "The Jury's In: Greed Isn't Good," *Newsweek*, June 24, 2002, 37; Keith Naughton, "The Mighty Fall," *Newsweek* August 5, 2002, 24–25; Keith Naughton, "Martha's Shrinking Act," *Newsweek*, November 4, 2002, 50.

8. Keith Naughton, "Mighty Fall."

9. *Public Papers of the Presidents of the United States: George W. Bush, 2001 (in Two Books), Book II—July 1 to December 31, 2001* (Washington, D.C.: United States Government Printing Office, 2003), 1549.

10. John Conyers Jr. to George W. Bush, August 13, 2002, folder 535045, FOIA 2014-0221-F: Records sent to, sent by, or received by President George W. Bush between January 2001 and December 2002 regarding Enron, Jeff Skilling, Kenneth Lay, and Andrew Fastow, courtesy George W. Bush Presidential Library, National Archives and Records Administration.

11. NBC/WSJ Survey July 2002, Robert Teeter Papers, box 88, folder "July 2002," Gerald R. Ford Library.

12. For example, see Tim Barry, *The Totally Unauthorized Enron Joke Book* (Vancouver, Wash.: IT Press, 2002), 87.

13. Morgan and Behr.

14. Conyers to Bush.

15. George W. Bush, State of the Union Address, January 29, 2002, National Archives, http://georgewbush-whitehouse.archives.gov/news/releases/2002/01/20020129–11.html (accessed March 27, 2016).

16. "The Enron Hearings," *New York Times*, January 20, 2002, LexisNexis Academic.

17. Michael Oxley, interviewed by James Stocker, Securities and Exchange Commission Historical Society, March 9, 2012, http://www.sechistorical.org/museum/search/?q=oxley& qop=any&record-type=type%3A%22Oral+Histories%22&from=&to=&sort=score+desc (accessed March 27, 2016).

18. Ibid.

19. Senate Commerce, Science and Transportation Committee, *The Collapse of the Enron Corporation*, 107th Cong., 2nd sess., 2002, 1; William Powers et al., "Report of Investigation by the Special Investigative Committee of the Board of Directors of Enron Corp.," February 1, 2002, 187–203.

20. Senate Commerce, Science and Transportation Committee.

21. Powers et al., 14.

22. Ibid.

23. Ibid., 15.

24. Though Fastow was undeniably crooked, I believe it would be a mistake to view these SPEs as somehow aberrant details in Enron's overall history. Rather, they are only the most extreme examples of the impulses Enron had been operating under since the early 1990s.

25. Powers et al., 15, 34.

26. See Kurt Eichenwald, "Enron's Many Strands: The Accountants," *New York Times*, April 10, 2002, http://www.lexisnexis.com, and Jonathan D. Glater, "Last Task at Andersen: Turning Out the Lights," *New York Times*, August 30, 2002, http://www.lexisnexis .com.

27. Dennis Jacobe, "Has the Time Come for Real Reform?" *Gallup Tuesday Briefing*, May 28, 2002, http://www.gallup.com/poll/tb/finanComme/20020528.asp. Oxley.

28. "President's Ten-Point Plan," 2002, folder: Corporate Governance Briefing Book: Summer/Fall 2002 [2], FOIA 2014-0373-F: Records on the Sarbanes-Oxley Act of 2002 to or from the Securities and Exchange Commission (SEC) or Congress, courtesy George W. Bush Presidential Library, National Archives and Records Administration.

29. Tom Daschle and Patrick Leahy to George W. Bush, July 1, 2002, folder 527657, FOIA 2014-0373-F: Records on the Sarbanes-Oxley Act of 2002 to or from the Securities and Exchange Commission (SEC) or Congress, courtesy George W. Bush Presidential Library, National Archives and Records Administration.

30. Oxley.

31. Zell Miller, "Floor Statement on Amendment to Require Corporate CEOs to Sign Tax Returns Remarks Prepared for Delivery," e-mail attachment, e-mail to Alex Albert from Alison Jones, "Re: Fwd [3]: Proposed Draft Attached," July 9, 2002, FOIA 2014-0373-F: Records on the Sarbanes-Oxley Act of 2002 to or from the Securities and Exchange Commission (SEC) or Congress, courtesy George W. Bush Presidential Library, National Archives and Records Administration.

32. Amendment Summary, Counsel's Office, White House, folder: Sarbanes Passed Bill [4], FOIA 2014-0373-F: Records on the Sarbanes-Oxley Act of 2002 to or from the Securities

and Exchange Commission (SEC) or Congress, courtesy George W. Bush Presidential Library, National Archives and Records Administration.

33. E-mail to Majority Leader's Office from Karen Hughes, Re: Free the Corporate Accountability Act, July 10, 2002, FOIA 2014-0373-F: Records on the Sarbanes-Oxley Act of 2002 to or from the Securities and Exchange Commission (SEC) or Congress, courtesy George W. Bush Presidential Library, National Archives and Records Administration.

34. Seamus Moore to Karl Rove, July 9, 2002, folder: 508471, FOIA 2014-0563-F: Records created by or sent to Roel Campos, SEC, courtesy George W. Bush Presidential Library, National Archives and Records Administration.

35. Anthony A. Tully to Karl Rove, June 30, 2002, folder: 508471, FOIA 2014-0563-F: Records created by or sent to Roel Campos, SEC, courtesy George W. Bush Presidential Library, National Archives and Records Administration.

36. Published volumes of the *Public Papers of the Presidents of the United States*, for instance, do not record any questions about Enron or Ken Lay during press conferences with the president in 2002 after January of that year.

37. Shelly Moore to George W. Bush, August 1, 2002, Folder 534518, FOIA 2014-0373-F, Records on the Sarbanes-Oxley Act of 2002 to or from the Securities and Exchange Commission (SEC) or Congress, Courtesy George W. Bush Presidential Library, National Archives and Records Administration.

38. "Sarbanes-Oxley Act of 2002, Summary of Key Provisions and Possible Action Items for Financial Institutions," American Bankers' Association, July 25, 2002, http://www.aba .com/aba/pdf/sarbanes_oxley_2002.pdf (accessed March 27, 2016). Sarbanes-Oxley was part of what Arjun Appadurai calls "immanent corporate ethics," a set of ideas and terms that separate corporate action from broader ethical systems. Arjun Appadurai, *Banking on Words: The Failure of Language in the Age of Derivative Finance* (Chicago: University of Chicago Press, 2016), 26.

39. Oxley.

40. See, for example, the letter Congressman Harold Ford wrote to the president. Harold Ford to George W. Bush, July 9, 2002, folder 535045, FOIA 2014-0221-F: Records sent to, sent by, or received by President George W. Bush between January 2001 and December 2002 regarding Enron, Jeff Skilling, Kenneth Lay, and Andrew Fastow, courtesy George W. Bush Presidential Library, National Archives and Records Administration.

41. Alan Greenspan, "Remarks Before the Institute of International Finance," April 22, 2002, folder: 509028, FOIA 2014-0221-F: Records sent to, sent by, or received by President George W. Bush between January 2001 and December 2002 regarding Enron, Jeff Skilling, Kenneth Lay, and Andrew Fastow, courtesy George W. Bush Presidential Library, National Archives and Records Administration.

42. Financial Crisis Inquiry Commission, *The Financial Crisis Inquiry Report* (New York: Public Affairs, 2011), 60.

43. Bethany McLean, "The Geeks Who Rule the World," *Fortune*, December 24, 2001, 93–94.

44. Benjamin Waterhouse, "The Corporate Mobilization Against Liberal Reform: Big Business Day, 1980," in *What's Good for Business: Business and American Politics Since World War II*, ed. Kim Phillips-Fein and Julian E. Zelizer (Oxford: Oxford University Press, 2012), 233–49.

45. Citizen Works, news release, February 27, 2002, http://lists.topica.com/lists/can-globe/read/message.html?sort=d&mid=1709739027&start=2 (accessed March 27, 2016).

46. "Nader Urges Corporate Curbs," CNN Money, April 7, 2002, http://money.cnn.com/2002/04/06/news/companies/nader.business.refor/ (accessed March 27, 2016).

47. Harvey Pitt to George W. Bush, November 5, 2002, folder: Harvey Pitt, FOIA 2014-0370-F: Appointment of SEC chairman Harvey Pitt, courtesy George W. Bush Presidential Library, National Archives and Records Administration.

48. Carl Levin to George W. Bush, November 1, 2002, folder: 544108 subject files FG249, FOIA 2014-0563-F: Records created by or sent to Roel Campos, SEC, courtesy George W. Bush Presidential Library, National Archives and Records Administration.

49. "Welcome to Layoff.com," Layoff.com, December 13, 2001, https://web.archive.org/web/20011213061930/http://www.layoff.com/ (accessed March 27, 2016).

50. "Ex-Employee Relief Fund Account," Layoff.com, October 6, 2002, https://web.archive.org/web/20021011100620/http://layoff.com/eerfa.html (accessed March 27, 2016).

51. "Welcome to Layoff.com."

52. "Layoff Survey," Layoff.com, April 7, 2002, https://web.archive.org/web/20020407151948/http://vote.sparklit.com/survey/559316?ns=16 (accessed March 27, 2016).

53. Dennis Jacobe, "How to Rebuild Investor Confidence," *Gallup Tuesday Briefing*, August 27, 2002, http://www.gallup.com/poll/tb/finanComme/20020827.asp; Kurt Eichenwald, "Enron's Many Strands: Overview," *New York Times*, October 3, 2002, LexisNexis Academic.

54. Kurt Eichenwald, "U.S. Indicts 11 Former Enron Executives," *New York Times*, May 2, 2003, LexisNexis Academic. Other parts of Enron, including international assets, seemed less attractive to buyers in part because Enron's strategy of pushing for places to deregulate meant that projects such as the Dabhol power plant were, despite their size, risky investments. Claire Pool, "Focus of Enron Auctions Goes Overseas," *Daily Deal*, January 18, 2002, LexisNexis Academic.

55. "Enron Founder Lay Indicted," *Facts on File World News Digest*, July 15, 2004, LexisNexis Academic.

56. George W. Bush to William H. Donaldson, June 14, 2005, folder: 664822, FOIA 2014-0357-F: Records created by or sent to William Donaldson, SEC chairman, courtesy George W. Bush Presidential Library, National Archives and Records Administration.

57. "New Business Ventures," Layoff.com, June 3, 2002, https://web.archive.org/web/20020609233017/http://www.layoff.com/nbv.html (accessed March 27, 2016).

58. Peter Carson, "Playboy's 'Women of Enron,' Cashing In on the Bare Market," *Washington Post*, July 16, 2002, LexisNexis Academic.

59. Oxley.

60. Martin Kaplan, "How Enron Stole Center Stage," *USA Today*, January 23, 2002, LexisNexis Academic.

61. Richard Lacayo and Amanda Ripley, "Persons of the Year 2002: The Whistleblowers," *Time*, December 30, 2002, http://content.time.com/time/magazine/article/0,9171,1003998,00.html (accessed March 27, 2016). "Interview: Cynthia Cooper, Sherron Watkins, Coleen Rowley," *Time*, December 30, 2002, http://content.time.com/time/magazine/article/0,9171,1003994,00.html (accessed March 27, 2016).

62. For example, in discussing the appearance of Watkins and Swartz's *Power Failure*, the publication notes: "Although it's possible that the reading public's interest in *Enron* has faded,

Watkins's name on this book's cover and the timing—a good six months after the rush of *Enron* books—will help sales." "Forecasts," *Publishers Weekly* 250 (March 24, 2003), http://web.ebscohost.com/ehost/ (accessed April 8, 2009). To a degree, it seems as though publishers' instincts were right. Though several titles did make appearances on the *New York Times* best sellers list, they were brief compared to the time they spent on *BusinessWeek*'s book lists. Three Enron narratives, *Power Failure*, *24 Days*, and *The Smartest Guys in the Room*, were all on that publication's best seller list in 2003 and 2004.

63. See Dean Starkman, *The Watchdog That Didn't Bark: The Financial Crisis and the Disappearance of Investigative Journalism* (New York: Columbia University Press, 2014), 93. As Leigh Claire La Berge notes, the 1980s were marked by the disappearance of such considerations from literature. Enron books represented a return to these larger issues. See Leigh Claire La Berge, *Scandals and Abstractions: Financial Fiction of the Long 1980s* (New York: Oxford University Press, 2015).

64. The movie was loosely based on the otherwise obscure book, *Anatomy of Greed*, which was written by Brian Cruver, who briefly worked for the company. Brian Cruver, *Anatomy of Greed: The Unshredded Truth from and Enron Insider*, (New York: Carroll & Graf, 2002).

65. Despite Eichenwald's obvious use of literary conventions, he did not see them as detracting from the book's basic truth claims. In defense of his decision, the author included an appendix, in which he announced that while some of the dialogue was taken from transcripts, the majority of dialogue was "reconstructed with the help of participants or witnesses to conversations, or documents that describe the discussion." After offering several such caveats, Eichenwald insisted that while the dialogue was not "a perfect transcript of events dating back some twenty years," it was "the best recollection of these events and conversations by participants, and more accurately reflects reality than mere paraphrase would." Even though the reporter clearly felt this technique was in need of a defense, this was not the only liberty Eichenwald took with reality in the name of "truth."

In addition to the author's statements regarding the use of dialogue, the appendix also addressed the issue of continuity. As Eichenwald explained: "For ease of reading, if a scene was moved a few days out of order to allow for a theme in one chapter to be completed, the next chapter moved back in time to an unrelated event, launching a new story line. Such instances are described in the notes." To be sure, that decision at least in part reflected the difficulty the writer faced in turning Enron into a coherent narrative. Complicating matters even further was the author's justification of his use of interior monologue. As he put it in the appendix, "When a person is described as having thought or felt something, it comes either directly from that individual, from a document written by that individual, from notes or other records of that individual's comments to a third party, or from others to whom the individuals in question directly described their experiences." Far from removing doubt about the narrative's truth claims, the appendix hinted at how shaky the concept of "truth" could be as far as Enron was concerned. Indeed, perhaps more than anything, Eichenwald's appendix laid bare the amount of agency the author had in fashioning the narrative. After all, individual memories fade, and people do not necessarily accurately perceive the thoughts and feelings of others. Finally, as some of the interviews with former Enron employees demonstrate, the role of the media and Enron narratives themselves proved to be powerful influences on the way these former workers thought about Enron after they had left the company. Kurt Eichenwald, *Conspiracy of Fools* (New York: Broadway Books, 2005), 447, 682.

66. Rebecca Smith and John R. Emshwiller, *24 Days: How Two Wall Street Journal Reporters Uncovered the Lies That Destroyed Faith in Corporate America* (New York: HarperBusiness, 2003), 107–8, 151, 146.

67. *The Crooked E: The Unshredded Truth About* Enron, DVD, directed by Penelope Spheeris (Echo Bridge Home Entertainment, 2003).

68. Robert Bryce, *Pipe Dreams: Greed, Ego and the Death of Enron* (New York: Public Affairs, 2002), 123, 14.

69. Mimi Swartz and Sherron Watkins, *Power Failure: The Inside Story of the Collapse of Enron* (New York: Doubleday, 2003), 292, 262, 350, 132.

70. Bethany McLean and Peter Elkind, *The Smartest Guys in the Room* (New York: Portfolio, 2003), 15, 17, 145. Rooted in a tradition of financial journalism focused on the arrogance and wantonness on Wall Street, McLean and Elkind had a firmly established model for writing about the outrageous slide into corruption and licentiousness as Skilling transformed the company into something closer to a financial services firm.

71. Ibid., 28, 55, 56.

72. The authors did not reserve all their scorn for Skilling alone. For instance, their portrait of Greg Whalley as a bully who considered his intelligence a license to treat the people around him badly was particularly unflattering.

73. McLean and Elkind, 212.

74. Ibid., 264, 268.

75. Ibid., 189, 197.

76. Ibid., 28.

77. *Enron: The Smartest Guys in the Room*, DVD, directed by Alex Gibney (Magnolia Pictures, 2005). Karyn Ball is one scholar who has noted how pervasive these images are in Gibney's film, writing that the "documentary zealously provides images for every referent, even the nearly dead metaphoric ones." See Karyn Ball, "Death-Driven Futures, or You Can't Spell *Deconstruction* without Enron," *Cultural Critique* 65 (Winter 2007), 6–42, 6.

78. Indeed, Reagan is only the first in a string of Republican politicians who appear in Gibney's documentary. Of course, the film spends most of the time discussing Enron's various connections with both Bushes. In particular, the Bushes are depicted throughout this documentary as providing a range of political favors for Enron. In effect, they operate as further rejoinders to Reagan's proclamation, revealing the hypocrisy and contradiction of laissez-faire economic policy. It is, of course, fitting that Gibney would spend so much time on the Bushes. Indeed, as he lingers on this relationship, Gibney again falls back on "reenactments," such as a briefcase opening to reveal stacks of money. *Enron: The Smartest Guys in the Room*. Cheryl Felicia Rhoads, "Traverse City Showdown," *National Review Online*, July 27, 2005, http://article.nationalreview.com/ (accessed November 22, 2009).

79. Michael O'Sullivan, "Where Enron Went Wrong," *Washington Post*, April 29, 2005, LexisNexis Academic.

80. Bruce Westbrook, "Enron Film Praised by a Tough Crowd: Ex-Workers," *Houston Chronicle*, April 20, 2005, LexisNexis Academic.

81. Richard Hofstadter, *Anti-Intellectualism in American Life* (1964; New York: Alfred A. Knopf, 1970), 19.

82. *Enron: The Smartest Guys in the Room* (film).

83. Interestingly, these are some of the ways in which Gibney's film, for all its outrage, fails to challenge capitalism on any systemic level. Rather, here, and much like some of the early press accounts, Gibney sees—on some level—Enron and the informational economy as an aberration and even a threat to capitalism.

84. For example, see Benjamin C. Waterhouse, *Lobbying America: The Politics of Business from Nixon to NAFTA* (Princeton, N.J.: Princeton University Press, 2014).

85. Statistics for *Enron: The Smartest Guys in the Room*, Box Office Mojo, http://boxofficemojo.com/movies/?page=weekend&id=enron.htm (accessed October 24, 2009).

86. Mary Flood, "Reel Exposure: Enron Caught on Film," *Houston Chronicle*, January 24, 2005, http://www.lexisnexis.com (accessed October 10, 2009).

87. As *Publishers Weekly* put it, "The larger question is whether positioning the book as a true-crime thriller can help it outperform the string of major Enron books that failed to earn back their large advances, including *Power Failure* by journalist Mimi Swartz and whistle-blower Sherron Watkins (Doubleday, 2003) and *The Smartest Guys in the Room* by *Fortune* reporters Bethany McLean and Peter Elkind (Portfolio, 2003)." "Broadway's 'Fool's' Gambit," *Publishers Weekly*, February 7, 2005, Academic OneFile, http://find.galegroup.com (accessed November 4, 2009). This is not to say that *The Smartest Guys in the Room* was ignored. On the contrary, *Publishers Weekly* pointed out that the book sold well, even if it did not recoup the hefty advance.

88. McLean and Elkind, 337, 418–49; *Enron: The Smartest Guys in the Room* (film).

89. Smith and Emshwiller, 378.

90. This reliance on the market as an arbiter of objective truth and morality is not unique to Smith and Emshwiller. Thomas Frank has identified this sentiment as "market populism" throughout the 1990s in his book *One Market Under God: Extreme Capitalism, Market Populism, and the End of Economic Democracy* (New York: Anchor Books, 2000). However, the idea that markets contain the seeds of objective truth is at least as old as classical economics. Adam Smith's notion of "natural" prices posits that merchants can only keep prices inflated for so long before the truth is revealed and the price of a commodity floats back down to where it properly should be in the first place. Adam Smith, *The Wealth of Nations* (1776; New York: Modern Library, 2000), 62–72.

91. "Famous Cases and Criminals: Enron," Federal Bureau of Investigation, https://www.fbi.gov/history/famous-cases/enron (accessed July 15, 2017).

92. Ken Lay, "Guilty, Until Proven Innocent" (speech, Houston Forum, Houston, Texas, December 13, 2005). Similarly, other conservative writers referenced Eichenwald, even borrowing phrases such as "Enron Myths" to protest the "criminalization" of the company. Tom Kirkendall, for example felt so moved as to write on his blog: "I am about halfway through *Conspiracy of Fools* and it is excellent. With more information and the benefit of more hindsight, Mr. Eichenwald's book will likely replace the earlier *Smartest Guys in the Room* as the best book on the Enron scandal." See Tom Kirkendall, "More on 'Conspiracy of Fools,'" *Houston's Clear Thinkers*, March 20, 2005, http://blog.kir.com/archives/2005/03/more_on_conspir.asp (accessed November 23, 2009).

93. See Per H. Hansen, "From Finance Capitalism to Financialization: A Cultural and Narrative Perspective on 150 Years of Financial History," *Enterprise and Society* 15.4 (2014): 605–41.

94. Jon Stewart, interview with Bethany McLean, *Daily Show*, January 15, 2009.

Conclusion

1. Sandra Lord, "Information About Ken Lay," 2006, box 2, folder, 74, Discover Houston Tours Records, Woodson Research Center, Rice University, Houston, Texas; Sandra Lord to Philip Azar, e-mail, March 13, 2006, box 2, folder 50, Discover Houston Tours Records, Woodson Research Center, Rice University, Houston, Texas; Sandra Lord, "Proposed Newsletter and Website Listing," 2006, box 2, folder 50, Discover Houston Tours Records, Woodson Research Center, Rice University, Houston, Texas; Sandra Lord, "Lifestyles of Houston's Rich and Infamous: The Enron Tour," April 22, 2006, box 2, folder 84, Discover Houston Tours Records, Woodson Research Center, Rice University, Houston, Texas.

2. Mark Fraser, "Enron—the Musical," unpublished manuscript, 2006, 49, 58, courtesy of the author.

3. Sandra Lord to Bruce Nichols, e-mail, March 28, 2006, box 2, folder 50, Discover Houston Tours Records, Woodson Research Center, Rice University, Houston, Texas; Sandra Lord to Kate Appleton, e-mail, February 22, 2006, box 2, folder 50, Discover Houston Tours Records, Woodson Research Center, Rice University, Houston, Texas; Sandra Lord, "Proposed Newsletter and Website Listing—Effective March 22, 2006," 2006, box 2, folder 84, Discover Houston Tours Records, Woodson Research Center, Rice University, Houston, Texas; Malcolm Gladwell, "Open Secrets: Enron, Intelligence, and the Perils of Too Much Information," in *What the Dog Saw and Other Adventures* (New York: Little, Brown, 2009), 151–76, 154.

4. Financial Crisis Inquiry Commission, *The Financial Crisis Inquiry Report* (New York: Public Affairs, 2011), 242–90.

5. Ibid., 339, 389.

6. Ibid., 372.

7. George W. Bush, quoted in "Transition 2008," https://www2.gwu.edu/~action/2008 /chrntran08.html (accessed March 21, 2017).

8. Financial Crisis Inquiry Commission, xvii.

9. Eventually, books such as Michael Lewis's *The Big Short* would be turned into popular movies. Michael Lewis, *The Big Short: Inside the Doomsday Machine* (New York: W. W. Norton, 2011).

10. Daniel Gross, "Enron on Broadway," *Newsweek*, May 3, 2010, http://www.lexisnexis .com.

11. Lucy Prebble, qtd. in Tim Adams, "'I Hate to Be Told Somewhere Is Out of Bounds for Women': Enter Enron . . ." *Guardian*, July 5, 2009, http://www.guardian.co.uk/stage/2009 /jul/05/lucy-prebble-playwright-interview-enron (accessed January 26, 2011).

12. Dominic Maxwell, "The Smartest Play in the Room," *Times* (London), January 7, 2010, LexisNexis Academic.

13. Lucy Prebble, *Enron* (London: Methuen Drama, 2009), 18, 63.

14. Ben Brantley, "Titans of Tangled Finances Kick Up Their Heels Again," *New York Times*, April 28, 2010, LexisNexis Academic. However, other outlets, such as *USA Today*, re-

garded the play as a morally serious treatment of "American excess." Elysa Gardner, "Exhilarating 'Enron' Is Anything but Old News," *USA Today*, April 30, 2010, LexisNexis Academic.

15. Busta Scam, *The Kingdom of Norne* (Rockville, Md.: Castle Keep, 2006).

16. Ibid.

17. Cindy Kay Olson, *The Whole Truth . . . So Help Me God: An Enlightened Testimony from Inside Enron's Executive's Offices* (Mustang, Okla.: Tate, 2008), 325–26, 330.

18. Robert L. Bradley Jr., *Capitalism at Work: Business, Government, and Energy* (Salem, Mass.: M&M Scrivener, 2009), 18.

19. Clayton M. Christensen, *The Innovator's Dilemma: When New Technologies Cause Great Firms to Fail* (Boston: Harvard Business School, 1997).

INDEX

ACKNOWLEDGMENTS

No writer can successfully finish a book without the help and support of many people.

Archivists at the Texas State Archives, the Dolph Briscoe Center for American History at the University of Texas at Austin, the DeGoyler Library at Southern Methodist University, the Southwest Collection/Special Collections Library at Texas Tech University, the Woodson Research Center Special Collections and Archives at Rice University's Fondren Library, the George H. W. Bush Presidential Library, the George W. Bush Presidential Library, and the Gerald Ford Presidential Library helped me tell a story that grew richer with every find. I am also grateful to the Hagley Library for a critical set of documents online.

As I developed the project, I benefited from the feedback on conference papers at the Business History Conference, Cornell University's Histories of Capitalism conferences, the German Historical Institute, and the American Studies Association. In addition to panel commentators, informal conversations at these meetings with colleagues and historians, including Jonathan Coopersmith, Kenneth Lipartito, Hartmut Berghoff, Louis Hyman, and Rick Popp, helped me think through important arguments. Numerous conversations with Roseanne Camacho have also been thought-provoking.

In the Department of American Studies at the University of Texas at Austin, Jeffrey Meikle and Steve Hoelscher, as well as Mark Smith, Brian Bremen, and Erika Bsumek offered ways to think about sources. This project also benefited from the department's singular academic community. Faculty members including Elizabeth Engelhardt, Nhi Lieu, Shirley Thompson Marshall, Janet Davis, Julia Mickenberg, Randy Lewis, Bob Abzug, Steven Marshall, and Cary Cordova all contributed to a friendly and intellectually stimulating environment. Of course, Austin would not have been nearly as enjoyable had it not been for my friends. In particular, Becky D'Orsogna, Rebecca Onion, and Stephanie Kolberg provided great advice and camaraderie while this book was in its formative stages. Irene Garza, Andrew Busch,

Marsha Abrams, Andy Jones, Eric Covey, John Cline, Katherine Feo Kelly, and Dave Croke were present to celebrate every milestone along the way. I could not have asked for a better place to start conceptualizing and working through the initial stages of this project.

After leaving Austin, I had the good fortune to receive a fellowship at the University of South Florida in Tampa. In particular, Catherine Connor, Anne Koenig, Julia Irwin, Steve Prince, Darcie Fontaine, Nadia Jones-Gailani, Phil Levy, David Johnson, Brian Connolly, and Fraser Ottanelli in the History Department provided a productive intellectual environment to help me begin the long process of reconceptualizing and reframing. In the Department of Humanities and Cultural Studies, Dan Belgrad, Scott Ferguson, Amy Rust, and Andrew Berish helped me rethink key ideas informing the book. This project similarly benefited from conversations with the other two members of my postdoctoral cohort, Roger Stanev and Mustafa Gurbuz.

My year at Southern Methodist University's Clements Center for Southwest Studies was crucial in helping me hone both my argument and prose. I am grateful to Julia Ott, Chris Castaneda, and Bill Childs for providing detailed and unsparing feedback on a draft of my manuscript. Wayne Shaw, Holly Karibo, and Ashley Winstead offered valuable insight during a manuscript workshop. I am grateful to have spent my fellowship year with Andrew Offenburger, Rachel St. John, and Doug Miller, all participants in the workshop, who formed a small but vibrant intellectual community. The center's directors, Andrew Graybill and Sherry Smith, and the irrepressible Ruth Ann Elmore provided support and advice throughout my time in Dallas. In 2016, the Clements Center generously funded a trip back to Dallas to look through records at the George W. Bush Library. I am also grateful to my colleagues in Boston University's College of Arts and Sciences Writing Program, who have been supportive as I finished work on the manuscript. Boston University's Center for the Humanities also provided support with a Publication Production Award. Portions of this book appeared in an article, "From Green Fields and Grey Pipes to Narrating Nothingness," published in *American Studies* 53.2 (2014) and in "The Follow-Through is the Key—Enron, Energy, and the Politics of Climate Change at the End of the 20th Century," a chapter in *The President and American Capitalism Since 1945*, an edited collection published by the University Press of Florida in 2017.

At the University of Pennsylvania Press, Bob Lockhart helped sharpen the book's writing and arguments. Noreen O'Connor-Abel helped me polish the book in its final stages. The series editors, Andrew Wender Cohen, Pamela

Walker Laird, Mark H. Rose, and Elizabeth Tandy Shermer, encouraged me to refine my arguments and prose. I am deeply indebted to Mark Rose, who has always been available for help and counsel. I am certainly not the only first-time author to benefit from his time and attention. Without question, this book would not have been possible without his help.

Most important, my family has been an invaluable source of encouragement throughout this process. My parents, George and Deborah Benke, and my brothers, Erik and Brendan, offered the sort of advice and support that can only come from family. Finally, I am eternally indebted to Stephanie Kolberg, who has offered a keen eye for every page of draft upon draft. But more than that, as I worked through revisions at coffee shops and the kitchen table, she has been what she remains—an endless source of joy in my life.